Terror and Irish Modernism

SUNY series, Studies in the Long Nineteenth Century

Pamela K. Gilbert, editor

Terror and Irish Modernism

The Gothic Tradition from Burke to Beckett

Jim Hansen

SUNY PRESS

Published by
STATE UNIVERSITY OF NEW YORK PRESS
ALBANY

Printed in the United States of America

For information, contact State University of New York Press, Albany, NY
www.sunypress.edu

Production by Eileen Meehan
Marketing by Michael Campochiaro

Library of Congress Cataloging-in-Publication Data

Hansen, Jim, 1968–
Terror and Irish modernism : the Gothic tradition from Burke to Beckett / Jim Hansen.
p. cm. — (Suny series, studies in the long nineteenth century)
Includes bibliographical references and index.
ISBN 978-1-4384-2821-5 (hardcover : alk. paper)
ISBN 978-1-4384-2822-2 (pbk : alk. paper)
1. Gothic fiction (Literary genre), English—Ireland—History and criticism.
2. English fiction—Irish authors—History and criticism. 3. Terror in literature. 4. Gothic revival (Literature)—Ireland. 5.Modernism (Literature)—Ireland. I. Title.
PR8807.G67H36 2009
823'.087290989162—dc22 2008054531

10 9 8 7 6 5 4 3 2 1

Contents

Acknowledgments vii

CHAPTER 1
Gothic Double Binds, Or, Irish Terrorists Confront an Unholy Union 1

CHAPTER 2
The Wrong Marriage: Maturin and the Double Logic of Masculinity in the Unionist Gothic 27

CHAPTER 3
The Revolution Within: Wilde's Gothic and the Confines of Convention 59

CHAPTER 4
Overcoming Allegory: Joyce's *Ulysses* and the Limits of the Irish Gothic 87

CHAPTER 5
Engendering a Cartesian Gothic: Generic Form as History in Beckett's Fiction 125

EPILOGUE
The Poetics of Fear: Gothic Inheritance at the End of Modernity 169

Notes 175
Bibliography 193
Index 205

Acknowledgments

I've learned that no book is actually written by a single author. This is not a theoretical insight akin to something that Roland Barthes might say. Rather, it's an insight that I've acquired through the very practical experience of writing. Very few of the ideas in any book are purely the author's, and this book is certainly no exception. In fact, this book is really the result of the constant intellectual and emotional encouragement that I received over the years from many colleagues, comrades, and mentors, and I'd like to take this opportunity to thank those who offered me both their support and their ideas.

I was extraordinarily lucky to run into three professors at the University of Notre Dame who helped me to formulate an intellectual project. About a decade ago, I walked into Jerry Bruns's office, and I told him that I wanted to write a book about philosophical hermeneutics, politics, and Irish modernism. He looked at me in complete silence for a few moments, and then he walked over to his bookshelf. He picked up a copy of Theodor Adorno's *Aesthetic Theory* and said, "I don't think you can do that, but why don't you read Adorno for a while and then we'll talk." The result of that conversation—and of the many, many conversations that followed—is the book that you now hold in your hands. Jerry is certainly the godfather of this study, and I am indebted to him for teaching me one of the most important lessons of my life, to think slowly. Professional academics in the humanities tend to pride themselves on being quick and on responding to inquiries and aesthetic problems with immediacy. Jerry taught me to slow down and think about the texts and contexts that I encountered, and I am eternally grateful to him. The readings in this book also reflect the way that Seamus Deane helped me to think through, understand, and interpret James Joyce. In fact, much of what I have to say about Joyce in this book has been culled from the notes I took when Seamus read the entire text of *Ulysses* to a graduate seminar in the fall of 1996. Seamus taught me about Ireland, and his readings of *Ulysses* and his comments on the historical and theoretical implications of Joycean modernism provided the foundation for much of what I have to say about Irish literary history. Ewa Plonowska Ziarek was quite simply the finest and most demanding teacher that I've ever had. She was never satisfied with writing that was merely clever, nor was she satisfied with writing that merely reflected hard work. She demanded that I produce pieces that were both clever and rigorous, and I am glad that she did. She has continually provided me with sound advice over the years, and I owe much of my success in the profession to her guidance and assistance.

During the last five years, I have been fortunate enough to find myself surrounded by a dynamic group of provocative, genial, and sympathetic scholars and critics at the University of Illinois. Joseph Valente has been a particular inspiration to me. I remember talking to him while I was having a bit of trouble finishing the Joyce chapter of this book. I told him about the various incommensurable ideas that I had about Joyce and the Gothic, and after a few seconds he said, in his own very emphatic way, "OK, get a pen. Write this down." Joe has an intellect as fecund as it is dazzling, and he's always proved capable of challenging my old-fashioned Marxist dogmatism. Jed Esty is a model of the professional intellectual. He offered careful, thoughtful, and generous criticism of this manuscript at every stage of its production. He's also one of the most rigorous dialectical thinkers that I've ever encountered, and I envy his capacity to think through social and intellectual contradictions. I can only hope that I've picked up at least a few of his skills. Most importantly, Jed has always been an extraordinarily reflective and supportive friend and colleague throughout my time here at Illinois. The debt that I owe to Joe and to Jed is a nearly incalculable one, and I imagine that it will take me the rest of my career to repay it. Michael Rothberg has also been a markedly circumspect and helpful reader of these pages. He has always offered thoughtful professional and intellectual advice, and he's always reminded me to keep reading new material. Julia Walker commented on nearly every chapter, and she offered constant encouragement and insight throughout the process. Jim Hurt has corrected many of my oversights, and he has always been an amiable friend and mentor. Peter Garret, Lauren M. E. Goodlad, and Ted Underwood provided much-needed commentary on the early chapters on C. R. Maturin and the Gothic. A number of other colleagues here at Illinois, including Rob Barrett, Anna Ivy, Gordon Hutner, Bill Maxwell, Stephanie Foote, Curtis Perry, Tim Newcomb, Lori Humphry Newcomb, Mark Christian Thompson, Dale Bauer, Matt Hart, and Bob Parker, helped me through this process with my sanity intact. I thank them for their help, their oversight, and their friendship. I'm particularly indebted to the Wednesday Winos discussion group that included Brett Kaplan, Rob Rushing, and Lilya Kaganovsky for helping to make the final stage of this project far less stressful than I ever imagined it could be.

The University of Illinois's Campus Research Board provided me with the release time necessary to bring this project to a successful—and at least somewhat timely—conclusion. My work has also been enriched by the Jewish Studies Workshop, which helped me to sift through much of the material on Midrash and Kabbalah relevant to Joyce. The students in the graduate seminars that I taught on Frankfurt School Aesthetics and Terrorism and Modernity helped me to articulate many of the questions that this book raises, and The Unit for Criticism and Theory here at Illinois also helped by providing me with several opportunities to discuss that sticky Marxist dialectic of form and history in a public forum.

I was also lucky to have found in James Peltz at the State University of New York Press an editor who was committed to and excited by the connections that this project attempts to make between theory, literary history, and politics. Christy Burns and Phil Wegner, my readers at SUNY, provided productive, valuable, and thorough criticisms of this book while it was still in manuscript form. They encouraged me to make this a more thoughtful and reflective study, and that seems to me to be precisely what the best readers should aim to achieve when they sit down to read a manuscript. This is a better book because of them. I'd also like to thank *Mosaic: A Journal for the Interdisciplinary Study of Literature*, for publishing an earlier version of some of the materials in chapter 4, which appeared in a special issue in the winter of 2001 (vol. 34.4, pp. 85–106), and *Studies in Romanticism,* for giving me permission to reprint sections of my article on Maturin in chapter 2 of this book.

Many of the close friends whom I met in graduate school contributed to this project in one form or another. Erich Hertz and Lara Vetter have always been very assertive and supportive comrades. They've both read every page of this manuscript, and they've both offered continual encouragement and good cheer over the last decade. What's more, they've always done so in a happy and engaged way. Ranen Omer-Sherman helped me to work through a good deal of material on Judaic conceptions of memory while we were both still graduate students at Notre Dame. My friends from Georgia State University, George Williams and Mike Duvall, along with Chuck Tryon, my oldest and most committed ally, have supported me emotionally and helped me intellectually whenever they could, and I am grateful to share so much camaraderie with them. Fergus Clinker, the arch-theorist of the Georgia State University crew, has also been a constant source of laughter through the years.

Neil and Becky Trilling have been remarkably faithful in their encouragement, and they've welcomed me cheerfully into their homes and lives. Amanda and Doug Clark also invited me into their lives and helped me to imagine that this project might someday come to completion. Their friendship has guided me through the process.

My parents did everything that they could to make this book possible. My mother, Connie Igneri Hansen, is one of the most demanding critical thinkers whom I've ever encountered. It is because of her that I learned to question the manifest. My father, Arthur Hansen, is a person of deep and abiding enthusiasms who can speak as intelligently about James Bond as he can about theology. His enthusiasms have very often become my own. My brother, Chris, is always willing to lend a hand and to help me think through intellectual and ethical dilemmas. My grandmother, Mary Agoglia Igneri, taught me to face even the most difficult of situations with humor and grace. I only wish she could have lived long enough to see this book into print.

My greatest debt is to Renée Trilling, whose companionship, warmth, courage, and guidance have been the pillars of my existence for the last ten years. I don't think I can begin to find the words to express what she means to me. In fact, I don't even think a writer as prolix as Joyce, as witty as Wilde, or as wise as Beckett could find the words. I hope that it suffices to say that she means everything to me. Finally, I'd like to mention the precious gift that my young daughter, Rowan Trilling-Hansen, has provided for me. Whenever I need to escape from the labor of this project—or from any labor at all—she is my most willing, cheerful, and fun-loving accomplice. She's also the best storyteller that I know. It is to Rowan and Renée that these pages are dedicated.

CHAPTER 1

Gothic Double Binds, Or, Irish Terrorists Confront an Unholy Union

> Real partisanship, which is the virtue of artworks no less than of men and women, resides in the depths, where social antinomies become the dialectics of form: By leading them to language through the synthesis of the work, artists do their part socially.
>
> —Theodor W. Adorno, *Aesthetic Theory*

IRELAND'S POLARIZED NATIONAL IMAGINARY

When Oscar Wilde checked in to the Hôtel de la Plage in Berneval, France, on 26 May 1897 under the name Sebastian Melmoth, he continued his ongoing work of converting himself into an *objet d'art*. As St. Sebastian, Wilde represents the terrorized, effeminate, young martyr who, though trapped and penetrated, survives. The famous painting of St. Sebastian by Guido Reni, which depicts a feminized, nearly nude saint penetrated with arrows and writhing in religious ecstasy, was one of Wilde's favorite works of art.[1] As Melmoth, Wilde stands in for the terrorizing, damned, occult nomad, the exile of his great uncle Charles Robert Maturin's Gothic novel, *Melmoth the Wanderer*. It seems tempting to interpret Wilde's *nom de voyage* as only an embodiment of his personal and authorial bipolarity. After all, his persona appears as a violent juxtaposition, an unholy marriage of the feminized victim and the manipulative victimizer. And Wilde certainly appears to us now both as a man who was martyred and destroyed by prejudice and as a decadent writer whose prose nearly always seemed dangerous and paradoxical.

From the perspective of Irish literary and cultural history, however, we should also note that Wilde's Sebastian Melmoth persona invokes the double binds that had come to dominate a great deal of Irish writing since the failure of the 1798 rebellion and subsequent rise of the Acts of Union in 1800.

In 1820, Wilde's Anglo-Irish uncle, C. R. Maturin, published *Melmoth the Wanderer,* which holds the paradoxical distinction of being called both the greatest of all Gothic novels and the swan song of the genre.[2] A deeply hallucinatory work built upon a notoriously byzantine stories-within-stories structure, *Melmoth* was written during the era of the Acts of Union that claimed Ireland as part of the United Kingdom of Great Britain. In the midst of the novel's manic instability, we witness a profoundly unholy marriage. The "Tale of the Indians," which constitutes the most protracted of the novel's vaguely interrelated stories, reaches its climax as the innocent former island girl, Immalee, moves to take the hand of the satanic wanderer, John Melmoth, in marriage. Throughout the tale, Immalee provides a powerful avatar of natural religion, à la Jean-Jacques Rousseau, but here we see her "enfeebled by terror beyond the power of resistance," as she begins to take her wedding vows in a Spanish graveyard (393). The lovers are married by the reanimated corpse of a Spanish priest, as the tale moves toward resolution, and Immalee joins hands with Melmoth.

Besides its obvious supernatural sensationalism, one of the odder things about this unholy marital alliance subsists in the fact that during nearly half of the "Tale of the Indians" the narrative actively desires this union. By manipulating the archetypical generic structure of the female Gothic romance—where a woman must be rescued from some confinement, find true love, and produce a male heir—Maturin has allowed us to imagine Immalee's apparent enslavement within the confines of the Spanish-Catholic Aliaga family household as somehow worse than a marriage to the demonic Melmoth. Melmoth himself becomes a rather paradoxical and unstable figure at this point in the novel. As a satanic Anglo-Irish landowner whose history dates back to Oliver Cromwell's 1648 invasion of Ireland, Melmoth constitutes the motivation for the storyline, the arch-villain who aims to trap the innocent female in an unnatural, but legally binding alliance, an unholy union. By becoming Immalee's heroic rescuer, however, Melmoth also transforms into her potential liberator and savior. Maturin imagines in the character of Melmoth, then, someone who appears constitutively doubled. Although the narrative is set against the satanic Melmoth, the social forces depicted in the novel also create a heroic Melmoth. Strangely enough, in Maturin's excessive novel, Melmoth is both the terrorizer and potential savior.

Like the Melmoth of Maturin's novel, Wilde appears constitutively doubled, but Wilde's version of this bipolarity clearly takes the problem much further. In Maturin's novel, Melmoth had become both the terrorizer and the heroic protector. Sebastian Melmoth signifies a subject position marked as both terrorizer and terrorized. Sebastian Melmoth actually comes to embody both a threatened, feminized innocence and the very demonic, masculine force that threatens it. Fleeing Pentonville Prison, the British Isles, and his scandalous trial under the guise of both martyred saint and satanic wanderer, Wilde represents the various Gothic antinomies of Ireland's unhappy union with England. The similarities and differences between John Melmoth and Sebastian Melmoth are significant ones. While the wanderer certainly embodies a contradiction, Wilde's persona internalizes, ironizes, and reflects on a contradiction. This study will concern itself with the similarities and differences between an Irish Gothic tradition that draws on a gendered and polarized conception of terror that we also find in one form or another in much of the prose fiction of the Irish modernist period. Leaving off for the moment the fact that Wilde's luggage had the suspicious initials "S" and "M" emblazoned on them, then, we might instead trace the relationship between the double binds that his suggestively aporetic pseudonym invokes and their historical inscription in and by a tradition of Irish Gothic fiction that stretches from the novels of Maturin through to the writings of Samuel Beckett.

I call the union itself an unhappy one because the 1800 Acts of Union were themselves figured in the newspapers, speeches, pamphlets, and political ephemera that followed the 1798 rebellion as a kind of marriage in which Ireland, a vulnerable "sister kingdom" threatened by the destabilizing violence of the French Revolution, would, as Britain's lord lieutenant claimed in a speech that preceded the first Union vote in Parliament, be joined to England in the "sentiment of mutual affection and common interest." The Union, he continued, would consolidate "as far as possible, into one firm and lasting fabric, the strength, the power, and the resources of the British Empire."[3] Speaking on behalf of the king, then, the British viceroy characterized the Union as a potentially happy marriage, devoutly to be wished. The fact that many of Maturin's own novels and plays, written directly after the ratification of the Acts of Union, continually represent both the terrors of unhappy marriages and the fractured, impossible social worlds engendered by failed domestic unions seems like more than a mere coincidence, then.

Even as far back as Edmund Spenser's 1596 "A View of the Present State of Ireland," the Irish appear characterized as a savage but strangely feminine race (175). Ireland's polarized national identity was not caused by the Union. Ireland had been referred to as a sister kingdom to England at least since Jonathan Swift, and the term *an t-athardha* (or *athardha*), used through the seventeenth century in Irish-language poetry to denote Ireland as a clannish (*clachán*) "Fatherland," had already disappeared, as eighteenth-century Ireland was continually referred to—in English—as a mythic and ideal "Motherland."[4] In light of this transformation, an Irish masculinity coded by the Western male/female binary as masculine also fell into the category of an overarching Irish identity coded as feminine.

After the era of the Union and the failure of the late nineteenth-century Irish home rule movement, however, Wilde refigured and writ large as the historical *Tableau Vivant* Sebastian Melmoth seems to summarize the confusion that followed the dichotomous logic of Ireland's unhappy domestic union with England quite well. That is to say that as an art object, Wilde comes to embody not only his own doubleness as de facto saint and supposed sinner but also what Theodor Adorno calls the social and historical antinomies that reside in the depths of the work of art.[5] Sebastian Melmoth becomes a figure not only for a feminized saintliness that remains confined, threatened, and finally penetrated, but also for a correlating masculinity so demonic in its desire and so unspeakable in its apparent savagery that it must be exiled from society. In the context of the colonized Ireland of the early nineteenth century or the decolonizing Ireland of the early twentieth century, the masculine stands as confined and exiled, terrorized and terrorist. It comes to embody both vulnerability and the threat to all things vulnerable. This is all to say that an Oscar Wilde reimagined in sheer literary terms as Sebastian Melmoth could fill both the roles of heroine and villain in a late eighteenth-century Gothic novel.

II. THE GOTHIC GENRE AND IRISH LITERARY HISTORY

This study, which offers a postcolonial reading of the Irish Gothic tradition, constitutes a work of literary history concerned with Ireland's national imaginary after the Acts of Union. Throughout, I will argue that the masculine gender anxiety that characterizes the fiction of Oscar Wilde, James Joyce, and Samuel Beckett grows out of and responds to the nineteenth-century Anglo-Irish Gothic's confrontation with Britain's colonial politics. Hence, I will explore more than a century of literary production, ranging from Edmund Burke's 1790 *Reflections on the Revolution in France* and the early Irish Gothic novels of Charles Robert Maturin up through Wilde's *The Picture of Dorian Gray,* Joyce's *Ulysses,* and Beckett's *Trilogy.*

After the 1798 rebellion in Ireland led by Theobald Wolf Tone and the United Irishmen, a great deal of political, social, and military anxiety revolved around what the British came to refer to as "the Irish Question." At the governmental level, the English Parliament worked to resolve this anxiety through the Acts of Union. Under the auspices of the Acts, Ireland would no longer be considered a nation separate from England. Instead, it would become part of the unified trade area known as the United Kingdom of Great Britain. At the cultural level, both the intellectuals and the popular press of the era began to represent the Acts of Union as a marriage between a protective England and a feminized Ireland. This marital union proved to be an unhappy one, particularly for the Irish, who usually responded to British rule with ambivalence or outright rebellion.[6] In the shadow of the Acts of Union, the Anglo-Irish novelist Maria Edgeworth, author of *Castle Rackrent* (1800), along with her near contemporary Charles Robert Maturin, began to appropriate and revise the basic generic tactics of the most popular novelistic form of the previous decade: the female Gothic. Edgeworth and Maturin found in the rudimentary confinement and rape narrative of the female Gothic—the genre popularized in England by Anne Radcliffe's widely read *The Mysteries of Udolpho* (1794)—a formal method for allegorizing the breakdown of the marriage between England and Ireland. Later in the century, Joseph Sheridan Le Fanu picks up on and revises this basic formal maneuver. Finally, the "Unionist Gothic" that these novelists helped to develop situates masculine agents in social and cultural spaces that the more familiar English Gothic novel had reserved only for its embattled yet passive female heroines. By Unionist Gothic, then, I mean to signify not only the era covered by the Acts of Union, but also the unhappy union-as-marriage metaphor and, as we will see, the symptomatic union of male anxiety and female-Gothic form that the Irish Gothic will come to embody in this study. The Unionist Gothic links colonialist politics to the destabilization of gender by translating the English female Gothic's generic confinement and rape story into a metaphor for colonial invasion that represents the entire Irish population—male and female—as vulnerable, feminine, and other.

During its heyday at the close of the eighteenth century, the female-Gothic novel was referred to by a reviewer for the 1797 volume of *Spirit of Public Journals* as "the Terrorist Genre" because, as the critic went on to claim, "it makes us fall in love with what we fear to look on" (323). So, in addition to the problems it presents for gender, the female Gothic's generic confinement story also manipulates the notion of terror at the precise moment in history when this concept discovers a political avatar in the Reign of Terror following the French Revolution. The "Terrorist" fiction written by Gothic novelists aggressively manipulates the reader's identification with fictive characters, but the narrative desire for conflict that animates these fictions also creates a divided reader who must rely on identification with both the terrorized and the terrorist in order to participate in the excitement and suspense provided by the genre. To this end, the very popular novels of Maturin, Edgeworth, and Le Fanu count on their reader's unacknowledged sadistic identification with the masculine terrorizer as much as they rely on a more overtly narcissistic and masochistic identification with the feminine victim.

In observing how this complex, double structure of identification continues to be deployed by subsequent writers in the Irish tradition, I want to engage with the ongoing problem of political terror and with how terror gets allegorized by the generic tropes of the Irish Gothic. As revisions of the female-Gothic form, the novels of the Irish Gothic tradition inveigh against colonial ideology only as they also betray a deep-seated fear of femininity. In fact, because of its melding of female-Gothic tropes and masculine gender anxiety, the Irish Gothic tradition sentimentalizes the feminine while representing any identification with femininity as the foundation of all terror. Its male protagonists, caught between an embattled, isolated femininity and the fearsome masculine anxiety it provokes, come to embody precisely the incapacitating contradictions of modern Irish masculinity. Terror comes from the feminine, and the male characters in the Irish Gothic tradition display great anxiety—and often, great violence—whenever they are identified with the feminine, the weak, or the maternal. Male characters like Maturin's Annibal Montorio or Bram Stoker's Jonathon Harker appear inescapably doubled because they remain as confined by their feminine identities and histories as they are terribly anxious to reject the feminine and its history entirely.

Building on the gender doubleness of the Unionist Gothic, I want to propose a dramatically new interpretation of Irish modernism: we must read the novels of Wilde, Joyce, and Beckett in relation to the fraught political dynamic of the Irish Gothic tradition. Each of these writers yokes together the unlikely combination of masculinity and domesticity, and each portrays this combination as not only isolating and dehumanizing but also as the social and structural cause for terror and violence. The Unionist Gothic allegorized male gender disorientation, the anxious state of at once being and not being a masculine subject. In the twentieth century, Irish modernism's continued obsession with male confinement constitutes a varied, often competing, series of epilogues to the Unionist Gothic's fusion of gender disorientation and colonial politics. Hence, in my reading gender disorientation, along with the political terror that follows from it, becomes something like the foundational condition of modern Irish political and cultural identity. In what follows we will come to see how the dialectics of gender confusion and domestic confinement begged by the Unionist Gothic persist and evolve into the fascination with personal, political, and aesthetic autonomy that haunts the fiction of Ireland's major modernist fiction writers, Wilde, Joyce, and Beckett. Rather than reading Irish modernist fiction as developing merely in response to European symbolist writing and to the late nineteenth-century home rule crisis, then, I read the modernist figures as building upon a series of tropes that had characterized Irish writing for over a century.

Situating Wilde, Joyce, and Beckett in relation to the Irish Gothic tradition allows us to perform two coextensive critical tasks at once. First, it provides us with a way to examine how literary genres, even ones that merely seem to respond to or allegorize a set of specific historical conditions, persist as nearly forgotten sign systems, formal operations, and modes of alienation in subsequent genres. In so doing, it also allows us to see how certain sociopolitical and sociocultural problems persist and develop in the face of historical, material, and stylistic change. We will observe, then, that even though Burke and Beckett were responding to differing contextual, material, and cultural pressures, features from Burke's analysis of political terrorism reassert themselves in powerful and relentless ways in Beckett's use of the Gothic. Even though the colonizing world occupied by the Anglo-Irish Maturin seems profoundly different from the decolonizing one inhabited by the Gaelo-Catholic Joyce, certain tropes from Maturin's Gothic continue to haunt Joyce's dynamically innovative prose experiments. Of course, Joyce and Beckett are not Gothic novelists in precisely the same way as Maturin, Le Fanu, Stoker, and even Wilde. Rather, I will argue throughout that Joyce and Beckett respond to an Irish political and literary unconscious characterized and saturated by the tropes of the Irish Gothic novel. As we will come to see, Joyce and Beckett each provide us with a different coda to the Irish Gothic generic tradition and to the sociopolitical regimes in which that tradition developed and flourished.

In the simplest terms, the critic and theorist Mikhail Bakhtin explains that genres provide us with something like a horizon of expectations for a given set of texts (288). Certain approaches, tropes, contextual concerns, and points of view "knit together" to constitute a genre, and we read that genre fully expecting to encounter precisely these elements. In fact, the English Gothic novel, with its fleets of unquiet ghosts, overly-sensitive confined women, usurping Catholic counts, and ineffectual suitors, provides what might well be the most lucid and flagrant set of generic tropes, approaches, and concerns in the history of modern English literature. The argument that I am making here, however, indicates that genres also participate in and signal the movement of historical dialectics. Literary genres participate in confronting and negating certain sociohistorical problems and, to some degree, in preserving those very problems in and for subsequent contexts. Novelistic genres persist dialectically. They accumulate in the structures of new forms of fiction. In *The Political Unconscious,* Fredric Jameson puts it another way. He claims that "the analysis of the ideology of form, properly completed, should reveal the formal persistence of such archaic structures of alienation—and the sign systems specific to them—beneath the overlay of all the more recent and historically original types of alienation" (100). Hence, form and history become dialectically intertwined in works of fiction, which often serve to reveal how fragments of the past are preserved, almost like ruins, in the landscape of the present.[7] In the sections that follow, we will come to see how the particular concerns about gender confusion, personal and political terror, and colonization peculiar to the Irish Gothic tradition endure as resonant—and sometimes as ironic—anxieties in novels generally interpreted as avatars of either a late-Victorian aesthetic decadence or of a fully realized aesthetic modernism.

III. POSTCOLONIAL IRELAND AND THE GOTHIC

Following the 1990 publication of Stephen D. Arata's "The Occidental Tourist," with its forceful account of the postcolonial dynamics at play in Bram Stoker's *Dracula,* we have witnessed a spate of academic criticism that finds in Gothic fiction analogues for the political and cultural complexities of a colonized Ireland. In his 1997 *Strange Country: Modernity and Nationhood in Irish Writing Since 1790,* Seamus Deane connects the Gothic's characteristics in Irish literature to the Yeatsian Literary Revival's nationalism and to its coextensive antiempiricist focus on the occult and the mythic as "saving forms of irrationalism" (110). Armed with a vocabulary that is part postcolonial theory and part negative dialectics, Deane's book, especially when set alongside his 1984 *Celtic Revivals* and his editorial contributions to the *Field Day Anthology,* helped to provide a sort of *elan vitale* for subsequent readings of the Irish Gothic that would find in figures like Maturin, Le Fanu, and even in Joyce the presence of a phantom discourse on nationalism buried in the Irish cultural imaginary.[8] Following this lead, Luke Gibbons has consistently argued that the historical references in Joyce's "The Dead" actually suggest a kind of Gothic vision of colonial history wherein the ghosts of a suppressed and repressed Irish Catholic past haunt the present day of Joyce's hemoplegic Dublin.[9] In fact, following Deane's *Celtic Revivals* has been a whole slew of postcolonial approaches to Irish literature, many of which observe how the ever-present "Irish Question" of the imperial age frames the convoluted history of modern Irish literature. Terry Eagleton's *Heathcliff and the Great Hunger* (1995) aided in this critical endeavor, particularly by revising Antonio Gramsci's conception of hegemony in order to nuance discussions concerning the cultural divide between a dominant Anglo-Protestant ascendancy class and a disenfranchised and disinherited Gaelo-Catholic peasantry.[10]

In the most basic terms, these approaches confront the structural dispossession—the active, historical disinheritance and disenfranchisement of political subjects by cultural, linguistic, juridical, and economic systems—experienced by colonized people. The postcolonial turn in Irish literary criticism often argues for the validity of an authentically Irish or nationalist perspective on the psychic and social difficulties faced by a dispossessed people. In essence, this criticism asks: How does a dispossessed populace deal with its own traumatic sense of lost identity? Do they imagine wrathful spirits who return to set things right, or do they instead imagine narratives in which the dispossessed are finally allowed a fair share of the spoils? Underlying many of these groundbreaking, markedly convincing, and politically savvy postcolonial readings of Ireland, and more recently, of Ireland's Gothicism, is what critic Walter Benjamin would doubtless see as an attempt to counter those histories, both literary and otherwise, written as tools of the imperialist and capitalist "ruling class" (1:255). For Benjamin, the history constructed by the ruling class always appears linear and progressive, and it always conceals its various injustices, inequities, and moral failings. Ruling-class history always simplifies and eliminates that which does not fit within its schema. But Benjamin also warns against counterapproaches that forsake consciously dialectical thinking and that simply attempt to appropriate and redirect the narrow, linear methodology of "ruling class" histories. He warns against histories that merely work to replace one master narrative with another master narrative. Recent Irish postcolonial criticism has occasionally fallen into this trap by following Daniel Corkery's aging thesis in positing a "hidden" and Gaelo-Catholic Ireland as something that seems to resemble the Lacanian Real of the nation while an opposing Anglo-Ireland becomes both its literal and symbolic *Lex Patris*.[11]

In the criticism, then, we often find a nostalgic longing for a kind of patriarchal Irishness untouched by British hands. In fact, some of the criticism, in following an inverted nationalist logic, has attempted to simplify characters as subtle, complex, and bifurcated as Joyce's Stephen Dedalus and redeem characters as unsavory and as violent as the Cyclops-Citizen of *Ulysses*.[12] This critical approach often imagines Anglo-Ireland as the lone name for colonial false consciousness, rather than as one hybridized component of a more complicated cultural and sociopolitical matrix that includes Catholics of the bourgeois, proletarian, and agrarian variety, a divided, declining Anglo-Protestant ascendancy, and an oft-overlooked Anglo-Protestant middle class. Furthermore, we must not forget that England's various ideological and political complexes had, at least since Prime Minister's William Gladstone's first Liberal Party Parliament in 1868, added to this already convoluted matrix by deflecting much of the criticism it received about the Irish situation onto the ascendancy class. Thus, while overlooking many of the disorienting ambivalences associated with and provoked by the complicated gender dynamics of Ireland's unionist marriage with England, a good deal of the Irish nationalist criticism published in the 1990s fails to read the modern Irish literary imagination as intractably hybridized and, in fact, produced by the double binds that this book will enumerate and explore. In focusing almost exclusively on the various problematics arising from an ascendancy hegemony, much of the postcolonial criticism concerning Ireland actually accedes to the terms imagined by an evolving and liberalizing British imperialism in the first place. Rather than arresting and disrupting a linear and "continuum" theory of history through dialectics, as Walter Benjamin and many of his cohorts in the Frankfurt School had hoped to do, these readings often tend to construct another singular and monolithic history that shares as it inverts the structuring logic of the histories written by the imperialist ruling class.

Deane's own criticism proves subtle, rigorous, and dialectical enough to resist the urge to characterize the Irish situation as a simple dichotomy. He is a careful enough reader of not only writers like Yeats and Joyce but also of critics like Theodor Adorno to see the negative formations dialectically enfolded into the overtly nationalist position and into what he has called the nascent, modernist "aesthetic of privacy" that began to constitute nationalism's other at the dawn of the twentieth century (*Celtic Revivals,* 15). But a mounting body of Irish nationalist-inflected scholarship tends to read the ideological divide and the subsequent terminology set up under the auspices of colonialism as colonialism-*an-sich* in Ireland.[13] By focusing on the racial and nationalist identities set up and, to a great extent, imagined by British colonial nationalism, these critics often end up accepting the simple, racialized, exclusive logic of nationalism constructed by imperial ideology. This is not to say, however, that the Anglo-Irish and the Gaelo-Catholics should be collapsed into or read as a single group. As L. P. Curtis's *Apes and Angels: The Irishman in Victorian Caricature* makes abundantly clear, a journalistic and pseudoscientific discourse that posited discrete and separate anthropological Irish racial entities certainly existed throughout post-Darwinian Great Britain. In teasing out the ideology constructed by the twin discourses of race and sectarianism, however, the scholarship often accepts the interpellated identities and the terms of difference as, in some sense, absolute. Consequently we find many critical approaches that simply replay as they redescribe the static political identities of the Victorian and Edwardian periods. The result is that some of the critical literature about Irish decolonization unwillingly—but by force of logic, necessarily—accepts the vocabulary of identity first put into play by imperialism, and, thusly, the language of imperial Britain and of the unhappy union always seems to carry the day. In this way, the criticism is liable to reproduce precisely the political stasis against which it inveighs.

Two notable exceptions to this trend are Joseph Valente's 2002 *Dracula's Crypt: Bram Stoker, Irishness, and the Question of Blood* and Margot Gayle Backus's 1999 *The Gothic Family Romance: Heterosexuality, Child Sacrifice, and the Anglo-Irish Colonial Order.*[14] Valente's narrowly focused book dissects the logic of latter-day Irish literary nationalism and its effect on the cottage "Stoker-as-Ascendancy" industry that developed in the 1990s. In problematizing Stoker's own convoluted ethnic heritage, foregrounding *Dracula*'s persistent and unconventional use of the doppelgänger, and interrogating the novel's concepts of gender and heroism, Valente begins by thumbing his nose at the accepted political wisdom about the novel and ends by offering a reading of Stoker that acknowledges the very real complexities of rethinking hybridity and cultural nationalism. Backus's study, which operates on a much grander scale, draws attention to those Anglo-Irish Big House writers such as Maturin, Le Fanu, and Stoker who attempt to allegorize the self-consuming isolation of the ascendancy class and to what she calls the "fundamental confusion between the public and the private spheres that the bourgeois family served to establish" (4). In her account, the insular questions begged by ascendancy hegemony lead outward to philosophical and Marxian questions concerning the heteronormative family values that support notions of Irish cultural difference. By bringing together the political concerns of the nationalists with questions provoked by what we might call the Irish Unionist gender troubles, *Terror and Irish Modernism* hopes to provide a dialectical analysis that observes how the dichotomous logic of colonial consciousness in Ireland actually produced Irish cultural identities that were structurally bipolar and, as a result, very often politically static. To my mind, the methodology best suited to provide this type of analysis is the allegorical and negative dialectical model provided by the Frankfurt School critics that I've mentioned several times already, Benjamin and Adorno. Because Adorno's dialectical thinking in particular allows the critic to observe both the revolutionary and the reactionary elements present in a work of art, it also provides us with a productive way to read the irreducible doubleness of Irish cultural and literary consciousness during the ages of empire, terror, and modernism.[15]

Of course, critical discussions of the Gothic "dark double," the second self of a novel's protagonist, have become pretty familiar terrain for readers who find in the Edward Hydes and Bertha Masons of the Gothic barely repressed truths about a text's main character. But by appending to it the term "double bind" in order to create the term "Gothic double bind," I mean to connect the genre's penchant for doppelgängers to instances in Irish cultural logic where the normative and ideological conditions for the construction of an identity like "masculine" or a concept like "terrorism" are materially, psychically, and structurally doubled and, subsequently, produce social contexts in which definitions are constituted by their own disjunction. So we end up with a modern Irish literature that reflects a Gothic double bind in which a gender identity—either a fearsome masculinity or a vulnerable femininity—is always already its own dark double. In order to avoid constructing yet another alternate, but nonetheless singular and monolithic, literary history of modern Ireland, I will read the literature produced during the Irish colonial period as cultural products that respond to and were triggered by a interrelated series of these gendered double binds.

If, like Sebastian Melmoth, the Irish male is characterized by the logic of the "union-as marriage" metaphor as both the masculine terrorist and the feminine terrorized, then the discourse of gender and domesticity that we find in the novels of the day reflects this ambivalent and impossible identity position. The Irish male depicted in this fiction experiences the internal incommensurability that follows from this apparently impossible dualism. Like the women of the female Gothic, he finds himself confined in Gothic houses, but if he attempts to escape, he is immediately coded as excessive, violent, and irresponsible. Irish masculinity finds itself in a Gothic double bind and, subsequently, incapable of wholly embodying either the masculine authority or the feminine passivity demanded by a dualistic and misogynistic Western culture. From one perspective, then, almost any action taken by the male protagonist in an Irish Gothic novel seems incoherent. Despite Maturin's overt religious moralism, for instance, his novels can never imagine a morally correct course of action for their various male protagonists because any action taken seems either excessively violent or excessively weak. In attending to the Gothic double binds instigated by the unhappy Union, I want to go beyond Valente's provocative analysis of Irishness and Backus's far-ranging critique of hetero-normativity and establish the dynamics of an Irish literary tradition that nearly always renders masculine anxiety in what would have been considered feminine terms. This volume, then, maps out the formation of an ideology of "domestic union" that was reimagined and represented in Irish Gothic fiction as a profoundly isolating and feminizing form of confinement.

IV. THE UNION AND THE TERROR

The dynamic rhetorical force of the language of the "domestic union," deployed in the first union debates by the British Viceroy in order to convert the political and economic assimilation of Ireland into the operative metaphor of marriage, extends as it borrows from a more complex argument for "domestic affection" initiated by Edmund Burke, Anglo-Ireland's most potent and convincing eighteenth-century political voice. In his 1790 anti-Jacobin opus, *Reflections on the Revolution in France,* Burke begins by staking out his own operative metaphors. Central to his argument is the English notion of patrilineal inheritance, which, he argues, establishes a tradition of liberty wherein any truly benevolent citizen looks backward to ancestry in order to look forward to posterity

(29). By forsaking the past, French revolutionaries unleashed a terror that would, subsequently, devour France's future. Conversely the British, Burke claims, in choosing inheritance as a standard, "have given to our frame of polity the image of a relation of blood, binding up the constitution of our country with our dearest domestic ties, adopting all our fundamental laws into the bosom of our family affection" (30). He goes on to argue that by always "acting as if in the presence of canonized forefathers, the spirit of freedom, leading itself to misrule and excess, is tempered with an awful gravity" (30). Simply put, good rule must come from benevolent rulers, from good fathers who inspire an affection in balance with the gravity of an inherited tradition that they must strive to represent and to embody.[16] In following this course of thought, Burke imagines a social and political world structured by the logic of the single, patriarchal family unit. With the burgeoning of the bourgeois public sphere in the eighteenth century, the family had become the ahistorical cynosure of English national identity. The bourgeois family, overseen by a benevolent and fully autonomous patriarch, came to represent both the symbol of England's cultural identity as it entered into the age of its greatest imperialist expansion and the apotheosis of the private individual's social identity and freedom. Moreover, by imagining the social world via the metaphor of domestic affection, Burke conflates the affective language of the intimate and domestic spheres with the practical and political language of the public sphere.

Of particular interest is the way that the domestic affection metaphor allows Burke to deploy the concept of terror itself. He depicts the terror in France as the inevitable result of barbarous ideologues-cum-"sophisters" who desire liberty over the affectionate and "chivalrous" familial system (66). In one of the most famous passages in the book, he characterizes terrorists as those who violate the hierarchy of affection so that "a King is but a man, a queen is but a woman; a woman but an animal, and an animal not of the highest order" (67). The patriarchal family hierarchy becomes the first and last victim of terror. Burke's arguments appear animated by the deep-seated fear that "private interests" will become the sole arbiters of "the Law" and that the solid, foundational affection for that larger family constituted by the nation will simply melt into air (68). Of course, this is a two-way street for the extraordinarily canny Burke, and as he had already claimed in his 1765 "Tract on the Popery Laws," and in his many letters opposing the Penal Laws in Ireland, bad governors invariably leave their citizen-families "justly discontented" (226). Burke recognizes the potential feeling of dispossession that comes with the patriarchal metaphor. He seeks to mitigate this feeling with a narrative of domestic affection that balances sublime masculine authority—the awesome responsibility and tradition of the patriarch—with the sincere feminine beauty imagined by the marriage metaphor. "To make us love our country," he goes on to explain, "our country ought to be lovely" (68).

Interestingly enough, in his 1807 *Memoirs,* the exiled United Irishman William Sampson offers a text, remarkably Gothic in its own right, that deploys the concept of terror in a manner that, at first glance, seems directly opposed to Burke's. For Sampson, those who seek liberty are certainly not terrorists. Rather, it is the English tyrants who not only resemble the terrorists of France, but actually out-Herod the French by executing the clergy and making the violation of "female chastity" a technique for controlling the rebellious population (162–3). Martin Burke claims that Sampson was among the first of the United Irishmen to imagine the rhetorical power that came from associating with "the vanquished, not the victors" (305). By comparing the 1793–1794 excesses of the French revolutionaries to the excesses perpetrated by the British government in Ireland in 1797 and 1798, Sampson deploys the rhetoric of the victimized in order to make a larger point about justice and equity.[17] As Sampson explains, when the British crushed the Rebellion and then policed the countryside with the Committee for Public Safety, the clergy were summarily put to death and women were regularly violated. In such a narrative, as Sampson seems to suggest, the Irish appear as a people for whom the ancient proverb "we are born to suffer" was written (162). Where Burke had opposed the concept of familial affection to terror in order to help craft and sustain the English system, Sampson evokes affection for the victimized in order to inveigh against an English system that is itself a form of terror. Although Burke remains more subtle in his approach, both men enact the binary of victim versus victimizer, and each characterizes his own side as the victim in need of justice. For Burke, the site of the greatest terror is the violation of Marie Antoinette. As Burke sets the scene, the queen is awakened from her bed by "a sentinel at the door, who cried out to save herself by flight" (62). As she flees, Burke tells us that "a band of ruffians and assassins, reeking with blood, rushed into the chamber of the queen pierced with a hundred strokes of bayonets and poniards the bed, from whence this persecuted woman had but just time to fly almost naked" (62). Without the shelter of a devoted and powerful patriarchal authority, the queen succumbs to the anarchic masses.

For Sampson, the great terror is the anonymous, government-sanctioned violation of female chastity. "I could never hear," Sampson explains, "that the most brutal of all ferocity, the forcible violation of female chastity, had made part of the system of terror in France; that it did in Ireland is too deplorably true" (163). In terms that almost seemed derived from the language, plot, and logic of an eighteenth-century Gothic romance, each side defines the binary in terms of lustful masculine aggression against virtuous feminine vulnerability. Both Burke and

Sampson finally depend on the idea that a benevolent patriarchal order would protect women and uphold justice. In articulating this gendered political logic, however, both men unwittingly underscore the dichotomous structure of post-1789 political terror as well. We have Burke's terror driven by the desiring masses confronting Sampson's terror driven by the desiring conqueror. Terror from below collides with terror from above. In each case, however, the feminized and victimized side also claims to be the more just. From a historical perspective the identity "terrorizer" or, if you will "terrorist," seems evacuated of any substantial meaning almost from the moment of its first invocation. By acting as the eternal other of one's own political cause, "terror" plays the simple and equivocal role of label in the modern political and social rhetoric of legitimation. In terms of British social doctrine, anyone called terrorist is always already an illegitimate political entity. More importantly, both political legitimacy and authentic fear reside with the position identified as feminine and threatened.

A confused and troubled dichotomy of terrorizer and terrorized, underwritten by a dialectical structure of desire, will appear again and again in the political disputes and cultural products of nineteenth- and twentieth-century Ireland. As the legal fallout from the Coercion Bills enacted by Parliament between 1795 and 1798 makes abundantly clear, the courts themselves were preoccupied with the idea of political terror, as nearly one-seventh of all prosecutions in Ireland were for political crimes such as conspiracy, oath taking, or assassination.[18] Throughout the nineteenth century, the disenfranchised Gaelo-Catholics will see themselves as the victims of the usurping, tyrannical Anglo-Irish, and the Anglo-Irish will see themselves as victims of barbaric Gaelo-Catholic agrarian violence and terrorism. Continually reconstructed versions of Defenderism and Whiteboyism will confront recalcitrant Orangemen while each side claims to be the victim in search of justice and social order. Both the Gaelo-Catholic and the Anglo-Irish become accused of and caught up in the double bind provoked by terrorism. The dynamic seems driven by what we might call the logic of the justified victim. Each side identifies itself always and only as terrorized in order to justify its own occasional terrorism

In his 1887 work *Zur Genealogie der Moral* [*On the Genealogy of Morality*], Friedrich Nietzsche provides us with a term that might help to elaborate on this logic. Nietzsche suggests that those seeking to discover how the contemporary logic of moral justice works might look into the concept of ressentiment. In the "Second Treatise" of his *Genealogy,* he goes on to define ressentiment as the hallowing of "revenge under the name of justice—as if justice were basically only a further development of the feeling of being wounded—and retroactively to raise to honor along with revenge the *reactive* affects in general and without exception" (48). For Nietzsche, ressentiment comes from the spirit of *reactive* consciousness, or, that is, from a consciousness incapable of acting on its own and defining itself, a consciousness predicated on its own fear, resentment, and envy of the other. From the foundation of ressentiment grows a whole societal structure based on the repression of difference, the principle that Nietzsche sees as "*hostile to life,* a destroyer and dissolver" (50). The cycle triggered by ressentiment can be endless and destructive. Nietzsche's ingeniously counterintuitive solution to this problem does not seek to do away with violent or bellicose action itself but, rather, to do away with the resentful weakness—the logic of the justified victim—that triggers it, for this logic is the real enemy of peace and justice. In the Irish context in particular, the apparently endless cycle of ressentiment, of reconstructed Defenderism and recalcitrant Orangemen, exposes as it replays the terrorist/terrorized binary that has remained central to the development and logic of the imperialist and neo-imperialist nation-state in modernity.

Following Burke's death in 1797 and the Rebellion led by the United Irishmen in 1798, the language of "domestic affection" and its subsequent marriage metaphor come to dominate the discourse of union in both Ireland and England. The opposing sides deploy the same language to differing ends. Hence, as the British viceroy's speech attests, the union figured as kind of a heterosexual marriage in which an English patriarch would and could care for its feminine sister kingdom. In collecting and describing many of the journalistic references to the union-as-marriage, Jane Elizabeth Dougherty indicates that the marriage metaphor was unequivocally a heterosexual one because it predicated itself upon fundamental gender distinctions that "denied and reified difference" as it promised the Irish "protection and legitimacy" (203). For scholars working in the academy today, particularly after the advent of Frantz Fanon, Edward Said, and postcolonial criticism, the feminization of a colonized people appears to be a standard component of imperial and capitalist assimilation strategy. But in the case of Ireland, as this phantasmatic ideology became a constitutive part of the political and social landscape and the proposed Union continued to be depicted as a marriage by both supporters and detractors, Irish intellectuals in each camp assented to and worked within the boundaries of this gendered logic in order to legitimate their respective causes. Both sides deployed the gendered marriage metaphor in order to justify the idea of civil union over and against the concept of inherent difference that marked much of the British and French rhetoric of colonization in places like India and Africa. The theory of alterity that underwrites the Irish colonial experience, then, relies more often on a Burkean notion of natural, domestic affection than it does on the assimilative discourse of civilization. As with Burke's notion of domestic affection, the marriage metaphor works to mitigate the sense of structural dispossession experienced by the colonized people.

During the Union debates in Parliament, Richard Brinsley Sheridan, himself a staunch antiunionist and a member of the Anglo-Irish Protestant ascendancy, decried the idea of dissolving Ireland's parliament and remonstrated that any "union" of the two kingdoms

> must not resemble those Irish Marriages which commence in fraud, and are consummated by force. Let us not commit a brutal rape on the independence of Ireland, when by tenderness of behavior we may have her the willing partner of our fate. The state of Ireland does not admit such a marriage; her bans ought not to be published to the sound of the trumpet, with an army of 40,000 men.[19]

Likewise, among the many political caricatures of the Union, one entitled "Carrying the Union," published in March 1800 by W. Holland, depicts William Pitt and Clare astride British lions as they carry off an unwilling, fainting Lady Erin while St. Patrick, John Foster, and Henry Grattan pursue them on Irish bulls.[20] Other pamphlets and political cartoons, published primarily in the Dublin papers and pamphlets of the time, depict the marriage as a rape or a murder or both.[21] The point of all of this, then, is not simply to restate the fact that representations of Ireland encoded the nation as the feminine sister kingdom and sometime wife to the British imperial husband, but rather that in the popular consciousness and in the literary imagination of the late eighteenth and early nineteenth centuries, the Union took on the character of a Gothic marriage. Ireland was continually characterized as the confined, threatened, terrorized female and England became—sometimes only potentially—her terrorizing, avaricious, and lustful captor-suitor. Encoded in these rather Gothic representations of the Union, we find the unconcealed fears and anxieties of a people whom Burke would doubtless see as "justly discontented" not only because their lands had been colonized by a British patriarch, but more precisely because they were imprisoned within the bonds of an unhappy domestic union with a failed, undeserving, and unwanted patriarch. From the perspective of an Irish political unconscious, the Gothic is born where the domestic-affection metaphor miscarries.

V. THE FEMALE GOTHIC, ALLEGORY, AND STRUCTURAL DISPOSSESSION

As I have already explained, the central claim of this book is that the generic boundaries of Irish Gothic fiction, and subsequently the entire genealogy of the canonical Irish modernist novel, should be redrawn around the central trope of the Gothic marriage. This new genealogy allows us to read the novels of Maturin, Joseph Sheridan Le Fanu, Oscar Wilde, Bram Stoker, James Joyce, and Samuel Beckett as working within, responding to, or extending Ireland's tradition of Gothic fiction. The most overt objection to this argument seems fairly clear. These writers are all male, and the literary features of the Gothic marriage derive from the subgenre of fiction that Ellen Moers dubbed the "Female Gothic," in order to classify those novels, written by women such as Anne Radcliffe and Charlotte Brontë, that thematize female confinement (90). But precisely because of the gendered logic of the Gothic marriage, Irish Gothic novels rework, reimagine, and blur the normal generic categories of the English Gothic tradition

The female Gothic remains a much-discussed and singular phenomenon in English literary history in no small part because it names the first novelistic form written by, for, and about women, with Radcliffe as the maternal *Arche* of this remarkably popular genre. As the typical Radcliffean female-Gothic story goes, a young, virtuous woman, either orphaned or, through meticulous and deliberate maneuvering, removed from the care of her particular friends, finds herself incarcerated in a castle, abbey, or monastery under the auspices of some "dark" nobleman, usually an Italian count, almost always a Roman Catholic. The logic of the narrative generally devolves upon this feudal patriarch, as he lays out an invidious plan to take the virtue and the ancestral lands of the heroine, to possess her—in every sense of the phrase—by guile, will, and, when necessary, violence.[22] And as I've already noted, a contemporary review of the genre, published in 1797 in the *Spirit of Public Journals,* calls Radcliffe's style "Terrorist" because it "makes us fall in love with what we fear to look on" (323). Hence, in a decade where the term terror was inextricably linked to events in France, the female Gothic becomes the novelistic subgenre that exploits terror by invoking a sadomasochistic structure of desire. In these sadomasochistically structured fictions, the desired objects not only manifest themselves as terrors to look upon, which would make them frightening enough, but they also invariably implicate their readers in both poles of the terrorist/terrorized dichotomy. If the kind of "terrorist" fiction written by the eighteenth- and nineteenth-century Gothic novelists manipulates the reader's identification with fictive characters, the narrative desire for conflict that underscores these fictions also imagines a doubled reader who must rely on identification with both the terrorized and the terrorist in order to experience the full thrill provided by the genre. The novels work at once to reproduce and to negate the dialectical logic of desire that underwrites the terrorist/terrorized double bind. Hence, they also provide us with a space to rethink the social, political, and historical problematics that attend this double bind. For the reader, the experience provided by the genre in some sense confirms Burke's fear that the pursuit of those beautiful liberties we so desire leads ineluctably and directly to excess and terror. In the elliptical logic followed by these novels, autonomy and liberty nearly always lead to vulnerability, violence, and excess. What's more, the reader must desire all of these conflicted experiences at once merely in order to finish reading a female Gothic novel.

The failed unions and marriages depicted in the female Gothic are always rather brutal and sensational affairs whose bans, to borrow Sheridan's terminology, are published by force, and the female Gothic itself reads as a double for the British model of domesticity that had grown out of the capitalist ideology of the private sphere. Of course, when we begin surveying the prose fictions of this period from the standpoint of Nancy Armstrong's assertions about the ideological structure of the British private sphere and the rise of the figure of the "domestic woman," we see in late eighteenth- and early nineteenth-century British fiction the groundwork for the construction of a new kind of woman.[23] We also become privy to the architecture of a modern bourgeois consciousness built upon the desire for domesticity and for the hearth rather than upon something as abstract as the individual's civil rights or as uncontrollable as regional, communal, or sectarian loyalty. In modernity, domesticity comes to serve as a central, foundational, and unifying metaphor for Great Britain's various ideological and colonial apparatuses. The autonomy promised by the separate spheres was, of course, only promised to men and corresponded to the ownership of private property.[24] At best, the domestic branch of the private sphere promised a kind of safe haven for the woman of the eighteenth century, but, as Kate Ferguson Ellis indicates in *The Contested Castle,* the Gothic novel, the most popular literary material for the woman reader of the period, also performed the paradoxical cultural work of embodying a "resistance to an ideology that imprisons [women] even as it posits a sphere of safety for them" (x). In the Gothic's more nuanced and reflective texts, like *Jane Eyre* or *Wide Sargasso Sea,* the female-confinement narrative unites an anxiety concerning the boundaries that demarcate Great Britain as a civilizing empire to the identifying mechanism that gender plays within the discourse of that civilization. Where English manhood becomes the mode of civilized subjectivity to be emulated, womanhood is coded as partial and often dangerously erratic. In the most overt sense, by structuring the boundaries of women's sexuality, confining it to the compulsorily maternal, heterosexual, corporeal, and vulnerable, these novels shore up the goals of English patriarchy and the burgeoning institutions of the bourgeois public sphere. Hence, the taking of the young woman's body in the novels is naturally mirrored by the taking of the property entailed to her. Both in the strict legal sense and in the social economy of desire imagined by Gothic novels, women figure as objects possessed, never as subjects allowed self-possession. And in the vast majority of these texts, anxiety concerning land-ownership resolves in the birth of an acknowledgeable male heir who must be allowed to inherit the ancestral land and, if only figuratively, to repossess the body of the mother.

The female Gothic, thusly, deals more directly with the problem of structural dispossession than any other form of domestic fiction. The male heir whose birth signifies a repossession of the land and of the mother's figural body appears, at least at first, as a kind of hybrid who embodies the union of masculine rational authority and feminine corporeal reproduction. The heir connects Burke's sublime masculine authority to the potentially dispossessed maternal line. But the novels themselves remain far more emphatic about patrilineal succession and about what Burke called the "awful gravity" and authority that this line of succession comes to signify. From the male heirs in Radcliffe's novels through to the multiply named male child of Jonathan Harker and Mina Murray in Stoker's *Dracula,* the masculine inheritor always points to the desire to ameliorate the structural dispossession that attends woman's position as object in the marriage contract. At the same time, even when we read him as a symbol of hybridity, the male heir reasserts precisely the male/female binary that his presence intends to smooth over. The Gothic male heir does not dispel fear so much as he signifies its shivering, uneasy presence beneath the deceptively placid surface of bourgeois domestic propriety. With the birth of the heir, the system might appear to have solved a problem, but in point of fact it has merely reaffirmed its initial social schema and returned to something resembling a status quo or, that is, to what a Hegelian-Marxist philosopher like Theodor Adorno would call the bourgeois ever-same.

By imagining its Emily St. Auberts and Mina Harkers as potential victims who fret over their respective positions within the private and intimate spheres, the Gothic novel obsesses about and worries over the cultural and social implications of structural dispossession in a more overt way than any other genre of fiction from the period. In so doing, the Gothic also allegorizes a historical problem, an anxiety concerning woman's confinement within the intimate and private spheres. It seems like no mere accident, then, that a revision of the female Gothic that represents the entire population of Ireland—male and female—as vulnerable, feminine, and other was also one of the most popular forms of nineteenth-century Irish fiction. The issue of structural dispossession lies at the heart of the domestic-affection metaphor, and in an admittedly shadowy, unsteady, and unsure way, the female Gothic points to the failings of domesticity as a model for understanding political authority. Moreover, when we read feminine confinement itself as a negative allegory of the autonomy promised by the notion of a private sphere, then we see dialectically enfolded into the female Gothic the social failings of the capitalist construction of the private individual. The promised autonomy experienced by the Gothic heroine is always already a form of enforced confinement rather than of liberation, and the sovereignty promised by privacy is paid for in the currency of quietism and social isolation. Simply put, then, the female-Gothic romance's favorite generic trope of female confinement constitutes the dark double of the nascent ideology of the domestic sphere, and, as we've already seen, as the "terrorist" genre, the female Gothic also invariably stages the terrorist/terrorized double bind by implicating its readers in a sadomasochistic structure of tabooed desire. In other words, the female Gothic allegorizes the historical problems faced by women at the closing of the eighteenth century and the dawning of the age of colonial expansion.

In his various discussions of allegory in *Ursprung des deutschen Trauerspiel* [*Origin of the German Mourning Play*], Walter Benjamin indicates that allegory itself often appears worn out, vulgar, and simplistic (175). After all, as a mode of literary representation, allegory constitutes an extended metaphor that allows for a character or object to represent a virtually unrepresentable idea.[25] A literary technique that intends to embody in a single character, object, or event a complex, historical phenomenon is bound to be reductive. The shape of Benjamin's intellectual career indicates, however, that by observing precisely the unpoetic and reductive elements of allegory, we may come to recognize the limits of human sense making. From a certain perspective, allegory reflects how artistic consciousness struggles to sum up a world, and in doing so, any given allegory reveals to us the failings and the transience of the material world from which it springs. Benjamin sums this all up by claiming, "Allegories are in the realm of thoughts, what ruins are in the realm of things" (178). If we can begin to read the female Gothic and its Irish equivalent as an allegory—a ruin—that attempts to summarize and criticize a historical phenomenon, then we can come to a better understanding of that phenomenon while also observing the Gothic's own limitations and reductive maneuvers.

Following Ellen Moers's lead, literary critics from Sandra Gilbert and Susan Gubar to Eve Kosofsky Sedgwick set the Radcliffean or female Gothic in opposition to a "male Gothic," written by men like Horace Walpole, Matthew "Monk" Lewis, and William Beckford, and predicated on dramatic Oedipal conflict and the dynamics of concealed homoerotic desire. Where female characters remain confined within the home, their male counterparts are expelled from it. These novels often read as anxious homosocial adventure stories about exiled characters, such as Don Raymond and the Wandering Jew of Lewis's *The Monk,* who traverse an inferno of loss and desire in an attempt to recover their usurped and discrete positions within a restored social order. Though the formal distinction between a male and a female Gothic might appear at first glance to be grounded in the logic of essential gender difference, Robert Miles indicates that critical studies of the Gothic complicate the basic male/female split to considerable effect, and it is easy to see that in the wake of the kind of queer theory pioneered by Sedgwick the division can become a supple dialectical tool for interrogating the ontological status attributed to gender difference in the first place.[26]

The metaphor of the Union as marriage brings into relief a certain genus of gender confusion. To some extent, the Unionist Gothic merely provided another embodiment of the problem that had marked Irish masculinity at least since Spenser's "A View of the Present State of Ireland." The unhappy Union allowed for yet another allegory in which Irish masculinity seemed both deeply savage and strangely feminine. The Union did not cause so much as it embodied and gave a powerful allegorical narrative to the condition of Irish masculinity in modernity. Following the dichotomous logic unfolded by Burke and Sampson, and embodied by Wilde as Sebastian Melmoth, the male protagonist in the Irish Gothic becomes both the threat and the threatened. As I said earlier, Sebastian Melmoth could be both the confined heroine and the terrorizing villain of a Gothic novel. The emphasis on an Ireland as ravished and confined female, an emphasis that we find not only in the words of Sheridan and in the political caricatures and cartoons of the time but also encoded in the political unconscious of Irish literature, certainly reflects the cultural strictures placed upon woman's self-possession. But this emphasis also underscores the Irish male's double affiliation to femininity.

Like the confined female of the Gothic, the Irish male is comprehended as an object to be transformed into an authentic subject through the contrivances of a British patriarchal order. The Irish male, like the Gothic female, must confront the issue of structural dispossession signified by this hierarchy. As a rule, Irish Gothic novels like Maturin's *Fatal Revenge* (1807) and Stoker's *Dracula* (1897) fear that systematic identification—and its affiliation of masculine figures with dispossessed and confined females—will result in a social world that can never accommodate a masculinity so ambivalently gendered. In the end, in fact, many of the male characters in the Irish Gothic novel find themselves cut off not only from the public sphere, but also from history itself. For instance, like many of the Gothic writers who came before him, Maturin wrote novels that remain eternally haunted by the specter of male usurpation. In *Melmoth the Wanderer* and *Fatal Revenge,* male characters who fear invasion, confinement, and the loss of personal autonomy always seem to believe that an appropriately patrilineal model of succession could fix their various social worlds, no matter how chaotic or supernatural those worlds might appear. But these male figures, particularly Annibal and Ippolito di Montorio of *Fatal Revenge,* can never look backward to ancestry nor forward to posterity because they can never really identify a true father nor produce true offspring. Domestic affection has abandoned them. They are both figurally and literally dispossessed by the social logic depicted in the novel. Unable to identify an appropriate patriarch until it is too late, the Montorios become incapable of situating themselves in any historical or linear narrative of inheritance. The novel's anxiety nearly always revolves around the male privileges that Annibal and Ippolito, continually confined in castles and monasteries, can never seem to claim as their own. Finally, they end up dispossessed of both land and autonomy and can see no way to ameliorate the situation. Their story concludes with bloodshed and with the deaths of two potential fathers. The novel ends with the family name of Montorio being "extinguished for ever" by legal decree as the Montorio lands devolve upon a shadowy, unknown state (3:487).

In much of the subsequent nineteenth- and twentieth-century Irish literature, an embattled and contained feminine identity becomes both the arch-figure for justice and the trigger for a corresponding and subsequent masculine identification with violence. The theme of structural dispossession that attends the Irish Gothic and the subsequent double bind concerning confinement and femininity reappears in a more nuanced form in modern Irish fiction. In the opening pages of *Ulysses,* we discover that Stephen Dedalus fears being feminized at the same time that he angrily labels Buck Mulligan a usurper. If a patriarchal masculinity becomes the exemplar for authentic autonomy, then reclaiming and reasserting the violence of phallic logic in order to attain autonomy is the response of a beleaguered and perpetually transgendered Irish masculinity. We see what might be the apotheosis of this logic in W. B. Yeats's 1902 play, *Cathleen Ni Hoolihan,* which represents a ravaged Mother Ireland whose mere identity draws her sons into the cycle of violence initiated in 1798. In the Gothic tradition, male characters identify with the confined female or mother as they also fear the loss of autonomy that corresponds with this identification. The genre itself subsists on this tension. In the Irish Gothic, then, the logic of the justified victim confronts its own ambivalence and ressentiment. Post-1798 Gaelo-Catholic identity always appears to suffer under the weight of this logic, but the enclosed and isolated big houses of the ascendancy class also appear as dark doubles for the domestic "safe haven" of British bourgeois isolation. As a result of this initial gender double bind, the Irish Gothic writing that I will discuss, though often replete with homoerotic and Oedipal dilemmas, mimics the tropological structure of its supposed other, the female Gothic, the terrorist genre about terrorized women. The genre itself becomes a space in which the Irish cultural imaginary pits the dichotomous logic of terror against the troubles provoked by the unhappy Union. A careful reading of the genre should help us to unearth and interrogate the structuring logic of this double bind while also allowing us to see its dialectical revision in the Irish modernist novels of Wilde, Joyce, and Beckett. Moreover, we will come to see that what Seamus Deane has referred to as Irish modernism's "aesthetic of privacy" actually constitutes a modernist response to Ireland's Gothic political unconscious.

Throughout, I will read the modernist figures who comprise the heart of this study via the logic of the Hegelian dialectic. In effect, Wilde's translation, through the figure of the aesthete, of the weakness of the Gothic hero into a new source of strength will come to represent the initial modernist stage of the narrative that I've put together here. Wilde's work constitutes a transvaluation of what had been a weakness, an attempt to reimagine a disempowering cultural and literary stereotype as a new mode of empowerment.[27] As a stylistic foray into high-modernist utopianism, Joyce's *Ulysses* effects a "negation" of Wilde's decision to work within the confines of generic conventions. Joyce's text, instead, affirms a new open-ended way of staging our relationship to the past, modeled, as we will come to see, on a Jewish tradition of hermeneutics. Beckett's major fictions will conclude this dialectic, offering a "negation of negation," a body of work that demonstrates how limiting, how structurally dependent, and how similar the identities of victimizer and victimized have become in modernity.

The second chapter of this book, "The Wrong Marriage: Maturin and the Double Logic of Masculinity in the Unionist Gothic," revolves around a reading of Maturin's seldom-discussed 1807 novel, *The Fatal Revenge, Or, The Family Montorio,* and details the political and cultural history of the Unionist Gothic from its beginnings in the novels of Maria Edgeworth through to its death throes in the writings of Le Fanu. Each of the subsequent chapters demonstrates how an Irish modernist writer appropriates the Gothic tropes concerning gender and confinement initiated by the Unionist Gothic in order to comment on the political and social problems that circumscribed Irish identity in the late nineteenth and early twentieth centuries.

The third chapter, "The Revolution Within: Wilde and the Confines of Convention," argues that the gender-disoriented confinement narrative that defined the Unionist Gothic is finally thematized in a most overt sense by Bram Stoker's *Dracula* and transformed into a proto-modernist theory of autonomous art in the life and work of Oscar Wilde. In their most famous prose fictions, both Stoker and Wilde connect issues of confinement to masculine identity. Through the Jonathan Harker narrative that begins *Dracula,* Stoker fuses the colonial adventure tale and the female-Gothic story. Stoker converts the feminine confinement narrative into a gendered and colonial one where a male hero finds himself in danger of being incarcerated and penetrated by a non-European other. Wilde's *Picture of Dorian Gray* borrows a great deal of its elliptical structure and manic imagery from *Melmoth the Wanderer* while also managing to follow Le Fanu's lead by embodying in the single character of Dorian both the satanic terrorist and the languid, feminized figure. Wilde finally transforms the structure of the female-confinement narrative into a decadent meditation on the freedoms provided by the artist's autonomy. For Wilde, acknowledging the confines of social and artistic convention ultimately allows the canny artist to work within and to frustrate conventionality itself.

Chapter 4, "Overcoming Allegory: Joyce's *Ulysses* and the Limits of the Irish Gothic," reads Joyce's most famous text as the premier mock-Gothic novel since Jane Austen's *Northanger Abbey.* By reading Stephen Dedalus and Leopold Bloom as figures culled from the Gothic tradition, I place Joyce alongside such writers as Anne Radcliffe, Maturin, Le Fanu, and Wilde. Stephen's patriarchal theory of artistic patrimony, which draws on Wildean aestheticism, betrays his unspeakable fear of identifying with the maternal and the cloistered. Like the captive woman of the female Gothic and the gender-disoriented man of the Anglo-Irish Gothic, Stephen appears deeply anxious about his relationship to the maternal, his perceived femininity, and his various confinements. Joyce deploys many of the tropes that the Unionist-Gothic writers had used to allegorize colonial politics, but in placing Stephen and Bloom side by side in *Ulysses,* he also takes great care to reveal the sectarian and patriarchal biases that underwrite and constrain the usefulness of these tropes.[28] Joyce presents us with a form of writing that brings together oppositions, a form that realizes and overcomes the Gothic allegory of dispossession represented in the works of the Unionist-Gothic writers. Finally, Joyce, a Gaelo-Catholic writer who remains at once inside and outside of the Anglo-Irish Gothic tradition he invokes, acts as the primary parodist and critic of that very tradition.

The final chapter, "Engendering a Cartesian Gothic: Generic Form as History in Beckett's Fiction," argues that Samuel Beckett's terse, caustic prose extends and ultimately annuls the Irish Gothic tradition. Despite the impact of such studies as Seamus Deane's *Celtic Revivals,* David Lloyd's *Anomalous States,* John Harrington's *The Irish Beckett,* and Eoin O'Brien's *The Beckett Country,* Beckett's texts are less often seen as exemplars of postcolonial writing than as versions of the metaphysical questions central to Western thought.[29] The fact that Beckett's writing struggles to show how these questions get grafted onto a social world populated by characters with names like Malone and Murphy, characters who continually complain about "the Island," and who, like many twentieth-century Irish political prisoners, often starve in solitary confinement, appears to be beside the point for most critics. Yet when we read Beckett's writing together with the genealogy of the Irish Gothic, we see how *Murphy, First Love,* and the *Trilogy* meditate on how the male figures who reside on "the Island" become identified as subjects homologous to the confined female of the Gothic. Finally, however, Beckett's work disavows the distinctions between terrorist and terrorized that characterized the Irish Gothic tradition. Where the Unionist Gothic had always attempted to clarify these two poles in order to articulate what an appropriately domestic political system might look like, Beckett depicts the poles as irremediably intertwined. In the end Beckett inverts the typical gendered hierarchy of Western and Cartesian dualist thinking by imagining a feminized corporeality as the universal category and masculine rationality as its failed other. What I will come to call Beckett's "Cartesian Gothic" actually constitutes an afterword to the Irish Gothic tradition. A rereading of Beckett that foregrounds his appropriations of the Ireland's Gothic political unconscious allows us to set the gendered and the postcolonial features concealed in his fiction at the center of twenty-first-century Beckett studies. We end up with an Irish Beckett whose nuanced, disciplined, literary rethinking of both the universal and the particular problems provoked by modernity has a singularly Gothic character.

As the specter of terror continues to haunt our political and social worlds, the double logic that plays out in the Irish Gothic, a logic that fears and fetishizes any identification with a feminized victim, continues to motivate our responses to the problem of terror. In a brief epilogue to *Terror and Irish Modernism,* I consider how the self-contradictory logic of the Irish Gothic speaks to our contemporary concerns about terrorism and its effect on culture.

CHAPTER 2

The Wrong Marriage

Maturin and the Double Logic of Masculinity in the Unionist Gothic

EDGEWORTH AND THE PREHISTORY OF THE UNIONIST GOTHIC

A rather persistent dilemma complicates many of the interpretations of *Castle Rackrent* (1800), Maria Edgeworth's Arch-Anglo-Irish big-house novel. Is Thady Quirk, the novel's Catholic Irish narrator, a "disingenuous" manipulator of the Anglo-Irish ascendancy he seems to serve, or is he a "transparent," good-natured follower who earnestly bemoans the disintegration of the family whose story he tells?[1] Although, as Mary Corbett indicates in *Allegories of Union in Irish and English Writing, 1790–1870,* the moment when Thady's son, Jason, assumes the Rackrent estate may be read as both a "return of the Gaelic repressed" and as Edgeworth's prescient analysis of the rise of a Catholic Irish bourgeoisie, few critics have been able to come to any satisfactory conclusion about the veracity of Thady's narrative voice (49). After all, while he certainly seems to identify his emotional and financial welfare with that of the Rackrent family and its storied nobility, Thady also seems inventive enough and subtle enough to play at being the "old family retainer," all the while promoting the interests of his son Jason and influencing the dissipated Sir Condy by misdirection and false loyalty. In some sense, the narrative's tension revolves around the ambiguity of Thady's identity and, subsequently, Sir Condy's.

Thady's contradictory loyalties serve as a starting place for discussions of the anxieties that inhere in the Anglo-Irish literary imagination following the 1798 rebellion and the era that followed the 1800 Acts of Union. The Union guaranteed the estates of the Protestant ascendancy only as it eliminated the Irish Parliament and consolidated the lands of the British imperial state. Catholic Ireland found itself completely disenfranchised, but the Anglo-Irish ascendancy, once identified as the colonizers, found themselves shut up in their own estates, incapable of running the affairs of their supposed homeland, and, in some strange way, converted into a simulacrum of the colonized. Having arrived in Ireland under the auspices of Cromwell's military incursion in 1649 and the Williamite confiscations of the 1690s, the Anglo-Irish now appeared either as absentee landlords or as a decaying class, enclosed within the confines of their own domestic spheres. *Castle Rackrent* lays out absenteeism, extortionate renting (rackrenting), and sectarian divisiveness as the animating but contradictory forces of late–eighteenth- and early nineteenth-century Irish culture and politics. The novel presents us with the collision of a set of Anglo-Irish landlords who often blithely live elsewhere and overcharge their tenants and a Catholic peasant class who appear stigmatized for their religious practices and driven to anger and civil unrest by material deprivation. As Edgeworth's novel depicts the collapse of a landlord class that has failed to retain any semblance of its noble heritage, however, it also portrays the rise of a coterie of unethical capitalists who are motivated by little more than their insatiable desire for money and property. Neither side seems to be a particularly attractive one, in other words, and as the novel concludes, we see Thady's once disenfranchised heirs change places with the Rackrent family. Sir Condy lives out the remainder of his short life confined to Thady's old shack, as Jason takes over the Rackrent estate. The novel's antagonist seems to have confined and effectively neutered the once powerful—if irresponsible—landlord. This capacity of the supposed antagonist and the would-be protagonist to change places, of one identity to transform into its other, marks both Edgeworth's key insight into the problem of Irish colonialism and one of her singular contributions to the fiction of the Irish literary tradition.

Literary critics and historians tend to figure Edgeworth's *Castle Rackrent* as an archetype for the kind of Anglo-Irish Gothic fiction that would come to be written later in the century by Charles Robert Maturin and Joseph Sheridan Le Fanu.[2] Though, generally speaking, Edgeworth's book stands before and outside of the Irish Gothic tradition proper, we can have little doubt that the formal tropology of the big-house story and the regionalist typology established in *Rackrent* act as literary antecedents for the Anglo-Irish Unionist Gothic's obsessive guilt-ridden ruminations on landlordism, its troubled representations of class, sectarian, and—eventually—racial difference, and its compulsive dread of the claustral. But the critical literature tends to overlook precisely how this literary language becomes complicated and inflected, however subtly, by the gender anxieties of the female Gothic tradition. In fact, when we borrow the language of the female Gothic romance to read Thady's ambiguous narrative voice, the problem for the post-1798 Anglo-Irish imagination transforms into one of determining precisely who is the masculine usurper and who is the confined female, or, that is, who ends up as the "terrorizer" and who as the "terrorized." In Edgeworth's novel we witness the moment in which a rising capitalism and a declining feudal aristocracy stand face-to-face. Has Thady's family, through misdirection and manipulation, imprisoned Sir Condy, or does Sir Condy's family remain culpable for the Cromwellian invasion, for the Williamite confiscations, and for provoking the various uprisings that followed? Who is confined and who confines? Moreover, can any palliative be discovered for the polemical identities engendered by the politics of a colonized Ireland? At first glance, the identities of colonizer and colonized that mark the discourse of Irish politics appear to line up in neat, parallel categories where the colonizer fills the role of the masculine usurper who confines the feminized usurped, but, as we see quite clearly in *Castle Rackrent,* the relationships can very quickly be imagined in reverse, and the masculine usurper can be converted into the feminized usurped in the mere turn of a page.[3] Edgeworth's novel seems, then, to speak of ambiguity, or, rather, of the inability to determine who violates and who has been violated that marks much of the post-1798 Anglo-Irish literary tradition. In her brief editor's afterword to *Castle Rackrent*, Edgeworth gives us another instance of this ambiguity when she asserts that "it is a problem of difficult solution to determine whether an Union will hasten or retard the amelioration of this country" (97). Finally, critical interpretations that work to situate Thady as either "transparent" and willfully usurped or "disingenuous" and willfully usurping miss the mark because the anxiety that underwrites the big-house and Gothic traditions that follow from Edgeworth's book always appears characterized by the irreducible doubleness of these Irish identities. The terrorizer nearly always seems to transform into the terrorized and, likewise, the terrorized into the terrorizer.

Maturin acts as one of the first writers in Ireland to suture the sociopolitical concerns that suffuse Edgeworth's novel to the manic suspicions of the English Gothic tradition that begins with Horace Walpole's *Castle of Otranto* (1764). That tradition finds its most noteworthy female avatar in Anne Radcliffe's *The Mysteries of Udolpho* (1794) and its male equivalent in Matthew Lewis's *The Monk* (1796). With Edgeworth the regional novel had come into being, and with Radcliffe's female-confinement narratives the Gothic had discovered both its most popular author and its most fashionable form. To some extent, then, Maturin hoped to discover the means to meet both his personal desire and material need for commercial success in the marketability of these two forms. In novels like *Fatal Revenge* and *Melmoth the Wanderer,* and even in a less overtly Gothic text like *The Milesian Chief,* Maturin joins the paranoid proliferations of the Gothic to the regional, political ambiguities that structured both Edgeworth's *Castle Rackrent* and the intellectual discourse surrounding the Acts of Union. The rather byzantine conundrum of ambiguity lies at the very heart of the Gothic genre itself. Unlike those novels from the eighteenth and early nineteenth century that we like to think of as more overtly literary—novels by, say, Henry Fielding, Laurence Sterne, Fanny Burney, or Jane Austen—the Gothic attempts to present a social world devoid of moral ambiguity. The villains always appear unrelenting in their villainy and inhumanity, while the heroes always seem to act heroically and on behalf of moral fortitude and civility. But when one deploys the Gothic's moral typology either to resolve or to represent the resolution of historical problems, that typology itself becomes convoluted and overdetermined. The more that the Gothic attempts to disambiguate the morality of the social order, the more it actually reambiguates that very order. We have only to call upon the wretched excesses that mark the climactic attack on the Convent of St. Clare in Lewis's male-Gothic novel, *The Monk,* in order to find an example. The bulk of the novel works to generate a great deal of authentic and unrelenting hatred toward the brutal, abusive behavior of the hypocritical Prioress, but when she is dragged from her monastery, murdered, and mutilated by an angry crowd, she is converted precisely by moral outrage into something that the text describes as even more "unsightly, shapeless, and disgusting" (356). The novel's readers are forced to witness their own moral judgments and desires realized only as those judgments and desires are themselves abased and stigmatized. In a sense, secure moral judgment acts as the Möbius band of the Gothic, the conceptual plane in which morality turns, subtly and imperceptibly, into immorality. In the Gothic, then, moral terror is often compounded by moral error, and moral clarity transforms into moral ambiguity. We might say that the Gothic can suggest a morally ambiguous vision negatively, or, that is, by attempting—and failing—to depict a world circumscribed by clear and unambiguous moral choice. As a literary form, the Gothic's definitions of the just, the right, and the ethical nearly always collapse.

When Maturin fused the complex big-house tropology and regionalist typology of *Rackrent* to the Gothic's schizophrenic moral vision in order to write texts like *Melmoth the Wanderer* and *Fatal Revenge,* he created that hybrid form—the Unionist Gothic—that desperately desires real-world moral clarity and resolution at the level of content as it also denies the very possibility of such cogency or resolve at the level of form. As I said in chapter 1, by Unionist Gothic I mean to signify the embattled era covered by the Acts of Union, the unhappy union-as-marriage metaphor that we examined earlier, and the symptomatic union of male- and female-Gothic forms that Maturin's work will come to exemplify in this chapter. By reading *Fatal Revenge,* the first Gothic novel written by Maturin, a male writer whose texts follow the path cut by Edgeworth's, this chapter will demonstrate and historicize how the doubleness of terrorizer and terrorized, of masculine usurper and feminine usurped manifests itself in the Unionist Gothic as an epistemological sense of gender disorientation, or, we might say, as a double logic through which ostensibly masculine identities are depicted as sliding, by dint of social force, into feminine ones. I'll conclude the chapter by considering how Joseph Sheridan Le Fanu's "Carmilla," the short story that marks the end point of the Unionist Gothic, reformulates this gender disorientation through the figure of an abject maternal identity. The social problem that manifested itself as a gender double bind in Maturin's work becomes sublimated in Le Fanu's as Ireland moved away from the Acts of Union and toward the home rule crisis that would come to dominate Anglo-Irish relations after 1875. As we will see, Le Fanu's "Carmilla" attempts to suggest that the movement toward national coherence and personal autonomy begins by defining a feminine and maternal inheritance as abject, retrogressive, and, finally, vampiric.

II. THINKING THROUGH THE ANTINOMIES OF MATURIN'S LITERARY REPUTATION

Much of the scholarship and criticism concerned with the novels of the Anglo-Irish curate Charles Robert Maturin (1780–1824) appears to agree on three of the central issues that mark him out as one of the major writers in the Gothic tradition. To begin with, though he wrote five novels and three plays, his literary reputation rests solely on *Melmoth the Wanderer* (1820), which critics generally name the "greatest" Gothic novel in English.[4] The scholarship also tends to assert that Maturin's work embodies the English-Romantic ambivalences regarding revolution, particularly when translated into a Catholic or Irish-colonial setting.[5] The final and most illuminating of these issues derives from the fact that as most critics see it, nearly all of Maturin's novels borrow their basic plot and thematic machinery from female-authored models such as Anne Radcliffe's *The Italian,* Lady Morgan's *The Wild Irish Girl,* and Edgeworth's *Belinda.*[6] Hence, the author of the most lauded of Gothic novels was at once deeply troubled by nationalist politics and an appropriator of the female-Gothic form.

If this list identifies Maturin's qualifications as one of the foremost Gothic writers in British literary history, it also points to several of the latent and competing tensions—call them the antinomies—that overwhelm his novels. For instance, *Melmoth* itself has often been described as a "Chinese-box" narrative, a text stitched together by such a precarious stories-within-stories structure that one of Maturin's earliest biographers was led to suggest that the "whole fabric of the work is nothing but a gigantic digression" (Idman, 263). Put another way, we could say that no story begun in *Melmoth* can come to a conclusion without necessitating yet another story. So it may be with Maturin himself. When we read Maturin's work in the context of a more politically astute literary history, one that depicts Maturin's Gothic novels as caught between colonial-nationalist dynamics and the enervating gender troubles that they provoked in the Irish context, then we can reimagine the list of issues surrounding his literary reputation as a series of wholly interdependent questions. This reimagined list of questions asks: If his work remains ambivalent about revolution, why is Maturin generally characterized as Jacobin in politics, and, for that matter, why are his heroes always Byronic and his sympathies always disposed to depicting the plight of the oppressed renegade (Watson, 117)? Why is he regularly read together with Matthew Lewis, Horace Walpole, and William Godwin as part of a generic "male-Gothic" tradition if his forerunners were nearly all female and if, as the preface to *Melmoth* clearly demonstrates, Maturin himself was terribly anxious about, if not embarrassed by, any comparison between his own work and that of the "Radcliffe-Romance" (5)? Finally, how can an only partially unified—if not to say lavishly disintegrated—text like *Melmoth* represent the high-water mark of a genre so obsessively and manipulatively structured? The first two questions situate Maturin and his work at the nexus of Ireland's post-1798 colonial-nationalist and gender-disorientating historical problematics, where the final one interrogates the formal structure of Maturin's writing. In order to see these questions as interdependent, I will read them as addressing a dialectical problem wherein the two historical questions find their synthetic realization in the final question of literary form.

I suggest that we begin to think of Maturin in terms of the unsynthesized sociohistorical antinomies that manifest themselves in the formal features of his various works. In turn, this series of interdependent questions helps us to fabricate a theory for rereading Maturin that takes the convoluted, unstable structure of his prose fiction as a locus of historical tensions and not just as a testament for or against his importance as a literary figure or stylistic innovator. If each of these questions pulls Maturin simultaneously in two opposing directions, if we see him as both a committed Irish nationalist and a guilt-ridden supporter of English rule, as both a writer of fiction in the male-Gothic and in the female-Gothic traditions, and as both the author of the great Gothic novel and of a semicoherent series of anti-Catholic digressions, then perhaps we might begin to think of his Gothic novels as representing the double binds—the incapacitating moments of double logic—that underscore the problem of Anglo-Irish political autonomy in the period following the Acts of Union. Again, we have here a dialectic in which a first set of historical questions is synthesized by a subsequent question of form. As I indicated in chapter 1, by double binds, I mean to point to instances in Irish cultural logic where the normative and ideological conditions for the construction of an identity, such as "masculine," or a concept, such as "nationalism," are materially, psychically, and structurally bipolar and, subsequently, produce social contexts in which definitions are constituted by their own disjunction. If we read Maturin through the lens of the double bind, then he becomes the historical allegorist of the doubly-embodied Unionist Anglo-Irish, a socio-ethnic group that Margot Gayle Backus describes as simultaneously identified with "the colonized and the colonizer" (132). As the Rackrents of Edgeworth's novel come to exemplify, Anglo-Irish identity seems to be constituted by its own disjunction, and post-1798 literary representations of the Anglo-Irish tend to reveal the subtleties, convolutions, and impossible social schemas generated by this bipolar identity. Through this lens, Maturin's decision to publish his first two books under the pseudonym Dennis Jasper Murphy indicates not only a desire to protect his professional persona as an Anglican curate, but also his inability to fully extricate that persona from the Catholic Irish other that it so fervently disavows. We are left, then, with a Maturin who, from the perspective of psychopathological loyalty, cannot really be read as an effective partisan for either the antiUnionist Irish rebels or the Unionist Irish Tories. His novels do not consciously allegorize a position but, rather, embody what we might call symptomatic allegories of a historical condition. This chapter will reinterpret Maturin's Unionist Gothic as the allegorical reflection par excellence of the connected nationalist and gender double binds that underwrite post-1798 Irish cultural politics. Through a reading of Maturin's seldom-discussed first Gothic romance, *The Fatal Revenge; Or, The Family of Montorio,* I'll demonstrate how these double binds are reimagined through the figure of the "wrong marriage" with all of its conflicted social and psychic loyalties.[7] If we begin by reading *Fatal Revenge* as the first embodiment of these double binds, then we should finally be able to return to Maturin's acknowledged masterpiece, *Melmoth the Wanderer,* and read it as a more refined, internalized, and formally complicated version of them. I'll conclude by articulating how the logic of Maturin's "wrong marriage" plot actually works to depict terror, in both its political and literary formulations, as an inevitable result of the gender anxiety that haunts the nineteenth-century Irish imaginary.

III. MATURIN'S GOTHIC UNION

Maturin's entire literary career, dating from the 1807 publication of his first book, *Fatal Revenge,* up to the 1824 publication of his final one, *The Albigenses,* can be framed by the Irish Acts of Union. When

Maturin died in 1824, it would still be four years until Ireland's Catholic leader, Daniel O'Connell, was elected MP of County Clare and five years until O'Connell's Catholic Board helped to achieve Catholic emancipation and to begin anything like an authentic movement for the repeal of the Union. In the era following the passage of the Acts of Union, the Irish Parliament was abolished, and the Union was continually depicted by the popular press as a "marriage" between the English patriarch and his Irish sister. As we've already seen in chapter 1, this marriage was depicted as a heterosexual one that promised to legitimate Ireland's identity as a modernizing country, but the marriage itself was often characterized by the press and in the pamphlets and political ephemera of the day as a potentially violent union, a marriage against instincts, or, that is, as a kind of Gothic marriage through which an English patriarch violated a feminized Ireland in order to possess her land and productive power. As with the wife in the bourgeois private sphere, Ireland was characterized as a nation incapable of achieving coherent sovereignty on its own.[8] Furthermore, neither side challenged the marriage metaphor. Both sides readily accepted the gendered marriage metaphor in order to suggest that a civil union between nations was preferable to the concept of inherent difference that came to characterize the British and French rhetoric of colonization in places like India and Africa.[9] Where the Unionists made the union-as-marriage trope into a strategy that supported the ideology of an adventurous, imperial English manliness, the antiUnionists suggested that a marriage between England and Ireland must simply be fully consensual.

The narrative of the terrors produced by the wrong or loveless or unholy marriage remains one of the more intricate and resonant obsessions of Maturin's Gothic. Such a narrative provides the engine for the plot work in *Fatal Revenge*, in *Melmoth*, in his short story, "Castle Lexslip," and in his remarkably popular 1814 play *Bertram*, all of which hinge on failed marriages, but this narrative also represents the space in which the various interdependent questions concerning Maturin's place in literary history collide. If the narrative arc of the "Radcliffe-Romance" always concludes with a happy, sanctified marriage, then the Maturin-Romance always allegorizes the terrors of its unhappy, unholy equivalent. In the space occupied by the wrong marriage, Maturin's writing nearly always manages the paradoxical feat of sympathizing both with unity and with fragmentation, with colonial order and with rebellion, with masculine gender anxiety and with the feminine sentimentality that in many cases produces it. In *The Contested Castle*, Kate Ferguson Ellis points toward this problem when she indicates that Maturin's Gothic generally depicts a "man stripped of the gender attributes to which he has, he believes, a right" (166). While the wrong-marriage plots of *Fatal Revenge* and *Melmoth* certainly represent the terror resulting from the breakdown of the domestic-affection model of governance, Maturin seems to accept the basic patriarchal premises that constitute this model. He also sees domesticity, defined broadly and metaphorically, as that which legitimates forms of governance, as growing necessarily out of an authentic, passionate, and sentimental attachment. To extort affection from the female subject shames and demeans both of the marriage partners. In fact, in the Catholic liturgical tradition, such a marriage is not binding and may be annulled. The desideratum of Maturin's texts always remains the blissful domestic union that social circumstance has rendered impossible. These social circumstances vary in kind, but generally speaking, they revolve around a female or feminized character who is forced by material deprivation or familial pressure into a marriage that is neither wholly sincere nor fully consensual. Finally, then, the vivid, paranoiac force of Maturin's imagination, which resides in its capacity to depict the anxious condition of at once being and not being a masculine subject, of possessing and being dispossessed of the index of one's own autonomy, allegorizes the post-1798 Irish condition and its attendant cultural politics of a "Gothic marriage" between England and an unwilling Ireland.

Many of the critical evaluations of *Melmoth* and even more particularly of *Fatal Revenge* actively work to fit the novels into specific political categories and to piece together, straighten out, and otherwise clarify plots that are anything but cogent and rectilinear.[10] It occurs to me that the partisan readings, in particular, err for the simple reason that they can be made very effectively on either side. For instance, in a novel like Maturin's *The Milesian Chief,* we could easily read Connel O'Morven, a character who cherishes his noble Catholic-Irish legacy only as he responds to an uprising similar to the 1798 rebellion by suggesting to his fellow rebels that Ireland could never subsist as an independent nation, as embodying both the bold energy of the Jacobin revolutionary and the anxious resignation of the guilty Unionist. The partisan readings of Maturin finally fail to take seriously the underlying historical and social antinomies that not only structure but actually provide the condition of possibility for his work in the first place. His work tends to allegorize a multifarious condition rather than a singular politics. With all of its digressions, narrative dead ends, and schizoid delusions, Maturin's Gothic offers us a glimpse at the experience of incommensurablity. If we read Maturin's texts as constitutively bipolar, then, in a rough way, we might say that at the level of content, his novels certainly foster structures like unity, colonial order, and masculine dominance while simultaneously undercutting them at the level of form through disruption, rebellion, and sentimentality. We witness a double move as certain ideologies are affirmed only to be very swiftly negated. Because he is always pulled in two directions at once by his historical context, Maturin writes a kind of Gothic fiction that actually pulls itself apart. When his texts attempt to work out insoluble social problems at the level of content, they end up falling apart at the level of formal unity. In this way, the novels embody the double logic of post-1798 Irish masculine identity.

Take, for example, one of the central chapters from the "Tale of the Indians," the most overtly Romantic, exoticized, and Radcliffean of the embedded narratives that make up *Melmoth the Wanderer.* In chapter 16 of the tale, the reader encounters a powerful hermeneutical quandary. At this late point in the text, we already know that the Wanderer has bargained away his eternal soul to the Devil in return for remarkable power, occult knowledge, and an exceptionally long life. In order to get out of the bargain, he must find someone to take his place. We also know that the Anglo-Irish Wanderer counted among his kin a brother who served under Cromwell during the 1649 invasion of Ireland, that this brother was evidently the first of the Melmoths to settle in Ireland, and that he staked his family's claim on land "confiscated from an Irish family" (26). During the "Tale of the Indians," we find the Wanderer discussing European culture with the supposedly Indian girl, Immalee, whom the text refers to as "a thing that nature loved" (281). In the scene, the Wanderer, who readily stands in for the colonizer, begins, against his own inclinations, to develop a sincere romantic attachment to Immalee, who comes to represent the novel's version of a female noble-savage figure. Thus, the novel allegorizes the uneasy intimacy between the colonizer and the colonized as a potentially beneficial and constructive confrontation between the civil and the natural.[11] Imagined in the typological terms of the Radcliffean-Romance, however, Melmoth comes to embody his own doubleness as Immalee's ardent yet ineffectual suitor and her nefarious, calculating premodern captor. He only desires her salvation as he works for her destruction. The Wanderer's tormented and tormenting romance with Immalee eventually leads to a profoundly unholy marriage performed by the reanimated corpse of a Spanish priest (394). During Melmoth's first attempts to seduce Immalee, however, he delivers a nearly chapter-length tirade against the bellicose evils of monarchy, the violently inimical character of European colonialism, and the excesses of a nascent capitalist class. Wherever Westerners go, he explains, they leave "behind them famine, despair, and execration" (300). In order to undercut this impassioned soliloquy, Maturin inserts a tellingly anxious footnote. "By mode of criticism equally false and unjust," he explains, "The sentiments of my worst characters [. . .] have been represented as *my own,* I must here trespass so far on the patience of the reader to assure him, that the sentiments ascribed to the stranger are diametrically opposed to mine, and that I have purposely put them into the mouth of an agent of the enemy of mankind" (303).[12]

By interrupting the narrative flow of the text itself, Maturin launches only to retract a rather pointed critique of Europe's colonial imperatives. Though many of the critical perspectives, including some very informed pieces by Norman A. Jeffares and Julia M. Wright, seem to agree with Nilo Idman's 1923 assertion that Maturin was "an ardent Irish nationalist who resented the Union," few take very seriously the revealing footnote that complicates the Wanderer's invective and points directly to the cultural double bind it invokes (8).[13] If the strained excesses of English colonialism in Ireland created a social position identified, to paraphrase Backus, as colonizer and colonized, then it follows that Maturin's writing testifies to this problem.[14] The passage and the accompanying footnote embody precisely the problem of moral clarity that we discussed earlier. Like most Gothic novels, Maturin's clearly wants to represent simple, unambiguous moral identities, but the bipolar social context of Anglo-Ireland prohibits any such easy identification. Thus, the "enemy of mankind," himself an Anglo-Irishman in Maturin's novel, comes to speak a truth about colonialism that must be immediately stigmatized by the footnote. In fact, truth, ethics, and justice themselves begin to take on the character of the occult in *Melmoth*. In Maturin, the anxiety to counter such Jacobin, anticolonial, or occult sympathies and to clarify the "real" moral truth leads to the overproduction of narrative, to the frantic need to tell more and more stories and to interrupt the stories being told in order to drive home the singular moral point of the initial tale. We see this technique recur throughout *Fatal Revenge* and *Melmoth*. The impossible social position that Maturin's novels come to allegorize appears constituted, then, by its desire for unity and for fragmentation, for colonial order and for rebellion, and for a rigorously self-possessed masculinity that also acts as a carefully protected and confined femininity. In the next section, I will demonstrate how *Fatal Revenge* allegorizes this anxiety by setting the logic of the wrong marriage next to the bipolar cultural identities that it engenders.

IV. THE TERRORS OF A MASCULINITY "BORN TO TREMBLE AND WEEP"

Jacqueline Pearson has argued that much of Maturin's work "cannot be fully understood except in the context of its purposeful borrowing from, resistance to, and remaking of, female-authored models" (635). Pearson seems particularly interested in Maturin's retrofitting of certain techniques lifted from the pages of Radcliffe, Edgeworth, and Sydney Owenson (Lady Morgan) and deployed by Maturin in order to strengthen his own literary reputation. She also goes on to argue that the masculine anxiety that underwrites Maturin's novels can be seen in his "persistent use of the image of transvestism or other forms of gender-reversal

[. . .] which may image Maturin's discomfort with his own transvestite role, as a male author adopting forms of female-dominated fiction" (640). Of course, in an essay published in an 1818 edition of *The British Review,* Maturin himself confesses his passionate enthrallment to what he calls the irresistible and dangerous delights of Anne Radcliffe's fiction.[15] In what amounts to an almost unwilling encomium to Radcliffe's work, Maturin focuses on her heroines, whom, he explains, have "no struggles of energy, no bursts of passion—[for] they are born to tremble and weep."[16] Annibal and Ippolito di Montorio, the heroes of Maturin's *Fatal Revenge,* certainly struggle with energies and passions, but, like Radcliffe's heroines, they are also "born to tremble and weep." One of the most lasting visions we have of the two brothers is that of them weeping uncontrollably in each others arms (3:290–91). The text continually stages each brother's separate narrative arc around that most Radcliffean of plot devices, solitary confinement, and as Father Schemoli's final letter explains, each brother comes to experience "a mind weakened by loneliness and fear" (3:439). From the novel's opening, the brothers are set up as doubles with Ippolito as the bold public figure who lives in Naples and refuses "inward cultivation" and Annibal as the "timid, gloomy" and introspective character who resides in the family castle at Muralto (1:9, 31). Read together, the brothers come to know the passion and energy of such Radcliffean ineffectual suitors as Vincentio or Valancourt, only as they also live through the privations and confinements that mark the life of Radcliffe's most famous heroine, Emily St. Aubert of *The Mysteries of Udolpho.* The Montorios experience a passionate desire for justice and vengeance while also experiencing a kind of life that makes it impossible for them to remain autonomous agents in the public and masculine spheres, and this impossibility is duly noted in the novel's concluding pages when the land, inheritance, nobility, and the very identity of the house of Montorio are all dissolved by legal fiat. As we are told near the end of the final volume, "The name, the title of Montorio [. . .] are extinguished for ever" (3:487). The loss of autonomy that sparks this conclusion is particularly marked by the fact that nearly every time Ippolito attempts to live out the masculine homosocial adventure story of the male Gothic, the action switches over to find Annibal shut up in the confines of its female Gothic equivalent writing letters about his forced solitude. The irreducible doubleness of the brothers, who must finally meet to weep and to work together to affect the text's ill-fated climax, provides the economy of tension in the novel. The fragmentary double text folds the homosocial male exile narrative into the trembling fear of the female-confinement narrative.

In the opening pages of *Fatal Revenge,* we learn that the present Count Montorio succeeded his own brother, who died along with all of his family in an unprecedented "domestic calamity" (1:3). The novel frames this rather abstruse discussion of "domestic calamity" by setting the action in or "about the year 1690" (1:1). Strangely enough, then, the text's "domestic calamity" is temporally linked to the Battle of the Boyne and the Williamite confiscations in Ireland. If, with R. F. Foster, we mark this date as the formal beginning of the modern Anglo-Irish ascendancy class, then the poetics of the wrong marriage in Maturin's text seem tied to the historical foundations of the modern history of colonialism in Ireland, to the penal era that preceded the Acts of Union by more than a century, and to one of the instantiating moments of Anglo-Irish identity.[17] Though the previous Count, Orazio di Montorio, was evidently much-beloved, the narrator goes on to describe him as "jealous, violent, and vindictive, even beyond Italian irritability [. . .] his credulity was without bounds, his rage without restraint, and his vengeance without remorse" (4). The main narrative begins in earnest after this brief introductory characterization of the family line, but the pressing terrors of this unseen "domestic calamity" haunt the novel's protagonists, Ippolito and Annibal, the sons and heirs of the new Count Montorio. Much of the text's brooding, inexorable sense of mystery lies in its capacity to obsess about without fully revealing this foundational domestic disaster. The pain of the moment serves as a defining and communal one for the family while, at the same time, remaining somehow unknowable, obscure, and sublime.

The convolutions fly fast and furious after this early point in the novel. Annibal becomes so consumed by the tale of Orazio's family that he searches the forbidden apartment and bridal suite of the former Count in order to discover its potential secrets. Annibal and an old family servant, Michelo, eventually discover a skeleton concealed in a passage behind the wall of the apartment. Annibal believes it to be the body of Orazio di Montorio, and the villainous Monk Schemoli reinforces this belief. Schemoli goes on to claim that the skeleton is his own, and that his is the spirit of Orazio, doomed to inhabit the body of a two-thousand-year-old man until his own murderer is killed and justice set to right. The murderer is eventually identified as the present Count Montorio, a dark usurper of a particularly Shakespearean stripe, and Ippolito and Annibal are continually confined, weakened, and harassed until each surrenders personal agency and, quite mechanically, works to commit parricide and to fulfill Schemoli's inhuman scheme.[18] In opposition to its Radcliffean predecessors, then, *Fatal Revenge* folds the issue of domestic confinement into the more overtly political problematic of usurpation, and these two elements finally represent the dialectical poles that define both Maturin's appropriation of the Radcliffean female Gothic and his recasting of its basic tropes in terms of post-1798 Irish cultural nationalism. The masculine-usurper/feminized-usurped narrative becomes an allegory for colonization in the era of the Union.

The novel's parricidal ending is a foregone conclusion by the close of its first and briefest volume, but one problem seems to trouble what would otherwise be a fairly predictable tale of paranormal vengeance. The skeleton concealed in the forbidden bridal suite is not that of Orazio. On the surface, the story seems to be a supernatural one that shores up a doctrine of divine, patrilineal succession, and in an overtly Burkean sense, for Maturin true order must have "the image of a relation of blood" that holds fast to dearest, patriarchal "domestic ties"(Edmund Burke, *Reflections,* 30). Let's admit from the outset that fratricide coupled to usurpation and compounded by parricide certainly disrupts what we might call our dearest filial and domestic ties. But Annibal's conclusion about Orazio's skeleton, a conclusion that determines the entire course of his narrative, is a false one. Moreover, Annibal's presumptions, which are paralleled by a more active false ending in which Ippolito, in a dreamlike trance, gazes into a mirror only to imagine that he sees himself murdering his own father, warn us not to jump the gun, not to read only in terms of the ending. Rather, we should read the text in terms of the colliding, self-interrupting double narratives of Ippolito and Annibal, of male and female forms. The teleological journey toward identity that the novel attempts to articulate is misleading, disrupted, miscarried. If Ippolito and Annibal cannot come to grips with their own identities because they are confined by historical circumstances, then the text itself also fails to move toward any conclusive or teleological narrative cohesion. One of the features of Maturin's Gothic that places it in opposition to that of other male writers like Lewis, Beckford, and even Godwin, is its inexhaustibly Radcliffean capacity to offer as it defers the immediate gratification of narrative closure. Its pleasure, or rather its narrative desire, lies in its ascetic facility for denying pleasure. Where Lewis's *The Monk* revolves around the lurid, carnivalesque fulfillment of every desire and temptation it entertains, Maturin's Gothic, even in an obsessively occult text like *Melmoth,* generally manipulates the reader with the dead end and the unseen rather than providing fulfillment. In fact, the method of false endings, which winds its way through *Fatal Revenge,* eventually becomes the main structuring principle of the stories-within-stories that make up *Melmoth the Wanderer.*

Pearson is correct to draw attention to the transvestism and gender anxiety that suffuses Maturin's writing, but her psychologizing account of Maturin's appropriations of the female Gothic finally converts the engagement into a conscious confrontation between a masculinist culture and the feminine other it seems determined to overmaster. But in the parallel stories of Annibal and Ippolito, *Fatal Revenge* shows a strange admixture of both the male- and female-Gothic formulas. Finally, the novel provides a reading of the two subgenres and an early attempt to create that remarkably paranoid hybrid third form that I'm calling the

Unionist Gothic, the purview of which is to represent the horrors of a social context that renders masculine subjects in the same language that has been deployed to define the boundaries of the feminine sphere. As I explained earlier, by Unionist Gothic I mean to signify the embattled era covered by the Acts of Union, the unhappy union-as-marriage metaphor, and the symptomatic union of male- and female-Gothic forms that Maturin's work exemplifies. In his discussion of the British Declaration of Right and the Magna Carta in *Reflections on the Revolution in France,* Edmund Burke claims that British liberties are founded on the concept of "*entailed inheritance,*" derived from forefathers and handed down to posterity (29). As Burke well knows, an entailment system relies on the goodwill of the patriarch because wives and daughters can readily be disinherited and dispossessed by such a system. The fear of just such structural dispossession lies at the heart of the Jane Austen novels, *Pride and Prejudice* and *Sense and Sensibility.* In merging the two gendered subgenres of the Gothic, Maturin's *Fatal Revenge* extends the disinheritances and dispossessions that inhere in the entailment system into the colonial sphere. The novel, then, helps us to see that models of governance rely on the domestic-affection metaphor as they also work to conceal the problem of structural dispossession.

Many of the critical takes on Maturin have actively worked to eliminate the complex dialectic of male and female forms by either simplifying or stigmatizing the form of *Fatal Revenge* itself. Nilo Idman's 1923 biography of Maturin appears to have set the tone for many of the subsequent scholarly studies of the novel. For Idman, the novel's plot "is sufficiently intricate to necessitate a commencement of the analysis from the end and to reveal the mystery at once" (21). Rather than recounting what the experience of reading Maturin's novel might be, Idman straightens out, while always acknowledging, the various convoluted twists and false turns of the plot of *Fatal Revenge* in order to unpack the narrative's teleology. In her own groundbreaking, tour de force reading of the gender politics of Maturin's work, Kate Ferguson Ellis begins by sketching—again, from the point of view of the novel's revelatory conclusion—the basic outline and shape of the book. Likewise, Dale Kramer's capacious overview of Maturin's career initiates a discussion of the book by claiming that its torturous digressions are best unpacked from the perspective of Monk Schemoli's infamous "confessional letter," which constitutes the novel's final movement (28). While all of these approaches serve to clarify a text that remains, as Edith Birkhead once complained, bewildering enough to confound and trap even the most dedicated reader in its labyrinthine "mazes," none of them takes the text's mazelike form itself very seriously as a structural problematic (82). The book methodically and resolutely unfolds the horrors of confinement and feminization as experienced by its young protagonists,

Ippolito and Annibal, while also managing to hold Father Schemoli, the text's apparently unholy, supernatural agent, responsible for all of those various and sundry horrors. In continually deploying such techniques as false endings, digressions, fragmentation, and dreamlike states of consciousness, not to mention such overused Gothic tropes as misidentified corpses, empty tombs, and bogus doors, the novel also works to structure the experience of its own reading as a similarly systematic and frenzied mode of confinement and feminization. Birkhead is certainly correct to assert that *Fatal Revenge* is a labyrinthine maze, but its system of traps articulates a process. Unlike previous critics who see it as either a symptom of the strictures of patriarchal culture or simply a futile attempt to imitate the Radcliffean Gothic, I interpret the novel's hybridizing form as offering a phenomenological look at the anxiety, fear, and fantasies of the breakdown of civil society that would result from male subjects being *subjected* to female confinements. *Fatal Revenge* deploys the structural trappings of the Radcliffean female Gothic in order to allegorize the historical problems initiated by the Acts of Union and by the gender disorientation that the Acts provoked.

V. FORM AND "DOMESTIC CALAMITY"

Like much of Radcliffe's work, the main action of *Fatal Revenge* takes place in Italy, and Maturin's depiction of Monk Schemoli, who continually manipulates the superstitious beliefs of the other characters, appears, if anything, even more anti-Catholic than Radcliffe's similar characterization of Monk Schedoni in her 1797 novel, *The Italian*. Like Radcliffe and the majority of his other English-language predecessors, Maturin situates the action of his Gothic novel in the most notoriously Catholic region of Europe. As several critics have been quick to point out, the similarities between *The Italian* and *Fatal Revenge* do not end there.[19] Like Radcliffe's novel, Maturin's offers a story structured by confinement, the threat of the Inquisition, and the nefarious schemes of a complex, seemingly unredeemable monk.[20] Annibal, as voracious a reader as any of Radcliffe's various heroines, continually finds himself confined within the various castles he visits, and, like Radcliffe's heroines, he tries to read the encoded signs—the portraits, books, and rooms—hidden in the recesses of the intimate and domestic spheres in order to find a way out into the more social, public world. Whereas Radcliffe's malevolent Father Schedoni initially stands in the way of the happy marriage and domestic bliss that marks the conclusion of *The Italian,* however, his near-namesake, Schemoli, appears to structure his entire plan as the consequence of a failed domesticity.

As we have seen, most critics tend, like Annibal and Ippolito, to begin reading the text from the perspective of the end, from its final revelations about Schemoli and the "domestic calamity" that initiated the entire tragic tale, but, formally speaking, the novel enacts a far more complex process of feminization, collapse, and redirection than that of its own simple revenge plot. As we witness Annibal's cycle of confinement from castle to dungeon to monastery paralleled by Ippolito's cycle of exile as he pursues and is pursued by both Schemoli and his father, we also see the narrative of the male Gothic collapse into that of the female. In fact, the novel's form, predicated on false endings, disruptions, and the double structure of the Ippolito and Annibal tales, offers a logical process whereby we observe male subjects fused to or trapped within Radcliffean-female narratives that render autonomy largely impossible and terror as the unavoidable outcome. As the text revolves around an amalgam of male- and female-Gothic tropes, it also allegorizes the horror of losing the privileges that attend patriarchal masculinity. In large part, the union-as-marriage metaphor works to affirm patriarchal masculinity as the ur-figure for authentic autonomy, but reclaiming and reasserting the violence of phallic logic in order to avoid the confines of femininity and attain autonomy appears to be the response of a beleaguered, perpetually transgendered Irish masculinity. The idea of being feminized and manipulated constitutes the tense and palpable fear of both Annibal's and Ippolito's narratives. But, if we follow the linear path set up by the novel, we hold on to some hope of a restored order. The leading, suspenseful structure of the novel allows us to believe that the brothers will be able to restore their own masculinity through violence and that the efficacy of patrilineal succession will finally triumph.

After the brothers' swords meet "in their father's body," we finally learn the truth about the Montorio family's foundational "domestic calamity" from the confessional letter that Schemoli writes while awaiting execution in the prisons of the Inquisition (3:328). "I am Orazio, Count of Montorio," he begins, "so long believed dead, and who rises from imaginary death only to bewail that *it is* not real" (336). Orazio's first death, like those endings witnessed by Annibal and Ippolito, was a misleading illusion. Orazio goes on to explain that his bitter and licentious brother desired both the title, Count Montorio, and revenge on the Count's young bride, Erminia, who had spurned the brother's affections. Hence, in Iago-like fashion, the younger Montorio concocted a scheme to make the prudent, moral, submissive, but nonetheless, diffident Erminia appear unfaithful to Orazio. Very early in her life, Erminia married and bore a child to a young soldier named Verdoni, whom she subsequently believed to be murdered by bandits. Under acute pressure from her father, Erminia agreed to conceal the child and to marry the wealthy Count Montorio in order to help secure her family's standing in the community. But, of course, Verdoni has not been killed, and when he returns and hears of Erminia's marriage, he determines to leave Italy forever. Meanwhile, Erminia has chosen to confess her history to Orazio's jealous brother. Though she certainly does not hate Orazio and is about to give birth to their third child, in her heart the more authentic marriage to Verdoni, built upon ardent passion, trumps the marriage of social convention that she shares with Orazio. Orazio, though jealous and overprotective, appears noble throughout the story. Hence, as with the cultural and intellectual discourses surrounding the Irish Acts of Union, we have in *Fatal Revenge* a marriage plot tailored to fit the problem of usurpation. In fact, the text's wrong-marriage plot deeply injures Erminia and Orazio and, eventually, everyone who comes into their sphere just as, for Maturin, the union-as-marriage has injured the Catholic Irish, the Anglo-Irish, and the English.

Erminia confesses to the brother that she cannot go on with the charade and that after giving birth to Orazio's child, she will enter a convent. The younger Montorio uses all of this information to manipulate Orazio into believing that he is being cuckolded by Verdoni, that the Countess maintains another family, and that the Montorios will soon become a public laughingstock. In a jealous rage, the Count confronts Erminia only to discover her in the act of saying her final farewells to Verdoni and her first child. Schemoli then writes, rather shamefully, that he immediately caused Verdoni "to be stabbed before her sight" (3:378). In fact, he goes on to exclaim, "I paused between every blow. I bid her listen to every groan" (3:379). Upon seeing her true love brutally murdered, Erminia's "heart burst[s]" open and she falls onto Verdoni's bloodstained corpse (3:379). The Count leaves Italy in a fit of madness, learns of his brother's misdeeds, lives the life of an isolated "savage," and journeys to the East where he eventually studies the occult and learns the art of hypnotism. In appearing to "go native," though, Orazio merely seems to give in to his true, violent, and uncivil instincts. In the terms set up by the novel, he may be noble, but he remains savage. From the opening pages of the novel, Maturin has prepared us to see this as part of the Count's boundless, Catholic "credulity" (1:4). In the depths of a solitude that he refers to as a "total amputation from life," Orazio becomes consumed by his desire for revenge (3:383). He deploys his knowledge of hypnosis to return to his castle and, through privation and confinement, to control the minds and actions of Annibal, of Ippolito, and, at times, even of his own usurper brother. Schemoli refers to his own actions at this point as "demonic," and the text stages his plan to recover his lands and name as an overtly terrifying act of mad revenge (3:404–5). Thus, Maturin associates Schemoli's decision, born of grief, trembling, and isolation, not with something like decolonization, but rather with yet another dehumanizing form of usurpation and control. The new Count Montorio may be a usurper, but to murder him and erase the will and autonomy of his sons simply replicates the same treacherous logic. The flaw in

Schemoli's planned revenge inheres in its fatal similarity to the duplicity of usurpation. His approach might appear to be justified, but it requires so much falsehood and malevolence that it comes to resemble precisely the twisted logic of usurpation that he reviles. In the terms of the novel, this simply makes Schemoli into "a villain with unimpaired conscience" (3:405). *Fatal Revenge* replays and reflects the endless cycle of usurpation. Though Maturin's novel attempts to side against usurpation, it can never fully take the part of the dispossessed rebel whose satanic energies drive the story. The novel heaps on so much complexity and so much minutiae in an attempt to balance the scales of justice that we come to see, once again, how Maturin's oeuvre overproduces narrative detail in order to find some brief instance of sympathetic moral clarity. The novel never produces the moral clarity it desires but, instead, imagines a villain who appears to transform into a heroic victim while somehow remaining thoroughly villainous. Even in his attempt to remake himself by the sheer force of personality, Schemoli/Orazio has merely made himself inauthentic. He has become a simulacrum of the terrorist personality that he would eschew. He does not reestablish his own agency, but rather accepts the powerful identity of the usurper as his own, or, that is, he accedes to the logic of usurpation in order to overcome a usurper. In effect, he becomes two personalities at once: the injured Orazio and the conniving Schemoli. At his very best, then, Schemoli/Orazio simply remains a villain of "unimpaired conscience." In focusing specifically on the experience of pain and loss, the tragic logic of the novel manages the remarkably incongruous feat of sympathizing and identifying with both villain and hero.

At this point in the text, Maturin has done much to convert the villain who has manipulated the entire plot into a justified victim, the terrorizer into the terrorized, and, moreover, when Schemoli becomes Orazio once again, the narrator begins to describe him in feminine terms and to depict him, oddly enough, as melancholy and maternal. To add insult to injury, Orazio comes to discover that Annibal and Ippolito are his own sons, and so he experiences the utter and damnable pain of having turned his sons into murderers. Upon realizing his culpability, Orazio is described by the narrator as hugging his children "with the shriek and grasp of a mother" (3:490). Like his wife, Erminia, he dies of a broken heart, and his blood pours out onto his sons, who are stained by and identified with his sin. Through the process of feminization and confinement, the brothers give in to terror, but in Schemoli, we seem to have a clear antagonist who acts as the agent of that terror. The text plays this out as a logical process, and in modern parlance it almost seems like a measurable sociological problem: being feminized produces personal and political terror. When we come to the novel's real conclusion, we discover that Schemoli is Orazio; that he has not been murdered and is not supernatural, but, rather, has had his title usurped and has experienced dehumanizing isolation, a fate coded as worse than death. The text does not allow for a restored patriarchal order, as Ippolito, who could have inherited the Montorio title from the usurper and set the system to right again, has become a murderer and social pariah stripped of the Montorio name and title (3:487). In coming through this experience, the reader has learned to sympathize with the sentiments, born of privation and joined to domestic confinement, that create the condition of possibility for terror as well. At this point Orazio, too, comes to be depicted in feminine terms. He, too, was manipulated. Despite, or perhaps because of, its melding of female- and male-Gothic tropes, the novel seems to sentimentalize the feminine as it also represents being identified with femininity as the foundation of all terror. Caught between an embattled and isolated femininity and the fearsome masculine anxiety it inspires, the main characters of *Fatal Revenge* metamorphose into men "born to tremble and weep," and in so doing they come to embody the incapacitating double logic of post-1798 Anglo-Irish masculinity.

While the patriarchal colonial order remains at the heart of this problem, the logic of the Unionist Gothic seems to articulate both a conscious desire to shore up this order and an unconscious critique of its cyclical, debilitating logic. In fact, this logical collapse, this capacity of one identity to slide inevitably into another, even seems implicit in Edmund Burke's famous defense of the coherence of patriarchy against the inchoate violence of the revolutionary in *Reflections on the Revolution in France*. When Burke claims that in the face of social upheaval, "a King is but a man, a queen is but a woman; a woman but an animal, and an animal not of the highest order," he only protects a masculine order as he demonstrates that its loss is also a collapse of identities, an inevitable sliding of the masculine into the feminine and then into the bestial (67). In the "Preface" to his second novel, *The Wild Irish Boy* (1808), Maturin, again writing under the pen name of Dennis Jasper Murphy, explains that the story of the Montorios "was said to be too defective in female characters and female interests" (1:ix). Maturin's first novel may be deficient in female interests and characters, but the masculine anxiety that drives the text fears nothing so much as the feminine, or, that is, as what Mary Corbett calls the "hierarchical opposition between English man and Irish woman" (3). This anxiety subsists in the Unionist Gothic's profound desire to imitate the authority of the patriarchal voice and its equally profound incapacity to do so. If we trace the dynamic of this anxiety as it courses through the paired narratives of Annibal and Ippolito and the final characterizations of Schemoli/Orazio, we find in *Fatal Revenge* a map of the breakdown of the marriage analogy for Irish colonization. In Maturin's first novel, the wrong marriage, a marriage that causes terror and the collapse of social order for all those involved, initiates this cycle.

VI. THE ALLEGORY OF DISUNION

This reading of *Fatal Revenge* allows us to rethink the formal problems of Maturin's final Gothic novel, *Melmoth the Wanderer,* which also remains tied to the theme of failed domesticity. In fact, with the exception of the novel's first embedded narrative, the "Tale of Stanton," all of the tales that make up the body of the text concern the terror that succeeds the breakdown of pure and ardent domestic affection. Again, like *Fatal Revenge,* the action of *Melmoth* becomes temporally associated with a singular date in the history of British military incursions in Ireland. Where *Fatal Revenge* begins in 1690, the Anglo-Irishman Melmoth's contract, his devil's bargain, begins with the Cromwellian invasion and the pro-plantation rules that seized land from Ireland's indigenous Catholic peoples. By the time that Cromwell began his campaign in Ireland, the English had been handing Irish land over to English investors for quite some time. After the 1649 invasion, many of the soldiers who fought in Cromwell's army were paid in the currency of Irish estates.[21] The expropriation of Irish lands punished the Catholics who stood against Cromwell while helping to build up the ranks of the English landed gentry in Ireland. Unlike *Fatal Revenge,* in *Melmoth* the story is no longer displaced onto the continent, and the contract from the distant past continues to haunt both the present-day setting of 1816 County Wicklow and the Wanderer's namesake descendant, young John Melmoth, a Trinity College student who has returned home to take over the estate of his dying uncle. Where Maturin's first Gothic novel had fragmented the male-Gothic story of Ippolito by playing it against the female-Gothic tale of Annibal, the entire text of *Melmoth* embodies a series of thematically linked fragments. In some sense, then, the disjointed stories-within-stories structure of *Melmoth* appears, as Chris Baldick indicates, as "a preposterously convoluted contrivance" (x). Following the argument that I have suggested throughout, however, we should read the unstable structure of Maturin's prose fiction as a locus for historical tensions, as embodying the unresolved antinomies that constituted Anglo-Irish autonomy following the Acts of Union.

Margot Gayle Backus's landmark study, *The Gothic Family Romance,* also locates in Maturin's work a persistent obsession with the collapse of domesticity, which, she argues, is figuratively represented in *Melmoth* by the recurrent child sacrifice motif.[22] For Backus, however, Maturin's work, along with Le Fanu's and Stoker's, reads as "an exercise in self-protective projection [. . .] decipherable as much through its denials as through its assertions" (109). While Backus certainly provides a subtle and dialectical formula for reading the Anglo-Irish Gothic, in situating *Melmoth* as a text that attempts to disavow its own guilt by setting its acts of cannibalism, vampirism, and parricide on the European continent, Backus obscures the extent to which all roads finally lead back to Ireland, back to the frame narrative about young Melmoth, and back to the very problem of inheritance that makes child sacrifice an issue in the first place (110). Predicated upon a Freudian meta-narrative of repression, Backus's study represents Irish and Anglo-Irish identities as psychic wholes injured by forgotten, or concealed, or refused histories. Like much of the undialectical criticism it labors to critique, then, Backus's work sets the idea of a "Hidden Ireland," a lost Catholic Ireland that resembles the plenitude of the Lacanian imaginary of the nation in opposition to an Anglo-Ireland that embodies its literal and Symbolic *Lex Patris*.[23] A true Mother-Ireland is juxtaposed against a false Father-Anglo-Ireland.

Like much of the scholarship that surveys *Fatal Revenge, The Gothic Family Romance* tends to overlook formal dynamics. A system of disruptions, fragments, and false endings structures *Melmoth*. The more that Maturin attempts to fold the male- and female-Gothic forms together, and the more he attempts to have the stories and even the characters themselves internalize the irreducible doubleness of male and female, terrorizer and terrorized, the more the teleological unity of *Melmoth the Wanderer* disintegrates. Where *Fatal Revenge* fails to keep the male- and female-Gothic forms separate because each inevitably slides into its other in the colonial context, *Melmoth* attempts to work through the double binds by integrating doubleness into each of its interpolated stories and, subsequently, into nearly all of its characters.[24] Stanton and Moncada embody exiled male characters who end up suffering confinements that deracinate and desexualize them; Immalee, the feminine noble savage, turns out to be Isadora, the lost daughter of the wealthy, Catholic Aliaga family; the Walberg marriage of the Guzman tale is torn between Protestantism and the vicissitudes of Catholic Spain; and nearly every descendant of the Mortimer family in the "The Lover's Tale" appears caught between the desire for a natural religion and the divisive sectarian wars of the Cromwell era. Finally, as we've already seen, Melmoth himself acts as both the lover who must save Immalee/Isadora from her heretical Papist family and the feudal usurper who plots her final destruction. Hence, interpreting the concealed politics of *Melmoth* becomes more than simply an act of reading the plot as an allegory of social antagonisms; we must read the novel's form itself as allegorical, as reflecting the historical problematic of an impossibly bipolar Anglo-Irish cultural nationalism. If *Fatal Revenge*'s attempt to keep the male and female forms separate ends up in a self-interrupting, parallel structure that appears convoluted, then *Melmoth*'s attempt to integrate the doubleness of the two forms into each of its stories ends up in a text that lacks real narrative coherence. In fact, we could say that the novel's unifying theme consists of its allegory of disunion.

Moreover, after the "Tale of Stanton" and the "Spaniard's Tale," the narrative force of the novel is wrapped up in the "Tale of the Indians" with the two subsequent stories, the "The Tale of Guzman's Family" and "The Lover's Tale," constituting interpolated stories that act as explanatory caveats spoken to Immalee/Isadora's father, Don Francisco di Aliaga, about Melmoth's character. Hence, the final two stories, which serve to interrupt Immalee's narrative at precisely the moment when she is about to wed Melmoth, are at once bound to and glosses of the unholy marriage depicted in the "Tale of the Indians." The novel itself collapses as it coalesces around the unholy marriage. At the moment when the tension rises to its peak in the "Tale of the Indians," as Immalee realizes that the priest's hand, which joins hers to Melmoth's, is "as *cold as that of death*," the narrative is interrupted by the story of Don Aliaga's voyage and the occasion of his learning of the "Guzman's" and the "Lover's" tales (394). We are left to wonder what has happened to Immalee/Isadora's marriage while the two subsequent tales are told.

The "Guzman's Tale" unpacks the horrors of a Protestant family who arrive in Catholic Spain only to find that they have been dispossessed of their expected inheritance. The overwhelming problems of material deprivation drive Walberg, the loving husband and patriarch, to the brink of insanity as he attempts to murder his children and his loving wife. In the Guzman story, we see an affectionate marriage turned upside down by the "agonies of famine," as, once again, Maturin depicts a social circumstance that poisons domestic bliss (429). Mrs. Sandal's lie about her son John's parentage in the "Lover's Tale" makes the true love that John feels for Elinor appear incestuous, and the arc of the story eventually leads to John's brief, unhappy marriage to Margaret and to his unnaturally foreshortened life. In the "Lover's Tale," we see true affection disrupted by duplicity and by the sectarian divisiveness of Cromwell's Puritan militarism. Both the Guzman tale and the lover's tale devolve from Gothic narratives proper into overtly sentimental fiction, as their various wrong-marriage plots drain the force from and distort the focus of the satanic frame narrative. In fact, the novel ends up replaying as it obsessively circles around the marriage that has been depicted as both desired and repugnant in the "Tale of the Indians." We have moved, then, from *Fatal Revenge,* a novel that sutures the male Gothic to the female Gothic form in order to articulate the cycle of violence initiated by masculine anxiety, to a text that actually presents two frame stories, one concerning the Anglo-Irishman Melmoth's return to Ireland and another that offers the complexly Radcliffean "Tale of the Indians," as overarching narratives that are interrupted by confrontational glosses and by each other. When we do finally return to the "Tale of the Indians" frame and learn that Immalee/Isadora has died, the novel resorts to the original frame narrative about the Wanderer's return to Ireland. The exiled male is ushered back into Ireland precisely by the female-confinement story. The usurper's narrative eventually collapses into its other, the Radcliffean narrative. In *Melmoth,* then, even the attempt to impose unity on the novel via a frame narrative becomes fractured by doubleness. The plots and forms of Maturin's Gothic remain ineluctably haunted and disrupted by each other. To appropriate Adorno's words from *Aesthetic Theory,* we could say that the collapsing hybridity of Maturin's Gothic constitutes the space in which "social antinomies become the dialectics of form" (232). That is to say, by bringing the male Gothic exile narrative and the Radcliffe romance together, first in *Fatal Revenge* and then in *Melmoth,* Maturin manufactures a hybrid third form that embodies the gender double bind that constitutes post-1798 Irish masculine identity.

As I indicated in chapter 1, a good deal of the postcolonial criticism written about Ireland over the last decade has failed to account for the incapacitating complications that attend this gender double bind. Anglo-Ireland has become the lone name for usurpation, for the hegemony of colonial false-consciousness, rather than a hybridized component of a more complicated cultural and sociopolitical matrix. Thus, while overlooking many of the issues provoked by the complicated gender dynamics of Ireland's colonial period, a good deal of the Irish nationalist criticism published over the last decade fails to read the modern Irish literary imagination as constitutively bipolar. Instead, the Anglo-Irish are inevitably depicted as usurpers and the Gaelo-Catholics as the usurped and feminized people. To some extent, by recasting this problem in terms of the wrong-marriage plot, Maturin's Gothic displays as it rearticulates this kind of logic by placing the usurpers in a position where they seem as confined, as feminized by the social world created by the Acts of Union as do the usurped peoples. Both sides are subjected to the politics of terror, and both sides become terrorist in order to efface such an abject identity. Here, we can see the problem of Irish colonialism as a cyclic one, the longevity of which relies precisely on its inability to determine which side is repugnant and abject.

VII. THE MATERNAL VAMPIRE AND THE FATE OF THE UNIONIST GOTHIC

Between the 1820 publication of *Melmoth,* Maturin's final Gothic novel, and the 1872 publication of *In a Glass Darkly,* Joseph Sheridan Le Fanu's ultimate collection of Gothic fiction, the force of Irish politics turned, quite resolutely, against the ascendancy class. In hindsight, the continuing furor over absenteeism, added to ongoing sectarian divisions and the fact that most of the wealth of the Anglo-Irish class was being funneled into business ventures in England or on the continent, makes it easy to picture Ireland headed for a political crisis by midcentury that reached epic proportions in the deprivations of the Great Famine.[25] The political conflicts engendered by the ascendancy class dovetailed with the political crises provoked by material deprivation. As founding members of the ascendancy, Le Fanu's family traced its descent back to Charles Le Fanu de Cresserons, who served under William of Orange during the Battle of the Boyne. During the 1830s, the Le Fanu family residence in County Limerick became caught up in the Tithe Wars begun by Catholic peasants who refused to support the Anglican Church of Ireland. During this period, Ireland saw the resurgence of the Whiteboy movement, which opposed the tithe and responded to the landlord culture that had developed since the Union with a great deal of bellicose rhetoric and outright violence. Throughout his career, Le Fanu, who wrote for such paragons of Irish Toryism as *Dublin University Magazine, The Guardian,* and *The Evening Mail,* while also serving as editor and proprietor of *The Warder,* was generally opposed to Daniel O'Connell's various repeal campaigns and to the more radical nationalism of the Young Ireland movement.[26] During his lifetime, Le Fanu, the son of a Church of Ireland curate, also witnessed Gladstone's disestablishment of that church in 1869, not to mention the Famine and the rise of violent republican separatist movements like the Fenian Brotherhood. The aftermath of the famine, the rise of a Catholic-Irish petit bourgeoisie, and the midcentury advent of European-style nationalism left the Anglo-Irish, a class that we saw doubly allegorized as both colonizer and colonized in Maturin's Gothic, not only cut off from the peasant class and from England but also in a state of irrevocable political and economic decline by the time that Le Fanu comes to publish *In a Glass Darkly.*

Even in his later texts where the action is no longer set in Ireland, Le Fanu's Gothic obsesses about decline and suicide, about the collapse of the domestic sphere, and about the haunting persistence of a repressed past. These issues very often coalesce around a young woman, Maud Ruthyn in *Uncle Silas,* Fanny Glenfallen in *The Wyvern Mystery,* or Laura in "Carmilla," who finds herself confined within her family's corrupt or occult history.[27] As Le Fanu himself was such a vocal advocate of Unionism and Irish Toryism, however, few critics have been concerned to connect the Le Fanu Gothic formula to the Romantic, Jacobin nationalism that characterized the thinking of most of the uprisings and revolutionary movements in Ireland after the 1798 rebellion.[28] In fact, both Julian Moynahan and Margot Backus, some of the finest readers of the politics of Le Fanu's Gothic, situate him as, at best, an allegorist of ascendancy guilt. Even the nuanced, circumspect, and thorough account of Le Fanu's life and work presented by W. J. McCormack in *Sheridan Le Fanu and Victorian Ireland,* locates the author very firmly in the tradition of Irish Toryism.[29]

I want to conclude this chapter on the Unionist Gothic by taking this basic political interpretation of Le Fanu a step further. I believe that by the time Le Fanu publishes "Carmilla," the terror and gender double binds that served to establish the cycle of confinement, feminization, and male anxiety that structured Maturin's Gothic have become so endemic, so internal to the functioning of the Anglo-Irish Gothic in general that the idea of an autonomy coded as masculine and active has become veritably unthinkable for the genre. The double binds and identity fissures that constitute the foundations of the Unionist Gothic have been subsumed wholesale into the structures and characters that define Le Fanu's fiction. As with *Melmoth,* a concealed and interiorized doubleness becomes the enigmatic formal principle of Le Fanu's later texts. In much of Le Fanu's later writings, we witness not only patriarchy's continual failure to protect the sphere over which it has dominion but also a peculiar rumination on the collapse of identity into abjection, or, rather, a collapse of the repugnant into the maternal. We still see the anxious fear associated with a feminized identity that we encountered in Maturin's work, but now that identity seems to pervade and circumscribe every experience. In a text like "Carmilla," Le Fanu's tale of vampirism and lesbian desire, we no longer need to discover a male character who has been feminized because the feminine itself has become the locus of terror, and the languid, submissive, confined female is also the savage, revenant terrorist. Read in terms of the female Gothic form then, by the time the Unionist Gothic reaches "Carmilla," binary identity formations like terrorist and terrorized are not only collected into a single character, they are also coded very explicitly as female. Furthermore, both the terroristic Carmilla and the terrorized Laura are now represented as confined. The feminine has actually become the site of the masculine double bind. Hence, I read "Carmilla" as a reflection of what we might call the horrified "feminization of history" that suffuses both the ends of the Unionist Gothic and its rather persistent, albeit fragmentary and parodic, afterlife in the writings of Bram Stoker, Oscar Wilde, James Joyce, and Samuel Beckett. In these writers, as in Le Fanu, lines of inheritance often appear fully arrested at the stage of maternal abjection. The horrified meditations on maternal lineage and the subsequent occlusion of autonomy that such a lineage triggers find embodiment in the Irish cultural imaginary not only in the vampiric figure of Carmilla, but also in the ghostly maternal history that Stephen Dedalus hopes to get shut of in the "Proteus" and "Scylla and Charybdis" episodes of *Ulysses,* and in the claustral "mother's room" where Beckett's psychically detached Molloy writes his disintegrating autobiography.[30]

The collection of stories published as *In a Glass Darkly* gathers together six of Le Fanu's short tales. The stories involve a bifold central conceit in that they all appear to be first-person accounts that document the interaction between the human and supernatural worlds, and that they have all been pieced together from the files of a German doctor named Martin Hesselius, who stands in as Le Fanu's version of a Swedenborgian metaphysician-philosopher. The very structure of the collection brings pseudoscientific testimony together with the occult in order to blur the line between reality and fiction just as Emmanuel Swedenborg himself had spent his career eroding the distinction between the material and the spiritual realms.[31] Likewise, "Carmilla," the final tale in the volume, continually collapses the distinction between reality and fantasy by setting much of the central action of its plot within the context of dreams. In fact, the traumatic nature of dream work drives the plot, as the latent dreamscapes of "Carmilla," the scenes depicting violation and desire, inevitably prove to be more real than the manifest surfaces of its material world. If Freud had not come to write his *Die Traumdeutung* in 1899, in other words, the readers of "Carmilla" would have found it necessary to invent it. The story also works as a near-perfect version of the generic Radcliffean or Richardsonian tale of confinement and seduction, but unlike other avatars of the female Gothic, "Carmilla" stages its confinement-seduction narrative between two young women, both of whom appear to have only just reached sexual maturation.

The story's narrator, Laura, begins by telling us of her father's heritage as an Englishman, of the family's displaced life in Austria, of her own isolation and desire for friendship, and, most importantly, of the early death of her mother. Laura's mother was a descendant of the Karnstein family, an Austrian noble line. As several critics have been quick to point out, the fact that Laura's father is characterized as an Englishman who purchased a "feudal" estate in a "lonely and primitive place" upon retiring from the foreign service marks the story out as an allegory of the basic Anglo-Irish colonial dynamic. Furthermore, Laura's want of a mother helps to define both her inveterate solitude and her devout longing for a female other who can reflect back to her a coherent and soothing maternal image. As with most proto-Lacanian romances, though, the desire to return to the *Real* that manifests itself throughout "Carmilla" remains only as an impossible and retrograde phantasy. Finally, Laura's trauma is not that she has lost a mother but that she must be saved from one, that her identity seems incapable of moving beyond the moment of abjection. In *Powers of Horror,* Julia Kristeva explains the psychoanalytic concept of abjection. For Kristeva, abjection, figured as a violent breaking away from the phallic mother, involves a "subjective diachrony" (13). Abjection actually precedes the constitution of identity and involves rendering the mother both desired and repugnant. Before becoming a subject homologous to or in imitation of the mother, the infant's originary relation with the mother is one of absolute identification. "Carmilla" acts as a text that works to render maternal inheritance itself as abject. The text locates the source of weakness and cultural hybridity not in the union of Laura's English father and Austrian mother, but rather solely in terms of the consuming horrors of *Amor Matris.* The traumatic childhood dream experience that Laura recounts near the very beginning of the text maps both the tale's troubled relationship to colonial polity and its coextensive fixation with maternal abjection.

Laura describes her traumatic nightmare experience as "one of the very earliest incidents of my life which I can recollect" (224). In the dream experience that she recounts, she appears to awake only to find herself, uncharacteristically, alone in her nursery. On the verge of tears, the child-Laura sees,

> a solemn, but very pretty face looking at me from the side of the bed. It was that of a young lady who was kneeling with her hands under the coverlet. I looked at her with a kind of wonder, and ceased whimpering. She caressed me with her hands, and lay down beside me on the bed, and drew me towards her, smiling; I felt immediately soothed and fell asleep again. I was awakened by a sensation as if two needles ran into my breast very deep at the same moment, and I cried loudly. The lady started back, with her eyes fixed on me, and then slipped down upon the floor, and, as I thought, hid herself under the bed. (225)

Though it certainly seems consistent with the logic of the story and of the historical period to read this reported dream experience as a heteronormative culture's encoding of lesbianism as child molestation, Laura's memory leaves us with a great deal of ideological symbolism to unpack. The rather striking passage balances Laura's desire for a mother—for a woman to reflect back to her a consoling and unifying *imago*—against the ominously suggestive counter-*imago* of a young woman who provides consolation only as she caresses the female child "under the coverlet" and eventually penetrates her.[32] Molestation and vampirism, therefore, get bound together with lesbianism and with maternity. When Carmilla, the lovely young girl who comes to stay with the family as a guest after her carriage mysteriously overturns outside the feudal Schloss, finally arrives, an eighteen-year-old Laura immediately recognizes this new acquaintance as the figure who attacked her in childhood (233). Laura feels instantly drawn to and frightened by Carmilla. As Victor Sage indicates in *Le Fanu's Gothic,* however, the text consistently preempts Laura's suspicions by allowing Carmilla to tell stories about her own dreams that "mirror" the horrific nightmares that Laura experiences nearly every evening.[33]

Upon meeting Laura outside the Schloss, Carmilla explains that when she, too, was only a child she had a dream that provides the mirror image of Laura's originary nightmare. We could say that through the reverse angle of mirroring, Laura's nightmare transforms into Carmilla's fulfilling dream, but even taken on its own accord, Laura's dream reveals the double logic of her desires. Laura wishes for a maternal other, for a nurturing face that can mirror her own, and Carmilla certainly provides just such a figure. Laura's wish invokes a connection to her maternal homeland in Austria, where her father resides as a foreigner and landowner. If, following the basics of Freudian dream analysis, the dream acts both as a wish fulfillment and the symbolic reconstitution of childhood trauma, then Laura's dream actually squares the Freudian circle by making the wish to rediscover and return to the maternal other into the condition of possibility for the subject's trauma in the first place. Where Freud casts the meanings of any given dream as invariably overdetermined and the work of analysis as, subsequently, circular and never quite complete, the dream work of Le Fanu's story remains intractably linear. Laura dreams of, and so wishes for, a mother, but in this case the wish itself initiates and embodies the trauma. To wish for a mother—to reconnect with the maternal or indigenous line—in this context is also to wish for self-annihilation. Far from providing the narcissistic spectacle that Laura craves, the maternal figure of Carmilla finally acts as a source of defilement, dehumanization, and abject terror, and by identifying with such a mother figure, Laura risks becoming the vampiric terror that she beholds. As Nina Auerbach indicates in *Our Vampires, Ourselves,* Laura begins to see her own face in the vampire's (67). The basic structure of this dream recurs in various forms three other times in the text, and following each dream experience, Laura feels a strange ambivalence, a feeling of being "drawn towards" the figure's beauty and, at the same time, "something of repulsion" (237). Even at the very end of the tale, Laura claims that the remembered image of Carmilla returns to her "with ambiguous alternations—sometimes the playful, languid, beautiful girl; sometimes the writhing fiend" (288). The language of the text continually locates the source of the double bind in the maternal figure itself.

Though it seems tempting to code Carmilla as simply a wrong mother in the same way that Maturin codes certain unions as wrong marriages, her genetic relationship to Laura remains more than merely symbolic. When Laura and her father examine some recently refurbished portraits from their family gallery, Laura discovers one that bears a "wonderful likeness" to Carmilla (246). The portrait of Mircalla, Countess Karnstein, is marked by the date 1698, and Laura explains that she is descended from the Karnsteins through her mother's line (248). The portrait's date, 1698, traces the maternal line to the general era of the Williamite confiscations and to the specific year in which Anglo-Irishman William Molyneux's *Case of Ireland* claimed that Ireland be considered a sovereign kingdom and that the English parliament had no right to legislate for the Irish people.[34] In Le Fanu's story, Carmilla and Mircalla are one, and Carmilla acts as the *materfamilius*—the big mother—of Laura's Karnstein lineage. Hence, Le Fanu depicts Laura's confinement within a matrilineal inheritance as a form of social and ethno-genetic regression, as a failure to move beyond the stage of abjection and toward subjectivity. The mother is converted into a figure for an undead past that must be rejected for the sake of a living future. If the Karnstein mother is beastly dead, the text asks, will her children follow her?

Victor Sage claims that the text stages an encounter between the Darwinian logic of late-Victorian imperialism and Christological superstitions. The Karnsteins, Sage explains, "repeat the sterile genealogy of a landowning class, which is nothing more than a heritage of suicide, destroying itself by preying upon the peasantry and then suicidally upon itself. In fact, the whole blood-line has committed suicide, and stolen its own future. It is a conspiracy to substitute repetition for development" (198). That Carmilla becomes a vampire as a result of suicide further underscores the terror and weakness inherent in the maternal bloodline. As a kind of sow who quite literally feeds on her own farrow, Carmilla prefigures Stephen Dedalus's misogynist depiction of Ireland as a self-betraying mother. Moreover, in moving from the model of the wrong marriage to the problem of racial heritage, Le Fanu converts what first appeared as a sociohistorical problem into an ontogenetic one. As Sage argues, the Victorian scientific discourses of racial and natural history that began with Darwin allow Le Fanu to depict the Carmilla who haunts Laura's nightmares as regressing into animal forms.[35] Thus, the unholy union that had worked as an allegory of political interaction in Maturin's Gothic transforms into a fully internalized and symbolic struggle between the self and its regressive ethno-genealogy in Le Fanu's. The text's move to internalize the conflicts of the double bind, to contain the cycle of terror by placing it in the realm of maternity, finds its dialectical reversal in the weakened, aging, ineffective patriarchal figures represented by Laura's own father and by General Spielsdorf, whose young ward Bertha was killed by Mircalla before the story began. Even though Le Fanu's tale finally equates the impurities of a maternal and indigenous racial line with autophagy, it cannot imagine a patriarchy that can supercede this infectious and destructive problem, for, as we are told in a prefatory note, Dr. Hesselius's informant, Laura, died shortly after sharing her narrative. Thus, we are left to ask whether Laura's traumatic experiences or her inherited Karnstein illness finally destroyed her. In either case, the powerful weakness of the maternal line cannot be contained by the weakened power of the paternal one. Through both its figural and formal maneuvers, "Carmilla" works to internalize the double binds of masculine anxiety, to find a rhetorical space in which to contain the disjunctions that mark the Unionist Gothic, but, much like *Melmoth the Wanderer,* Le Fanu's story finally ends up being structured by the desire for bipolarity that it works to overcome. Though "Carmilla" certainly holds together better than *Melmoth,* its formal unity is always built around antinomies like dream/reality, desired/ repugnant, and mother/devourer. Despite the fact that the text seeks to contain all of these bipolar terrors within the figure of a maternal past, terror inevitably bleeds out onto and stains all of the other identities in the story.

For the most part, Le Fanu acts as a transitional figure. Though his later Gothic fiction takes up many of the gender anxieties that, more than a half century earlier, had characterized Maturin's post-1798 writing, Le Fanu also lies at a different threshold in Irish history. As we have already seen, he lived through the Famine, the advent of Fenianism, and the slow, melancholy withdrawal of Anglo-Irish political power. When he died in 1873, it would only be two years until Charles Stewart Parnell would be elected to Parliament and six years until, with the assistance of Michael Davitt, Parnell would help to nourish the nascent Land League and to permanently change the terrain of the Irish question by supporting the concept of home rule. With the death of Le Fanu and the emergence of Parnellism and the home rule crisis, the engines of the Unionist Gothic seemed to grind to a halt. The marriage metaphors engendered by the Union had evolved into the questions of personal and national sovereignty implicit in the idea of Irish home rule. But Le Fanu's conversion of the male/female Gothic binary into the single figure of the maternal revenant continued to haunt the cultural imaginary of late-Victorian and modernist Ireland. If the social and historical antinomies of post-1798 Irish masculinity migrate into the formal features of Maturin's novels, then Le Fanu's Gothic evinces a powerful desire to reimagine masculine anxiety through the avatar of a languid maternal figure who must be rejected for the sake of future growth. For Le Fanu an older, more feminine social world must be rejected.

In the next chapter we will observe that, to some extent, in their most famous prose fictions both Bram Stoker and Oscar Wilde begin by exploring issues of confinement and masculine identity. Through the Jonathan Harker narrative in *Dracula,* Stoker re-envisions and fuses the colonial adventure tale and the female Gothic story. Like Maturin, Stoker converts the feminine confinement narrative into an invert and colonial one in which a hero, now expressly male, is in danger of being incarcerated and penetrated.[36] Wilde's *Picture of Dorian Gray* borrows a great deal of its structure and imagery from *Melmoth the Wanderer* while also managing to follow Le Fanu's lead by embodying in the single character of Dorian both the Satanic terrorist and the languid, feminized figure. Dorian becomes both the threat and the threatened. More importantly, however, Wilde transforms the tropological structure of the female-confinement narrative into a rather decadent meditation on the autonomy of art. In *De Profundis,* his final piece, Wilde takes the opportunity of his literal confinement at Reading Gaol to reflect more fully on the potential failings of any social system based on privacy and solitude. *De Profundis* reveals the dialectical problems that inhere in Wilde's own decadence and in capitalism by casting them both in a language that resonates quite clearly with the terrors embodied by the confinement narratives of the female Gothic. The male exile as female confinement narrative that was continually refined, rearranged, and refurbished by the Unionist Gothic, finally becomes thematized in a most overt sense by Stoker's *Dracula* and transformed into a proto-modernist theory of autonomous art in the life and work of Oscar Wilde. In terms of literary history, then, it is precisely in the space between male anxiety and female privation that Irish modernism's aesthetic obsession with autonomy was conceived.

CHAPTER 3

The Revolution Within

Wilde's Gothic and the Confines of Convention

> Giving form to antagonisms does not reconcile or eliminate them.
>
> —Theodor W. Adorno, *Aesthetic Theory*

> Aesthete of Aesthetes
> What's in a name?
> The Poet is Wilde
> But his Poetry's tame.
>
> —"Swinburne on Wilde," *Punch,* 25 June 1881

After completing his sentence of two years' hard labor and leaving Pentonville Prison in May of 1897, a frail, physically worn Oscar Wilde headed to Dieppe, France, under the pseudonym Sebastian Melmoth. During Wilde's stay on the continent, the English Impressionist painter and sometime "Jack the Ripper" suspect Walter Sickert sketched in chiaroscuro what amounts to one of the most striking portraits of Wilde. In the sketch, entitled "Sebastian Melmoth (OW)," the subject appears to be reclining into a reflective, distant, and self-protective posture. His face is neither that of the noble, young, aesthete Wilde depicted in the famous Napoleon Sarony photographs taken in 1882 nor the highly feminized, rotund, squinting Wilde represented in Max Beerbohm's notorious caricatures or Henri Toulouse-Lautrec's late portrait. Instead, the figure portrayed in "Sebastian Melmoth (OW)" appears at once gaunt, embittered, and defeated and, perhaps paradoxically, dangerous, macabre, and vampiric. His eyes are neither squinting nor invisible but, rather, dark, fathomless, forbidding. Though longish hair hangs down around the face in a way that certainly betrays the aesthetic zeal of the youthful, Wildean dandy, Sickert's Sebastian Melmoth seems to have lived on for centuries and to have had his life slowly, inexorably drained away. The figure remains both threat and threatened. In this fashion, Sickert's sketch captures precisely what Wilde's Sebastian Melmoth persona had itself intended to represent: the paradoxical image of a supposed terror who has been terrorized, a potential victimizer who has also been the victim of his own symbolic and precarious life.

Sebastian Melmoth appears as a captive of his own carefully forged identity. Quite obviously, any figure who intends to bring together the masochistic beauty of Sebastian, the young saint bound and penetrated by arrows, with the satanic and sadistic force of C. R. Maturin's famed wanderer, Melmoth, also intends to foreground how our separate private and public personas invariably militate against each other, no matter how much care we take in crafting them.[1] The saintly persona is held captive—trapped—by the demonic only as the demon remains confined by the saint. In fact, in the strange case of Sebastian Melmoth each persona, that of terrorized saint and terrorizing demon, works to contain its other while also holding to the impossibly contradictory idea that the two antithetical personas might somehow end up striking a balance or being complementary. The tension between these two mutually imprisoning personalities characterizes more than just Wilde's posttrial identity. It also characterizes an entire literary-critical tradition that has persistently depicted Oscar Wilde himself as both the heroic self-creator and the tragically stereotyped hedonist. So, even from the perspective of literary history, Wilde has become something like his own double. In this fashion, as we saw in chapter 1, Sebastian Melmoth provides the apotheosis, the embodiment par excellence, of the Gothic double binds that characterized post-1798 Irish masculinity. Wilde's persona puts pressure on that double bind by very consciously evoking the image of a rationally impossible individual who occupies the position of both terrorist and terrorized.

In late nineteenth-century Ireland, of course, this type of contradictory and ambivalent identity was certainly not peculiar to Wilde. An infamous political cartoon entitled "The Irish Vampire," published in 1885 in the English newspaper, *Punch,* depicts Ireland's National Land League as an ominous vampire bat with a face peculiarly reminiscent of Charles Stewart Parnell's, Ireland's most noteworthy Victorian-era political leader, descending upon a young and helpless maiden. In a curiously antipathetic extension of the postUnion gender double bind that we've seen played out again and again, Lady Erin, depicted here as resolutely helpless, finds herself threatened by a vampiric, Irish masculine terror. The terror here is from within Ireland itself. In 1879, Michael Davitt had established the Irish Land League, and Parnell quickly became the organization's first president. A particularly harsh winter coupled with a long stretch of damp weather in 1878 placed Ireland's rural population in its worst economic position since the Great Famine of the 1840s. Davitt, the rather vocal leader of the Irish Fenians, felt strongly that a land agitation group would help to support tenant farmers while also giving voice to the concerns of liberal home rulers and republicans alike. Finally, like Parnell himself, Davitt imagined that an aggressive program of land agitation might help to facilitate Ireland's movement toward independence and, at least in some sense, create a much-needed political consensus among the Irish people. The league received wide national approval in Ireland and a great deal of funding from expatriate Fenians in America.[2]

In his analysis of the Irish Free State movement, *Britain and Irish Separatism*, Thomas E. Hachey claims that the league's primary purposes were to halt evictions, reduce land rents, and "ultimately, to make tenant farmers the owners of their land" (22). Parnell and Davitt wanted to oust the exploitative inheritance and ascendancy class systems overseen by the British and the Anglo-Irish landlords. Though the league's primary function was to use boycotts to achieve its ends, in following the basic structure of nineteenth-century Irish political engagement, it often resorted to violence against the offending landlords and their farms. Gladstone's Parliament in London offered a conciliatory bill. When Parnell rejected it, he was imprisoned under the auspices of the British Coercion Bill, and, in 1881 the Land League was outlawed. "The Irish Vampire" cartoon's translation of Irishness into the figure of an embattled, threatened, penetrable female and, simultaneously, into the figure of a monstrous vampire bat seems rather telling. Like Sebastian Melmoth, Ireland appears as a self-threatening and divided entity, an entity that in this case remains coded as both a vulnerable woman and a vampiric man. Unlike the "Irish Vampire," however, Wilde's Sebastian Melmoth identity was self-imposed. Where Irish writers like W. B. Yeats and Irish politicians like Davitt and Parnell had been fighting to unify Ireland through Celtic myth, through the home rule movement, and through the Land League, Wilde purposefully adopted a paradoxical identity, an identity divided against itself. Moreover, Wilde's pose as Sebastian Melmoth adopts both the vulnerable and delicate femininity implied by the confined beauty of Saint Sebastian and the violent and bellicose masculinity implied by the sublimely demonic Melmoth. In this way, Wilde embraces the political and personal tensions from which his Irish contemporaries seemed to flee. As in his aphorisms and in much of his work, he presents paradox as a truth that one might just be able to realize, work through, and embody. Finally, however, even though Oscar Wilde's thought and writing revel in the contradictory, we see in the persona of Sebastian Melmoth and in Sickert's sketch of that persona, someone for whom contradiction ended up as a rather lethal lived experience.

Over the last decade both gender theory and Irish studies have taken up Wilde's cause by attempting to make some sense of Wilde's various fin de siècle personas and of his fate as either the martyr of homoerotic desire on the one hand or an ambivalently colonized subject on the other. Though both the gendered approaches (primarily queer theory) and the Irish postcolonial ones end up portraying Wilde as a kind of urbane, tragic hero, an inveterate wit who was destroyed by contrasting social pressures, in each case Wilde's life, along with the personal and professional experiments that attended it, appears to have failed for different reasons. For the most part, that is, the gender and the Irish studies approaches disagree on precisely why Wilde's experiments in prose and personality failed. For the gender and queer studies approaches that follow the path cut by Ed Cohen's *Talk on the Wilde Side* and Alan Sinfield's *The Wilde Century,* both of which are basically Foucauldian genealogical studies, Wilde comes to embody an ambiguously desiring subject who was subsequently reconstituted by public pressure, by media discourse, and, indeed, by his own status as self-produced icon into the *ne plus ultra* of homosexual otherness.[3] The poststructuralist and queer theory approach readily accommodates Wilde's penchant for contradiction by making all of his art exemplary of his personal and erotic desire to refute binaries and embrace paradox. In this version of things, Wilde appears far too radical for his historical moment, and, in the end, the prejudices and limitations of that historical moment finally appear to have destroyed him.

The postcolonial impression of Wilde has taken a different route. In his *Short History of Irish Literature,* Seamus Deane, perhaps Ireland's most celebrated literary historian and postcolonial critic, claims that in nearly all of Wilde's drama, the plots remain highly conventional and "the subversive element is almost entirely contained by the dialogue" (136).[4] In this version of things, Wilde never seems quite radical enough. In the narrative of Irish literary history constructed by Deane and a host of others, the role of radical will be played by someone like W. B. Yeats or, even better, by James Joyce. Oscar Wilde will fill the role of precursor, fit to start a scene or two. Though most postcolonial critics would certainly agree that Wilde has a keen ear for the fecund possibilities of language and a profound sense of the malleability of persona, he appears confined by literary conventions and merely sets the stage for the more crucial, more revolutionary work to be done by the colossal, decolonizing figures of Yeats and Joyce.

The gender approaches and the postcolonial ones do seem to concur on one central problem. For both, Wilde appears trapped by powerful and intransigent conventions. The gender studies take imagines Wilde as the figure through which bourgeois consciousness came to develop and imagine the divide between hetero- and homosexuality. In this instance, Wilde, an author who actively embraces contradiction and multiplicity, gets trapped within the singular, sexualized identity that marked both the precedent for the criminalization of certain forms of male sexuality in fin de siècle England and the foundation for modern conceptions of decency and indecency. To the Irish studies contingent, Wilde appears confined by the conventions of English dramatic and prose forms. In the *Field Day Anthology of Irish Writing,* in fact, Deane goes so far as to claim that in all of Wilde's work, "the subversive, even radical, critique of society that is implicit in what he has to say, finds no release within the linguistic conventions which he mocked but by which he remained imprisoned" (721).[5] When we read these gender and postcolonial approaches side by side, however, the central feature of Wilde's art and life becomes precisely the tension between his overtly subversive persona and aesthetic instincts on the one side and his highly sentimental and apparently bourgeois works of art on the other. In either case, however, Wilde himself seems to struggle against that most Gothic of all literary tropes: confinement.

In an attempt to balance the Irish postcolonial and gender studies approaches to Wilde's life and work, Vicki Mahaffey writes in *States of Desire: Wilde, Joyce, Yeats, and the Irish Experiment* that "Wilde's fall came about largely because of the way he was troped (and trapped) by caricatures, but Wilde's writings express values that are diametrically opposed to such labeling; they endorse a methodology that is anti-representational, self-contradictory, and dynamic" (37). Mahaffey goes on to claim that "what ruined Oscar Wilde was, ultimately, an image, a representation, a stereotype (disseminated largely through satirical plays and the popular press, especially in cartoons in *Punch*); he was *textualized* (41). So, for Deane, Wilde was trapped within the conventions of an English—and so, of an imperial—aesthetic ideology, an ideology with which, try as he might, Wilde could never fully break. For Mahaffey, Wilde was trapped within the stereotyped identity formulated to describe the salacious details of "indecent" behavior and to inscribe the supposed moral truths of normative, "decent," heterosexual conduct. In Deane's version, Wilde remains trapped within formal conventions; in Mahaffey's, he remains trapped within cultural ones. From another perspective, for Deane, Wilde's extratextual identity does not really matter at all because, whatever else Wilde may have been, he was primarily a famous playwright, and he must be judged by the standards set by his work. For Mahaffey, on the other hand, since Wilde played so openly and so often with writing, identity, and persona, nothing about him could possibly be considered extratextual. After all, he was, and in some sense sought to be, as Mahaffey tells us, "*textualized.*" This leads Mahaffey to claim that Wilde's work was "antirepresentational." Despite my desire to see in Mahaffey's take on all of this a careful balancing of the postcolonial and the queer theory Wilde, something about Deane's apparently brusque yet thoroughly dialectical formalism seems right here. After all, Wilde's plays—even *The Importance of Being Earnest*—certainly operate primarily at the level of romantic, if not to say bourgeois, sentimentalism, despite the pyrotechnics of the dialogue. Moreover, though Wilde's one novel, *The Picture of Dorian Gray,* certainly entertains personal experimentation, narcissism, and nonconformity at the level of content, it also seems to be profoundly moralistic in tone and, setting aside the self-contradictory "Preface," a fairly conventional revision of the tropes we find in late-Victorian Gothic revivalism.

Much like the Anglo-Irish Gothic of his great uncle Maturin's *Melmoth the Wanderer,* Wilde's *Dorian Gray* operates primarily at the level of moralism, deploys the supernatural to ironic effect, and ends with the apparently deserved death of its titular antihero. Wilde's aesthetic experimentalism almost always appears contained within the confines of very recognizable conventions. By confining the experimental within the conventional, however, Wilde's *Dorian Gray* evolves into something more than a mere repetition of Gothic conventions. In the previous chapter, I claimed that the Gothic itself nearly always attempts to present a morally unambiguous social world. Gothic villains always appear inhuman, and Gothic heroes always act heroically. But, as we've seen very clearly in the writings of Maturin, when a writer deploys the Gothic's moral typology in order to resolve historical problems and to restore order, that typology itself becomes so convoluted and overdetermined that the distinction between good and bad, between right and wrong, actually breaks down. The more that Gothic novels like *The Mysteries of Udolpho, The Monk, Fatal Revenge,* or *Melmoth the Wanderer* attempt to clarify and disambiguate the morality of the social order, the more they actually obfuscate and reambiguate that very order. Their villains are often so petty and excessive that the novels can only respond to and punish them with equal amounts of pettiness and excess. Wilde's invocation of Gothic conventions in *Dorian Gray* certainly makes the novel moralistic, and Wilde himself proclaimed in his letter of 26 June 1890 to the *St. James's Gazette* that *Dorian Gray* was "a story with a moral. And the moral is this: all excess, as well as all renunciation, brings its own punishment" (339); but Wilde's tale actually realizes and emphasizes the ambiguous moral tensions that previous Gothic novels had attempted to conceal or eradicate. Wilde certainly accepts the boundaries and conventions of the genre, but he also uses his knowledge of those boundaries to open up new possibilities within the genre itself.

In response to the problem posed by Deane's assertion and by my own reading of Wilde's work, then, a question strikes me: can Deane's conclusions about the repressed conventionality of Wilde's art somehow line up with Mahaffey's conclusions about the irrepressible unconventionality of Wilde's life? When we reimagine this question in the form of a Wildean paradox, we might find that we can bring the gendered and postcolonial approaches to Wilde together by claiming that Wilde's work always seems, at once, all too radical and not quite radical enough. Wilde's most innovative contribution to literary and social history lies precisely in his capacity to invoke and borrow conventions, then. Similarly, in his 2003 *Tame Passions of Wilde: The Styles of Manageable Desire,* Jeff Nunokawa argues that Wilde attempted to imagine and represent desire itself as something both "safe and sensational" (2).[6] The central tension in Wilde's work always involves finding a balance between the social or aesthetic conventions that one must invoke and the innovative, autonomous genius that one must strive to embody. In order to sustain this claim, we'll have to look not only at the way that Wilde deploys and alludes to a conventional form like the Gothic in his writing, but also at how Wilde's work, very explicitly, accepts and embraces the confines of conventional forms in an effort to rethink, mock, and manipulate those forms. In a sense, then, Wilde's literary conventionality acts as a commentary on social conventions, an attempt to stretch conventions to their most extreme limits yet still maintain them, an endeavor to make a space within conventionality for the unconventional. By placing Wilde's writing, most particularly the rumination on artistic self-creation in *The Picture of Dorian Gray,* adjacent to the two other major nineteenth-century texts in the Irish Gothic tradition, *Dracula* and *Melmoth the Wanderer,* this chapter will explore how Wilde's texts consciously invoke and accept certain conventions from the Irish Gothic literary tradition. If we begin, however, by looking at the basic strategies of Wilde's forcefully counterintuitive style of writing, what we might call his "immanent dialectics," then we'll see how Wilde actually imagines accepting the confines of conventionality as a revolutionary aesthetic—and by extension social—activity.

II. WILDE'S IMMANENT DIALECTICS

Throughout Wilde's work, confinement acts as a potent metaphor. Dorian Gray works very hard to reject the social conventions that confine him, but the very literal confines of the picture frame that contains his portrait symbolize those constraints placed upon his identity which he has fully internalized. The dandies and aesthetes in Wilde's various plays find their social identities to be so intensely confining that they must find ways to revise and rewrite the world around them. Finally, some of Wilde's most powerfully affecting pieces of writing, "The Ballad of the Reading Gaol" and *De Profundis,* point to his own deep sensitivity to the literal confinements of prison life and the figural confinements provided by social interaction and societal norms. That is to say that Wilde's dramatic and prose pieces actively thematize the confines of convention as something that the aesthete characters—the Lord Henry Wottons, Dorian Grays, Lord Gorings, Lord Darlingtons, and Algernon Moncrieffs—must acknowledge, face up to, and in some strange, egocentric fashion, try to manipulate. They may succeed or fail in profoundly different ways, but they always work within the confines of conventions in an attempt to play with and revise those conventions. As it turns out, the method through which Lord Henry manipulates social gatherings with his countless witticisms and verbal paradoxes and the way that Algernon manipulates his own social persona via the dissimulating act he refers to as "Bunburying" both signify markedly individual stylistic choices that accept the constraints provided by social convention as necessary while at the same time reworking and mocking those very conventions. Although Lord Henry certainly enjoys appearing scandalous, he readily accepts the basic principles of social convention. In this way his witticisms and paradoxes merely mark his place and his social identity within his culture. He is the urbane wit who never truly offends or violates the social world that he pretends to detest. Lord Henry could not appear scandalous if his society actually changed. Algernon accepts convention by inventing a friend/persona, Bunbury, through which he can maintain his acceptable identity as the future Lord Moncrieff and still flout conventions when he chooses to go "Bunburying." In this fashion, the dialectic that animates Wilde's thought is always a dialectic that places an individual stylist like Lord Henry or Algernon and his or her personal "meaning" directly inside of a certain conventional structure. These characters subsist within convention. For Wilde, being confined does not necessarily entail being limited to a singular or a fixed identity so long as one understands and can influence the boundaries of the confining social conventions. His aesthetes and dandies find or manipulate meaning from the inside. In fact, we could go so far as to say that the Wildean dialectic is always an intensely internal or immanent one. The key to the immanent dialectic of Wilde's style subsists in his ability to present us with characters who might flirt either with exceeding the boundaries of social convention or with capitulating fully to social demands, but the most successful of Wilde's characters always manage to accede to the demands of society while also opening up a space in which to perform their personal and aesthetic experiments.

I have taken the term "immanent dialectic" from Theodor W. Adorno's first book, his *Habilitationschrift* entitled *Kierkegaard, Konstruktion des Asthetischen* [*Kierkegaard: Construction of the Aesthetic*]. Adorno's text is a provocative and thoughtful interrogation of the nineteenth-century Danish thinker Søren Kierkegaard and the German phenomenological and existential philosophies that were informed by his writings in the 1920s and 1930s. In his review of the 1989 English-language translation of Adorno's *Kierkegaard,* Peter Fenves draws attention to Adorno's use of the term "*wörtliche Metapher*" or "literal Metaphor" (104). Adorno claims that in reading Kierkegaard's metaphors literally, "the mythical content of his philosophy breaks through" (12). For Adorno, analyzing the metaphorical language that a writer uses demonstrates how the basic prejudices of the material world, those things that we might call foundational, ideological myths, limit even the most radical thinkers. Simply speaking, then, the metaphors that Kierkegaard deploys betray both his background and the social world in which he wrote. Literal metaphors are, as Fenves explains, "phenomenalized figures, figures reduced to their phenomenological content and, to this extent, divorced from the systematic, rationalistic, and idealistic intentions to which they were put to use. Literalization [is] the reduction of each figure to its original lexical position" (104–5). Kierkegaard's philosophy works to isolate the most basic elements of the individual—elements like personal desire, choice, and, most importantly, style—from the conformity implicit in what he refers to in *Concluding Unscientific Postscripts,* as the "great masses" that make us feel that we have some extrapersonal meaning or collective identity in life. For Kierkegaard, the true individual, the subjective thinker, has a form "for his communication with other men, and this form constitutes his style" (*Concluding Unscientific Prospects* 319). By formulating an intensely personal and eccentric style, the subject begins to discover his or her inner meaning. Meaning, then, is discovered for Kierkegaard via inwardness and interiority and not by looking out into the world and the conformist masses that populate it.

Adorno seizes in particular on Kierkegaard's use of the concept of the interior in "Diary of a Seducer." Kierkegaard uses the metaphor of a specific room in a bourgeois home to describe the way a subject should order, stylize, and control his or her private meaning. Here, as Adorno is quick to point out, "the material goes beyond the intention of the metaphor" (43). The bourgeois living space, the room of one's own, becomes the psychic symbol for subjective thought. This room is furnished, as Kierkegaard describes it, with the kind of carpet, lighting, and décor that give the individual comfort and personal satisfaction (*Either/ Or* 384–85). On the one hand, Kierkegaard's approach attempts to renounce that subject-object dialectic that has controlled philosophy—whether philosophers refer to it as a Platonic binary, Cartesian dualism, or Hegelian dialectic—by preferring a fully internal relationship between an entirely isolated individual and his or her personal meaning. In this kind of thinking, the material world is very forcefully renounced, and the subject formulates an "immanent dialectic" with his or her own meaning. The most revolutionary act, then, is to turn within, to seek the truths of the self within the self. Kierkegaard's tactic provides for a powerful way of removing the individual from the conformity implied by the masses or by any sort of collective identity that erases specificity and difference. On the other hand, Kierkegaard unconsciously draws on a conformist metaphor—the bourgeois interior, the intimate space decorated to one's taste—in order to prescribe the structure of this supposedly nonconformist, existential subjectivity. For Adorno, this move signifies Kierkegaard's entrapment within the very historical and social conditions that he seeks to overturn. The bourgeois space becomes both the model for the renunciation of conformity and the site of reification. The whole notion of an interior unconsciously accepts certain bourgeois social conventions about space and privacy on the way to staking out the location of individuality. From this, we can also conclude that one's internal or personal style, no matter how different, individualized, and eccentric it might appear, has to accept certain norms and conventions in order to be recognized as rhetorically effective in the first place.

Like Kierkegaard's then, Wilde's is an immanent dialectic, one that, whether we like it or not, readily accepts certain social and aesthetic conventions in order to make a space for personal style and autonomy. Likewise, Wilde's literal metaphors are always culled from bourgeois society. Central to Wilde's basic stylistic maneuver, however, is a counterintuitive reversal of conventional morality or wisdom. The trick here is that Wilde's counterintuitive reversals actually accept the ends of the conventional while simply substituting unconventional means for achieving these ends. This maneuver at the level of content mirrors a similar one at the level of form. Here, as someone like Seamus Deane would have it, Wilde certainly accepts conventional principles—that the Gothic must thematize confinement, that the drawing room comedy must conclude in sentimentalized romance, that an essay on social change must finally reaffirm some already accepted moral truth—but Wilde also deploys unconventional formal means in order to achieve these ends. His Gothic confines men instead of women, his drawing room romances redeem the manipulative and languid characters, and his essays realize socially accepted moral principles only through paradox.

In the dramas, Wilde achieves this formal and structural effect by imagining in dandy characters like Lord Goring of *An Ideal Husband* a playwright within the play. Such characters influence the action by rewriting letters, controlling discourse, and manipulating objects in order to bend the social world depicted in the plays to their respective wills. This is the kind of action that Shakespeare had allowed villainous characters like Iago and Don John or ambivalent figures like Prospero to perform. In Wilde's plays, two coextensive issues make the figure of the playwright within the play appear, at once, problematically conformist and singularly innovative. First, a character like Lord Goring never really intends to forsake society or its various rules. His revolutionary power does not consist in his desire to either abjure the social world, as a Nietzsche or a Kierkegaard might suggest, or change it irrevocably as a Marx might demand, and in the end Lord Goring's marriage to Mabel Chiltern merely confirms his status as haute bourgeois gentleman and prospective patriarch. Secondly, however, by manipulating Robert Chiltern, Lady Chiltern, and Mrs. Cheveley, Lord Goring actually rewrites and rethinks their desires, and he does so with unrivaled artistry and inimitable style. So as a figure who recognizes the rules of society—recognizes the basic formal conventions that build and destroy reputations and social positions—Lord Goring deploys those very rules and conventions in order to trigger the effects he chooses. He is an artist whose material is the social world. He reads social forms as if they were literary forms. The trick here, and in plays like *The Importance of Being Earnest* and *Lady Windermere's Fan,* is that the playwright within the play manipulates and rewrites the action in order to keep society running as it had before the play began. Both a pragmatist and an opportunist, the playwright within the play may be a powerful manipulator, an aesthete, and a narcissist to be sure, but he is also an advocate of the status quo and the ever-same. He has accepted the confines of society so that he may manipulate them. These confines provide him with something akin to a language that he has so thoroughly mastered that he can deploy its various puns and rhetorical tropes more effectively than anyone else.

We see another example of Wilde's immanent dialectic in his masterfully counterintuitive 1890 essay, "The Soul of Man Under Socialism." Wilde begins the essay by asserting that "the chief advantage that would result from the establishment of Socialism is, undoubtedly, the fact that Socialism would relieve us from the sordid necessity of living for others" (1079). Rather than rehearsing the predicable defense of Socialism—that it would create a more equitable and collective society—Wilde reassures his readers that Socialism would actually free us of such concerns and create a utopian world of self-interested individuals. Wilde defends a radical social agenda by fitting it within the accepted ends of capitalist conceptions of individualism. He has imagined from within the moral and social program of liberal capitalist democracy a way to make Socialism into the purest realization of Adam Smith's invisible hand. In such a society, Wilde explains, people will be free to generate their own styles, their own minds, and their own personas without having to "meddle with others," and, furthermore, such self-interest will create a more colorful, differentiated, vibrantly liberated, and, finally, moral world (1084). Socialism, then, would affirm rather than deny the personal and cultural achievements of bourgeois society. In "The Decay of Lying," of course, Wilde puts this kind of claim another way. There he has Vivian say that a true artist like Renaissance portrait painter Hans Holbein "compelled life to accept his conditions, to restrain itself within his limitations, to reproduce his type and to appear as he wished it to appear. It is style that makes us believe in a thing—nothing but style" (989). In challenging Aristotle's major aesthetic claim that art is the mirror held up to nature, Wilde actually accepts the world and its various social and natural forms as givens that the true artist must bend to his or her will. In Wilde's dialogue, as in his essays and his plays, the aesthete works within a convention, often a very conservative, bourgeois artistic or cultural convention such as "portraiture," "social order," or "individualism," in order to show how his or her radical style fits within that convention and actualizes its already accepted and acknowledged moral, political, and social ends. In this way, the dialectic that animates Wilde's thought always places the aesthete stylist inside of a conventional structure that he or she must acknowledge, influence, and finally realize. From within a convention, then, the aesthete constructs new and innovative meanings. Hence, Wilde's immanent dialectic allows him and many of his dandy characters to appear at once all too radical and not quite radical enough.

III. WILDE AND THE ANGLO-IRISH GOTHIC TRADITION

Up to this point, the writers of the Irish Gothic tradition whom we have studied have represented and allegorized what I have referred to as the logic of the justified victim. We see in the writings of Maturin and Joseph Sheridan Le Fanu an intensive investigation of how, following the 1800 Acts of Union, Irishness itself becomes confined and feminized, and, moreover, how the confined or victimized side in any social debate also claims to be the more just. In an odd way, then, both political legitimacy and genuine fear become embodied in the position identified as feminine, threatened, and confined. When we trace out the political and social implications of this logic in nineteenth-century Ireland, we see groups like the Defenders or the Whiteboys claiming, often quite accurately, that they have been confined and victimized by social injustice. Such a claim also serves to justify the Whiteboys and the Defenders as they attack the Anglo-Irish landlord class. Violent Anglo-Irish groups like the Orangemen follow the same logic by insisting that they are threatened and that they only seek after justice. Each side identifies itself always and only as terrorized in order to justify its own acts of terrorism. Thus, in the work of the Gothic writer Maturin, we see men like the Montorio brothers of *Fatal Revenge* who are trapped within feminized identities and who must break with those identities through violence.

In chapter 1, I suggested that this kind of thinking unwittingly confirms Friedrich Nietzsche's insights about ressentiment. In the "Second Treatise" of his 1887 work, *On the Genealogy of Morality,* Nietzsche describes ressentiment as the hallowing of "revenge under the name of justice—as if justice were basically only a further development of the feeling of being wounded—and retroactively to raise to honor along with revenge the *reactive* affects in general and without exception" (48). For Nietzsche, ressentiment is born of a reactive or conformist consciousness, of a consciousness incapable of acting on its own, of defining itself. From the fearful, disempowering roots of ressentiment grows a whole sociocultural system based on the suppression of difference. In essence, then, the logic of the justified victim provides the condition of possibility for social and political violence and repression. Finally, the social, political, and personal cycle triggered by ressentiment proves to be hostile to life for a philosopher like Nietzsche. But Nietzsche does not seek to do away with violence itself. Rather, he wants to do away with the resentful, fearful weakness that triggers it. As a thinker, Nietzsche never simply treats symptoms but chooses, instead, to attack causes.

The Anglo-Irish Gothic writers Maria Edgeworth, Maturin, and Le Fanu continually represent and replay this problematic binary. Their Gothic novels thematize and allegorize the social confinements experienced by the Irish peoples and, subsequently, the Gothic double binds that determined Irish masculine identity in the nineteenth-century wake of the Acts of Union. All of these novelists attempt to find a way out of this cycle. For them, any world in which men appear to be as confined as women invariably comes to a very violent conclusion. In the Anglo-Irish Gothic, violent conclusions work to cleanse the social sphere and to re-establish it upon a foundational ethic of patriarchal inheritance. In this re-established order, men are identified as the rightful and benevolent heirs, and justice reigns. Where Maturin, Edgeworth, and Le Fanu merely represent this binary, however, the Gothic as deployed by Oscar Wilde realizes it. Through the immanent dialectics of his style, Wilde not only acknowledges the confinements and the double binds allegorized by the Irish Gothic tradition, he actually embraces the confines of those social and aesthetic conventions. Wilde converts a problem that had always manifested itself in the content of the Irish Gothic into one of the central formal features of his work. In essence, the conventions allow him to inhabit both poles of the Irish sociopolitical and cultural identity. In this way, Wilde's fin de siècle Gothic stands in bold contrast to that of his nearest Irish contemporary, Bram Stoker.

Undoubtedly the most famous Gothic novel of the decade, Stoker's *Dracula,* published in 1897, evokes the Irish Gothic tradition of gender reversal and confinement as well. Following the 1990 publication of Stephen D. Arata's "The Occidental Tourist," a host of scholars ranging from overtly postcolonial thinkers like Seamus Deane to poststructuralist critics like Joseph Valente have argued that *Dracula* registers many of the anxieties that surrounded Irish decolonization in the home rule era inaugurated by Davitt, Parnell, and the Irish Land League agitation. In fact, when we read *Dracula* in light of "The Irish Vampire" cartoon from *Punch,* the endangered young Lady Erin beset by the Irish Parnellite vampire finds a strange, literary analogue in the figure of Jonathan Harker, Stoker's male hero whose journey toward selfhood seems far closer to the female protagonist of Richardson's *Pamela* than it is to any late Victorian notion of masculine self-fashioning. The novel begins and ends with the fictive journal of Harker, a proper, orphaned Englishman who, after having successfully worked his way up to the position of clerk, hopes to acquit his country well as he journeys to the outside world. [7] Unlike the Victorian orphans in a Dickens novel, however, Harker already knows his rightful place in bourgeois society and simply seeks to fulfill his, and consequently his nation's, manifest destiny. His diary enacts the tension between confinement and external threat that animates other Irish Gothic texts, but it also displays a great deal of anxiety about itself, about its own material presence.

Harker's journal continually extols the virtues of Great Britain as he slowly begins to realize that he has become a prisoner in Castle Dracula, an English subject trapped outside the safe interior of London's Greenwich Mean Time and within the walls of a temporally and historically regressive precapitalist state. On the first page of his journal, Harker records that departing from England gives him the feeling of leaving "the West and entering the East" (1). Furthermore, he writes, "it seems that the further East you go, the more unpunctual are the trains" (2). As Harker leaves the safety of a London where, presumably, the trains always run on time, he notices the world beginning to slow down. Outside of the ordered and punctual capital of modernity, time seems to creep along at a petty pace and at some point to stop altogether. This causes Jonathan no small amount of anxiety, for, as a clerk he reckons losing time with missing appointments and upsetting clients. The veiled condescension toward the "East" in the journal, presented through empirical insights into the tardiness of non-Western transit systems, reflects both the self-important nationalism of Victorian travel writing and Harker's own training as a law clerk, a meticulous cataloger of all that counts as real and legal. Outside of thriving, cosmopolitan London, a sphere ruled by civility and exchange, lies a world of lost time and superstition, a premodern, emotionally ignoble and barbaric society that Count Dracula himself characterizes as the realm of "the hunter" (18).

Most importantly, Jonathon displays a great deal of anxiety when either his letters to England or his diary is in danger of being read by the Count. When Harker explores Castle Dracula, all the while writing down his experiences, he always takes great care to hide his diary, to "replace the book and pen" in his pocket (36). Ownership of the book stands in for possession of the soul, and the text must be kept from the clutches of the soulless Count and his legions, for they are not the intended, or more potently, not the modern audience for Jonathan's subjectivity. The Count can damage Harker physically, but as long as the Englishman can privatize the written self, the internal remains safe from all permanent threats. This textual vessel gives Jonathan a kind of "sanctuary" from the terrors that haunt him, and he even writes in a coded shorthand in order to further protect the self written in the journal from interpretation and consumption by any outsider.

Jonathan's journal acts as the little piece of modern England that stands in contrast to the earthy, mundane piece of feudal Transylvanian soil that accompanies the Count when he is away from home. Like Wilde, then, Stoker fixes on the Gothic's capacity to thematize confinement. Unlike Wilde's, however, Stoker's Gothic seems far more anxious about the subject. Despite all of its proto-modernist convolutions, *Dracula* finally follows the basic structure of Gothic fiction by imagining confinement in largely Manichean terms. Here, dark or malevolent confinement always comes as a result of the social and economic intercourse between the domestic front and the international, occasionally premodern, world. Being locked up in the castle of a feudal-era Count remains as bad in Stoker's novel as it was in the eighteenth-century novels of Anne Radcliffe or "Monk" Lewis. By contrast, light or benevolent confinement comes from protecting one's self within the domestic safe havens of England proper, or, failing that, some little piece of modern England that can be imagined as a symbol of domestic safety. Following the generic conventions of Gothic domestic fiction, then, *Dracula* begins by representing Harker as a feminized central character who seeks a safe haven. In the female Gothic pioneered by Radcliffe's *The Mysteries of Udolpho,* the fiction always seems to move through stages. A female heroine begins in confinement and hopes that a proper marriage and reproduction will secure her both the protection and the autonomy that she seeks. Like the haven sought out by Radcliffe's Emily in *Udolpho,* Jonathan desires a home in which to house and protect his physical body, but, unlike Emily, he also seeks out a private space for his soul or, that is, for his metaphysical self. Where Emily cannot reproduce herself through acts of intellection and writing, Jonathan Harker, a modern, civilized man, certainly can.

So, at the fin de siècle, the historical moment succeeding the Parnellite home rule movement and preceding the revolutionary upheaval of early twentieth-century Irish politics, Stoker and Wilde, the most noteworthy Anglo-Irish Gothic writers of the period, both pen Gothic novels that obsess about feminization and confinement. Perhaps more importantly, both imagine in these texts a form of autonomy that responds to and, at least in some sense, ameliorates these problems. In Stoker's case, Harker's need to create a journal that signifies personal autonomy and metaphysical impenetrability points to the very real-world fear of being confined within a space or an identity that one has not chosen for one's self. Autonomy amounts to choosing a further mode of confinement, a space that remains one's own and, subsequently, virtually impenetrable to and uninterpretable by any outsider. In fear of confinement, Stoker's Jonathan Harker chooses more confinement in order to maintain his autonomy and the idea of a unified, thoroughly individualized, self. Wilde's notion of autonomy takes a vastly different direction.

In Wilde's aesthetic, the autonomous artist represents an iconoclast who operates within the confines of social, political, and aesthetic conventions. Finally, Stoker's Gothic maintains the fearful and binarist anxieties about confinement that we saw in Edgeworth, Maturin, and Le Fanu. The modern characters in *Dracula* want to escape confinement and binary identity on the way to envisaging a unified and unifying identity. The multiply named child of Jonathan and Mina Harker whose birth marks the novel's conclusion signals just such an attempt at a unified, inheritable, patriarchal identity. In naming the child after all of the modern male characters in the text, Jonathan and Mina have made him into a figure for a transnational Western unity that speaks with an English accent. On the other hand, Wilde's writing evinces something of a brazen affirmation of the confines of social convention. Wilde's Gothic fears neither confinement nor permeable, doubled identities. If autonomy is first and foremost acknowledged as a social and cultural activity, as an activity that depends upon the presence of others and on the social conventions that others invariably bring, then, for Wilde, autonomy is always already a kind of negotiation with preexisting social conventions. The aesthete's style derives from as it rebels against its social sphere. The autonomous aesthete's style needs confines—needs conventions—merely in order to appear new or innovative. Likewise, to be feminine, or, in more aestheticized and Wildean terms, effeminate, no longer seems disempowering. Quite the contrary, effeminacy has the power of style, the power to rearrange, reshape, and occasionally disrupt the bourgeois interior. Wilde's writing, then, views confinement as the space in which to imagine style, and hence, as a way to revolutionize society from within.

Wilde nearly always casts the character confined by social convention in the role of social manipulator and aesthete. Finally, he turns confinement itself into a strategy for articulating the power of the aesthetic and of the aesthete. In *The Picture of Dorian Gray,* Wilde converts the political unconscious of a popular aesthetic form like the Gothic novel into an aestheticized political consciousness. As Donald Lawler claims in "The Gothic Wilde," "Wilde required a form that emphasized powerful engagement of reader reaction through his manipulation of imagery, symbols, legendary or mythic structures and secondary or imagined emotions. Traditionally, appeals of this kind have been especially suited to the Gothic" (262). Wilde's characters, as we'll come to see, appear to embrace and adore confinement and, in balance, to turn it to their advantage. They realize that the position of the confined, threatened, and feminized individual generally appears to be the more beautiful, more affecting, and more justified social position. The more authentic dandies in Wilde's plays and fiction consciously realize that they can only continue to commit acts of terrorism by accepting the confines of a repressive social order. As illustrated most clearly in *The Picture of Dorian Gray,* however, these dandies and aesthetes must balance accepting social conventions with becoming self-stylized, innovative artistic commentaries on those conventions. They can only consider themselves radical, then, if they exist within the conventions they necessarily and readily accept but against which they languidly and noncommittally inveigh. Wilde does not overcome the Nietzschean problem of ressentiment so much as he realizes it and uses it to subvert the social and artistic conventions that he accepts and deploys. Without precisely reconciling or overcoming them, Wilde gives form to the antagonisms that we have seen embodied in the Irish Gothic tradition.[8] In the various discussions about aesthetics that wind their way through *Dorian Gray,* Wilde attempts to lay out precisely what kind of confined aesthete figure actually counts as an autonomous innovator.

IV. CONTAINING NARCISSUS WITHIN ECHO

Originally published in 1890 in a single issue of *Lippincot's Monthly Magazine, The Picture of Dorian Gray* operates as a novel about a work of artistic representation that becomes the preoccupation of the represented figure, about an artist's obsessed with how his artwork has altered and been altered by the subject that it represents, and, finally, about how a self-creating narcissism can appear as lethal as it is liberating. In his essay, "Oscar Wilde's Aesthetic Gothic: Walter Pater, Dark Enlightenment, and *The Picture of Dorian Gray,*" John Paul Riquelme claims that Wilde's novel provides one of the first instances of what T. S. Eliot would eventually come to call "the mythical method," a method for appropriating mythic stories and recasting them as allegories of modern sociohistorical and literary phenomena (617). Riquelme holds that just as Joyce's *Ulysses* appropriates the mythic structure of *The Odyssey,* Wilde's *Dorian Gray* invokes and revises the Echo and Narcissus myth (617). In Ovid's account of the myth in Book III of *The Metamorphoses,* Echo, who speaks incessantly, can only repeat what others have already said. Echo loves the young boy Narcissus, who overlooks and rejects her, choosing instead to fall in love with the image of himself that he sees reflected in a pool of water. In the case of Wilde's novel, it is quite easy to interpret Dorian Gray, who obsesses over his own beauty and over his picture, as Narcissus and to read Sybil Vane, the actress who repeats lines written by Shakespeare with such apparent authenticity that audiences find her performances mesmerizing, as the latter-day Echo whom Narcissus must reject. But Riquelme also implies that the novel's innovative use of Gothic doubling makes Dorian, who readily repeats the epigrammatic claims of Lord Henry, into a kind of Echo figure as well. Dorian himself comes to embody a Gothic double bind. Both Echo and Narcissus, Dorian's double persona—his desire to imitate and to innovate—seems to militate against itself. In the end, we can conclude that the tension between imitation, the burden of Echo, and innovation, the self-obsessed desire for narcissistic autonomy, animates the entire novel.

Riquelme seems quite correct to draw together Wilde's novel, Ovid's version of Echo and Narcissus, and the problem of Gothic doubling, but I want to examine this triangulated relationship in light of Wilde's obsession with aesthetics and convention. In fact, buried within this triangulation of the novel's plot, the mythopoetic structure that drives it, and the Gothic doubling that complicates that structure lies an exemplar of precisely the Wildean aesthetic theory that I have been articulating thus far. If, as we've seen in examining the immanent dialectics of Wilde's style, innovation and self-creation must be balanced with an informed and strategic understanding of conventionality, then we can safely say that in Wilde's works of art themselves, ingenuity must be poised against, or rather confined within, an already existing conventional structure. Too much of one side of the equation violates the other and ruins the aesthetic impact of the whole. Following Wilde's stated claims to the *St. James's Gazette*, just as too much capitulation to convention runs the risk of looking complacent and mundane, so also too much radicalism runs the risk of appearing excessive and vulgar.[9] *Dorian Gray* invokes Ovid's story by asserting that the aesthete's persona must finally contain Narcissus within Echo. To differing degrees and with differing ends, the aesthete characters in the novel—Basil Hallward, Lord Henry Wotton, and Dorian—attempt to embody this cautious balancing of mythic extremes.

As an artist, Basil finds himself both fascinated and terrified by his compulsive interest in the young Dorian.[10] He claims that his portrait of Dorian reflects more of himself, more of the artist, than of the represented object, but Basil also states very explicitly that from the moment he first gazed upon Dorian Gray, he feared that the young man's personality and image "would absorb [his] whole nature" (21). Despite his claims, for Basil art is, following Aristotle, "*e teckhnê mimeitai ten physin,*" an imitation of nature. He finds himself absorbed by the objects that he depicts, and his art reflects his fascinated desire for the world of those objects. Basil's persona, his fear of his own attraction to Dorian, his fear of his artwork's failure to control Dorian, coalesces around his earnest—but nonetheless, morally complacent—responses to the social world. Driven primarily by fear, he is too much of an earnest imitator to ever be much of an inspiring innovator. In the novel, he represents the thematic extreme of Echo. In contrast, Lord Henry is never very earnest. In fact, when Basil says to Lord Henry, "you never say a moral thing, and you never do a wrong thing," the doomed artist summarizes the decadent dandy's life quite succinctly (20). Henry, the lover of paradox and wit, finally has the greater influence on Dorian. Even though Lord Henry recognizes that everything is a pose, that "the aim of life is self-development," he never truly or actively violates social norms (29). He appears too excessively decadent, languid, and, finally, too narcissistic to imagine himself as a work of art, and near the conclusion of the novel Lord Henry himself acknowledges that he has never really attempted to fashion an art of life. His self-interest is far too languid and far too acquiescent to make him a perfect figure for balance. So, Basil apparently errs on the side of being too much of an imitator, and Lord Henry on the side of being too self-involved.

In *The Wilde Century,* Alan Sinfield argues very convincingly that Dorian himself must be read as a synthesis of Basil and Lord Henry. In this reading, Basil comes to represent what Sinfield refers to as the "intense and sincere" artist who precedes Wildean aestheticism while Lord Henry comes to represent the dandy who represents leisure-class decadence (99). For Sinfield, Wilde's novel certainly acts as an attempt to balance these two opposites, to imagine in a single figure someone for whom decadence has become an aesthetic identity. The problem for Sinfield consists of the fact that neither Basil nor Lord Henry combines artistry with decadence. Dorian, on the other hand, who is in some sense imagined by Basil's painting, the picture that names the novel, and is enthralled by Lord Henry's decadent Hellenism, supplies us with a character who synthesizes the two extremes. He transforms into a character who makes an art of life itself. From Sinfield's perspective, Basil appears too conventional to create a radically new *Lebensästhetik* or aesthetic of life, and Lord Henry appears too insouciant and decadent to be an artist. Dorian becomes Sinfield's model, albeit a partly flawed one, for the balance that neither Basil nor Lord Henry can achieve.

Though Sinfield provides a forcefully compelling reading, he has to neglect both the novel's mythopoetic structure and its use of Gothic conventionality and moralism in order to do so. The plot and characters of the novel come to represent social problems very directly in Sinfield's reading. Basil, Lord Henry, and Dorian all come to embody singular principles. Despite all of his talk about "form," then, Sinfield reads the novel primarily in terms of content and plot (99). Finally, Sinfield also has to overlook the fact that even at the levels of content and plot, Dorian never manages to strike a balance between artistry and decadence. In fact, throughout the novel Dorian oscillates between moral and artistic complacency and self-involved decadence as it suits his mood and his fearful sense of civil discourse. Though he moves between these two poles, he certainly never embodies their synthesis. From Sinfield's perspective, Dorian might appear to synthesize artistry and decadence, but the novel's capacity to foreground the Gothic's failed moral clarity also makes Dorian's attempts at self-creation appear aesthetically unbalanced, vulgar, and, worst of all, painfully unoriginal. As an artist, moreover, the work he creates, the *Lebensästhetik* graphically depicted in his changing and devolving portrait, grows increasingly ugly as the novel proceeds. By bringing together the Echo and Narcissus myth with the Gothic's overdetermined use of moral binaries, however, Wilde begins by inviting us to look at the novel in terms of each aesthete character's attempt to successfully balance Narcissus with Echo, but he also goes on to ask us to look at how the novel's form itself balances the confines of borrowing with the autonomy of self-obsessed innovation.

The problem with Dorian, his final and most resolute moral and aesthetic failing, is not that he's too much Narcissus, too much of a vain, self-obsessed vanguardist, but rather that he is also too much Echo, too much of a copy. After all, as Wilde once said, his aim in writing the novel was never to "run vanity down" (*The Picture of Dorian Gray,* 336). In fact, Dorian's narcissism and vanity only underscore his status as a copy. To begin with, his character is imagined by Basil, who claims to have projected or deposited "too much" of himself into his portrait of Dorian (25). Further, Dorian steals his witticisms and personal philosophy from Lord Henry. So, in fact, we have in Dorian an artwork fashioned by two artists.[11] Where Basil forms Dorian's image and character, Lord Henry writes his dialogue and shapes his motivations. Like his picture, Dorian himself represents a text written by someone else, and his plagiarized textuality—his inauthenticity—becomes even clearer when he reads Karl Huysman's *Against Nature,* the great nineteenth-century primer for decadence. After Dorian reads Huysman's novel, the narrator explains that Dorian "could not free himself from the influence of the book. Or, perhaps it would be more accurate to say that he never sought to free himself from it" (102). In fact, we are told that Dorian sees in the book's decadent antihero "a kind of pre-figuring type of himself" (102). By this point in the novel, Dorian Gray's image, his dialogue, and his plot arc have all been fashioned by someone other than himself. So when Dorian eventually imagines himself as the embodiment of a "new scheme of life," we should be quick to recall that his character arc is neither very new nor very original but, rather, always borrowed or counterfeited, always conforming to some previously determined "scheme of life" (104). The novel has telegraphed this moment of failed mythopoetic balance from the start. When he first meets Dorian, Lord Henry warns that being written or influenced by another makes one's sins "borrowed" (29). The influenced individual "becomes an echo of some one else's music, an actor of a part that has not been written for him" (29). Henry goes on to say that these latter-day Echoes are weakened precisely because they "are afraid of themselves" (29). Finally, when Dorian fears that the portrait, which bears the marks of age and villainy that he appears to have escaped, will betray him as too ugly, as too dangerous, as, in a word, different, he works tirelessly to conceal it in order to maintain his position in society and, supposedly, his freedom. Even in murdering Basil, Dorian has merely moved to maintain his position within society. He never loves himself as much as he fears himself and the world around him.

At the same time that he claims to abjure society's confining rules, Dorian shuts up the evidence of his true self in a very literally confining attic room, and thusly accedes rather complacently to the confines of his social world. Dorian's very conventional, very bourgeois fears about civil society actually force him to hide from and within that society. Dorian continually dances to the tunes that others have already played. He continually lives out a textual existence that others have already written. At the novel's conclusion, he dies while attempting to destroy his own echo, his portrait. He ends by being murdered, quite literally, by a copy. It is not merely his narcissism that seems excessive, but also his status as copy, or, that is, his conventionality and complacency. Like the latter-day Echoes decried by Lord Henry, Dorian Gray is written by others and his sins are all borrowed from one extant text or another. Lord Henry, the only dandy to survive the novel, the character whose moral culpability and influence over Dorian has been endlessly debated by critics and scholars, actually comes far closer to balancing narcissism and imitation than either Basil or Dorian. Henry embraces paradox and immorality, but he does so, as Basil reminds us, without ever doing a "wrong thing." Much like Wilde himself, Lord Henry speaks in witty paradox, paraphrases and borrows insights from Walter Pater's aesthetic theories, and consciously works to fashion a space and an identity for himself within his society.[12] Only Lord Henry proves capable of reading his position, his character, and his personal meaning as dialectical in any sense. Where Dorian and Basil become victims, Lord Henry's capacity to speak immorally while acceding to society's demands brings him a bit closer to balancing Narcissus within Echo than the characters who err more overtly on the side of imitation. Despite his profound influence on the novel's plot and its characters, however, Lord Henry also seems too idle to control or manipulate the story's dénouement. He simply turns away from Dorian near the novels' conclusion, and, so, he fails to restructure and redirect the action. Basil and Dorian appear to be too often on the side of fear, moral complacency, and imitation, and, even though Lord Henry's finely-tuned narcissism allows him to survive, his indolent approach to life finally inhibits his capacity to embody anything like the lively and vivifying energy required of the artist. After all, the artist of life, the master of the *Lebensästhetik,* must deploy his narcissism in order to reshape the internal structures of societal and aesthetic convention. Despite the text's obsessive oscillation between Narcissus and Echo, then, Wilde does not actually provide us with a character who fully contains narcissism within conventionality in the novel. Instead, he makes the novel's formal structure itself into the figure that artfully contains innovative autonomy within the confines of borrowed conventions.

V. IMITATION AND THE REVOLUTION FROM WITHIN

Through the Echo and Narcissus myth that underscores the symbolism in *Dorian Gray,* Wilde demonstrates how one can become too much of a complacent copy or too much of a languorous narcissist, but he also demonstrates in the book's structure and style how one can balance convention with innovation in a wholly ingenious and aesthetically productive fashion. The novel's form itself becomes an exemplar of the intricate and careful balance that its characters finally fail to strike. In "The Decay of Lying," Wilde had already explained that the "self-conscious aim of life is to find expression, and that Art offers it certain beautiful forms through which it may realize that energy" (992). For Wilde, art formulates and reveals certain kinds of patterns; it imagines narratives and conventions that, in turn, beautify and make sense of life and of nature. As both the form and the content of *Dorian Gray* demonstrate, then, the confines of convention are neither to be casually thrown off, nor thoughtlessly embraced. They must be carefully analyzed, however. As Wilde had Gilbert explain in the 1890 dialogue, "The Critic as Artist," the highest criticism "fills with wonder a form that the artist may have left void," and, so, the critical reader becomes creator (1030). Recognizing the patterns and conventions of art allows the critical artist to rework them, to reinvent them, and, in so doing, to reinvent himself. For Wilde, one must finally work within conventional confines in order to revolutionize the artistic, social, and natural worlds, and in *The Picture of Dorian Gray,* Wilde presents us with a text that combines its innovative narcissism with its borrowing from that most conventional of all novelistic genres, the Gothic. Beyond its mythopoetic structure, then,

Dorian Gray actually borrows a great deal of its conventional and thematic material from a Gothic novel: Maturin's *Melmoth the Wanderer.*

In the autumn of 1803, Maturin married Henrietta Kingsbury, sister of Sarah Kingsbury who, of course, gave birth to Wilde's mother, the poet and sometime Irish nationalist, Speranza (Lady Wilde). Wilde's family seemed particularly proud of this literary relationship, and when Maturin's Gothic masterpiece, *Melmoth the Wanderer,* was reissued in 1892, the editors actually thanked both Wilde and Speranza for supplying them with the biographical information about Maturin.[13] *Melmoth* had remained a powerfully inspiring text for French bohemian and decadent writers late into the nineteenth century. Charles Baudelaire had praised Maturin's novel and had planned to translate it into French. Honoré de Balzac, one of Wilde's favorite novelists, had gone so far as to write a sequel entitled *Melmoth Reconcile. Melmoth the Wanderer* appears to have provided the kind of inspiration for the French decadents that Huysman's *Against Nature* had provided for Wilde's Dorian. That *Melmoth* was important to Wilde also seems apparent in his choosing it as his postprison surname, and even though the intertextual relationship between Wilde and Maturin has never been the locus of a great deal critical interest, it none the less remains at the very heart of Wilde's invocation of the Gothic in *Dorian Gray.* In fact, as Edouard Roditi had noted in his 1947 critical biography, *Oscar Wilde,* some of the most distinctive allusions and themes in Wilde's 1890 novel were culled directly from the pages of Maturin's *Melmoth.*

Melmoth the Wanderer, the picaresque and fragmentary story of John Melmoth, a damnable Anglo-Irishman who arrives in Ireland around the time of Cromwell's 1649 invasion only to trade his soul for demonic power and for 150 years of youth. Reflecting many of the anxieties of Ireland's union with England, Maturin's novel is part supernatural Gothic adventure, part Radcliffean confinement tale, and part anti-Catholic invective. The character of Melmoth has the power to appear anywhere at anytime—hence his *nom de voyage,* the wanderer—and whenever he shows up, he is accompanied by strange, unearthly music. But Melmoth has a problem. He no longer likes the deal he's cut with the forces of Hell, and he wants out. Luckily enough, his contract has an escape clause. In the event that Melmoth can find someone who is willing to trade his or her soul for a similar deal, the wanderer can die cleansed and, potentially at least, ascend to heaven. Melmoth deploys his power of ubiquity to appear to individuals in dire straits—a monk imprisoned in a monastery, a young woman confined by the retrograde beliefs of her Catholic family, a Protestant father who cannot manage to feed his family in Catholic Spain—and to offer them a way out if they agree to take his place as the signatory of his devil's contract.[14] Not one of Melmoth's intended victims ends up being gullible or desperate enough to buy into the deal, and, in the end, the hopeless wanderer perishes when he falls off the cliffs near his ancestral home in Ireland. He is, quite literally, abjected from an Ireland that refuses to bear his satanic presence.

The novel has a fairly notorious stories-within-stories structure, complete with a contemporary frame setting in circa 1816 Ireland. The frame narrative, which bears a number of parallels with Wilde's *Dorian Gray,* concerns the wanderer's young namesake, a Trinity College student referred to throughout as young John Melmoth, who has returned to the ancestral home in county Wicklow to witness the death of yet another Melmoth, a miserly old uncle who has spent his life hoarding the family's riches and guarding its unholy secret. While attending to his uncle's various needs and final requests, John enters a closet in the dilapidated old estate only to find, concealed amidst his uncle's possessions, the portrait of a middle-aged man with fiery, piercing eyes. The figure's fierce, charismatic, demonic gaze draw young John Melmoth in with an impulse described as "equally resistless and painful" (18). Inscribed beneath the portrait are the words: "Jno. Melmoth, anno 1646" (18). A few hours later, young John catches a glimpse of the picture's still living original, Melmoth the notorious wanderer, who even in 1816 does not appear to have aged since he sat for the portrait well over 150 years earlier. The wanderer's picture provides the framing device for the entire novel. It dates the actual, temporal beginning of the story, the instance of the wanderer's "devil's compact," and it also marks the Anglo-Irish "big house" in which young Melmoth resides as the site upon which the entire convoluted tale of the wanderer will be reconstructed and resolved. As in Wilde's *Dorian Gray,* the picture also provides us with the image of a man with penetrating features who has traded redemption for the appearance of eternal youth. As Marie-Noëlle Zeender claims, "The picture of Melmoth is seemingly invested with a monstrous and autonomous life, and it even gives the impression that inanimate things can watch the living" (434). Hence, we have as the central character of *Melmoth* and of *Dorian Gray,* a Byronic hero who would give up his soul to be always young and who dies a presumably deserved death at the conclusion of the text. We also have this character's haunting, and in some sense haunted, portrait, which reveals the hidden truths concerning his origin and his hallucinatory, yet necessarily concealed and closeted, story.

To some degree, then, Wilde's *The Picture of Dorian Gray* might appear to be a textbook example of borrowing. After all, the narrative is framed literally and figuratively by a portrait, and the main character strikes a devil's bargain for eternal youth. But Wilde's novel avoids the kind of one-to-one borrowing that marks Dorian's relationship with Huysman's *Against Nature.* In fact, by actively thematizing the problem of borrowing with the invocation of the Echo and Narcissus myth, Wilde converts his version of the Melmoth narrative into a self-reflexive exploration of the recurrence of certain narrative forms and tropes. In contrast to Dorian himself, Wilde repeats and copies narrative and formal patterns in order to rework and reinvent them. Dorian has no real will of his own, so his desires inevitably become attached to objects and structures that were imagined and desired by others. In contrast, the true Wildean aesthete bends the world around him to accommodate his will and his desires. The autonomous aesthete reshapes the conventions as they stand into conventions that accommodate, even celebrate, him. Maturin's novel provides Wilde with the image of a work of art so compelling that it has developed the capacity to look back at and reshape the world and the subject that it reflects. For a thinker like Wilde, who wants to reverse the Aristotelian conception of mimesis and claim that "life imitates art," such an image is the perfect avatar of the work of art.

In Maturin's novel, Melmoth has a lengthy affair with the innocent and apparently orphaned island girl, Immalee. When Immalee's Spanish Catholic family reclaims and renames her as Isadora, Melmoth the demon becomes Immalee's potential liberator, and the moral clarity of Maturin's novel, built on a firm distinction between demonic evil and salvific innocence, begins to break down. Melmoth, who has knowledge and ubiquity on his side, transforms into the only character who can save Immalee from the confining beliefs that her family's Catholicism comes to represent in the novel. Maturin thusly provides us with a character who is, at one and the same time, a potential terror and a potential savior. In appropriating the Melmoth narrative in order to make a variety of claims about self-fashioning autonomy and aesthetic borrowing, Wilde imagines in the single figure of Dorian a character who is not only a potential terror and a potential savior, but someone who is also the potentially terrorized and fearfully feminized character. Recognizing the ambiguity implicit in Gothic moralism, Wilde makes Dorian into a confined individual who, paradoxically, has all of the narrative's power in his hands. Were Dorian a more careful and inventive reader of Gothic literature and of the narratives that have come to us from the past, were he a critical and aesthetic self-fashioner who could see the voids left open in the work of other artists, he would be able to recognize the patterns that have helped to shape his own life, and he would find himself in a position to revise, rework, and manipulate those patterns. Unlike the dandies and aesthetes in Wilde's plays, however, Dorian lives too closely to his own narrative, and he merely sees the texts that come to him from the past as figures to be reproduced or copied and not as textual and cultural themes that one might invoke, vary, and influence. For Wilde an iterated text can be imprinted with the stamp of a new personality. In the most aesthetic sense, a work of art that repeats as it reworks the formal features of a previous work opens up the possibility for reshaping the past and rethinking the conventions that mark the present. Although Dorian fails to do this, the novel itself actually deploys convention to stretch conventionality to its limits and to make a space within Gothic conventions for a proto-modernist *Kunstleroman* about borrowing and innovation.

In appropriating first the Echo and Narcissus myth and then the Gothic forms and conventions of *Melmoth the Wanderer,* Wilde lays the foundations for the kind of appropriative method that will characterize the more overtly modernist work of James Joyce and W. B. Yeats. Wilde's rewriting of the Melmoth story in *The Picture of Dorian Gray* aims to place the problem of narrative itself—of stories about individuals, communities, and nations that shape our identities and give us anterior structures and patterns to observe—into the hands of the canny, autonomous artist. Though Dorian, Basil, and Lord Henry all seem to have failed to contain narcissistic innovation perfectly within a borrowed structure, the novel itself, which borrows its thematic material from Ovid and its plot twists, framing devices, tone, and Byronic hero from Maturin, provides us with an exemplary case of how the artist must work to fit genius within convention. It also provides us with yet another illustration of the immanent dialectic that serves to characterize Wilde's work as, at once, all too radical and not quite radical enough.

VI. WILDE AMONG THE MODERNISTS

In *Minima Moralia,* his epigrammatic book of reflections on the catastrophes of modern history, Adorno claims that "the medium of irony itself has come into contradiction with truth" (210). As Adorno sees it, irony, along with its most favored child, satire, "usually acted on behalf of older strata threatened by more recent stages of enlightenment. [. . .] Its inexhaustible theme was the decay of morals" (210). Beginning with writers like Voltaire, however, Adorno argues that irony became a powerful tool on behalf of the oppressed. Adorno finally asserts that, "as a prisoner of its own form," irony "never entirely divested itself of its authoritarian inheritance, its unrebellious malice" (210). The social manipulator in Wilde's plays and his fiction, the dandy character who manages to so artfully contain innovation within convention that he or she appears to mock anyone who has an inferior understanding of society's rules, seems to embody what Adorno refers to here as irony's "unrebellious malice." Never fully a revolutionary, a character such as Lord Henry Wotton, Lord Darlington, Lord Goring, or Algernon Moncrieff always remains content to mock and manipulate others while he also attempts to show them some sort of compassion and understanding. In this way, Wilde's aesthetes personify the problem of modernist irony. Neither fully rebellious nor entirely reactionary, the ironic modernist aesthete, whether he's Wilde's Lord Henry, James Joyce's Stephen Dedalus, or Samuel Beckett's Murphy, always appears torn between his languid ability to manipulate social and aesthetic convention and his attentive sensitivity to others. He will nearly always choose manipulation over sensitivity. Ironizing the excesses of vulgarity on the one hand or the complacency of the everyday on the other, however, may merely reify the binary distinction that bourgeois culture would like to make between the two. It mocks certain identities and cultural positions without seeking to alter those positions. Joyce, Beckett, and a host of other modernist writers have continually been the subjects of political debate. Are they apolitical, and so, quietly on the side of the status quo, or are they hyperpolitical, and so, cautiously on the side of the revolutionary? The irony that characterizes and circumscribes Wilde's work in *Dorian Gray,* in the essays and dialogues, and in the plays puts him very firmly in the same camp—no pun intended—as these modernists.

I began by claiming that for the gender and queer theorists, Wilde appears too radical for the historical moment in which he finds himself trapped while for the postcolonialists, a Wilde who always appears imprisoned by literary conventions never seems quite radical enough. From the postcolonialist perspective, this assertion helps to shore up the essentially progressive and Hegelian aesthetic claim that holds that the most experimental, innovative works of art herald radical innovations in political and social thought. From the perspective of artistic vanguardism, then, Wilde seems to fall short. He never seems as dissonant or as innovative an artist as someone like W. B. Yeats. Neither does Wilde seem as careful, capacious, and reflective an artist as someone like Joyce. Wilde may be fit to set the stage, fit to write pieces like "The Decay of Lying," which inspired the young occultist Yeats to investigate aestheticism, fit to introduce paradoxical wit and aesthetic posturing to a writer like Joyce, but he is never really characterized as an important figure for Irish modernism. If, however, we read Wilde as a writer who cautiously deploys mythopoetic symbolism, who revises and expands generic forms like the Gothic, then Wilde becomes one of the original innovators of Irish modernist fiction. The Irish Gothic seeks to overcome the structural dispossession experienced by the feminized, usurped, and colonized figure. It does so by finding in the male heir someone who heals and overcomes the dispossession experienced by the feminine. But the modernist writers who deploy Gothic tropes actually parody and criticize this effort. Following Wilde's "The Critic as Artist," they look to the failings in the form left there by the Gothic's writers. One of the major distinctions to be made between the Gothic novelists that we have studied thus far and the modernist ones that we will go on to explore consists in the simple fact that the Gothic writers allegorize social and political antagonisms that they also hope to overcome while the modernists are never quite so optimistic. The modernist venture remains more of a critical one, and the modernist artists invoke conventions precisely in order to challenge and stretch the confines of conventionality. From this perspective, it seems difficult to avoid reading Wilde as one of Ireland's arch-modernist writers.

The next chapter explores how James Joyce's *Ulysses* deploys the structures of the Unionist Gothic in order to move beyond the political limits of the Gothic's allegorical technique and to suggest an alternative approach to politicizing art. Over the last two decades, Joyce criticism, which had once offered us the image of Joyce as a thoroughly apolitical modernist, has begun to propose that texts like *Ulysses* and *A Portrait of the Artist as a Young Man* actually present allegories of a postcolonial nationalism.[15] By exploring Joyce's use and abuse of the Unionist Gothic in *Ulysses,* I'll situate his work as a response to Irish literary history and suggest that Joyce's overcoming of allegory provides us with a dialectical model for thinking about politics that is neither merely apolitical nor strongly nationalist. Joyce never invokes the Gothic in quite the same way as Stoker or Wilde but, instead, responds to an Irish political unconscious that seems overwhelmed by the tropes of the Gothic. In opposition to the nostalgic, patriarchal nationalism of the Unionist Gothic, Joyce's mock-Gothic offers us a prototype for transnationalist conceptions of identity. A Gothic *Ulysses* proposes an aesthetic that accumulates multiple and conflicting identities rather than merely fixating on the singular, disinherited identity that lies at the heart of the Unionist Gothic's political allegory.

CHAPTER 4

Overcoming Allegory

Joyce's Ulysses *and the Limits of the Irish Gothic*

> What is overcome is not thereby reduced to nothing. Nothing is *immediate;* what is overcome, on the other hand, is the result of mediation. [. . .] It still has, therefore, *in itself* the *determinateness from which it originates.*
>
> —G. W. F. Hegel, *Science of Logic*

> What was Stephen's auditive sensation? He heard in a profound ancient male unfamiliar melody the accumulation of the past.
>
> —James Joyce, *Ulysses*

STEPHEN DEDALUS AND THE FAILURE OF GOTHIC ALLEGORY

At the beginning of book 4, chapter 7 of Anne Radcliffe's arch-female-Gothic novel, *The Mysteries of Udolpho* (1794), Emily St. Aubert, the book's perpetually sensitive and melancholy protagonist, appears trapped in a tower that overlooks a solemn, morning sea. She reads and contemplates poetry and gives herself up to the painful "remembrance of past times" (558). As she sits looking out over the sea, Emily worries about a usurper who holds her in confinement. Gothic villain par excellence, Count Montoni, a wicked lapsed-Catholic nobleman who plans to usurp Emily's landed estate, reigns as the lord and guardian of Udolpho Tower. Unless she can discover the "mysteries of Udolpho" and separate herself from Montoni, Emily fears that she will be dispossessed of her inheritance, of her autonomy, and perhaps even of her life.

Oddly enough, we discover a markedly similar scenario at the opening of James Joyce's arch-high-modernist novel, *Ulysses,* which begins by offering us an equally sensitive and melancholy figure who appears trapped in a forlorn tower overlooking the morning sea. Stephen Dedalus moves through the Martello tower on the morning of 16 June 1904 pondering poetics, haunted by the painful remembrance of past times, and concerned about separating himself from Buck Mulligan, the vulgar lapsed-Catholic who seems somehow to guard Stephen's tower-prison. If he cannot separate from Mulligan, Stephen fears that he will be dispossessed of his figural inheritance and of his literal autonomy. *Udolpho*'s usurping Count Montoni continually mocks and derides Emily's feminine weakness. *Ulysses* begins with Mulligan mocking and feminizing Stephen by linking arms with him and promising, in a camp allusion to Oscar Wilde, that together they might "Hellenise" Ireland (7). Finally, the first episode of *Ulysses* concludes when Stephen's momentary stream-of-consciousness monologue dubs Mulligan, "Usurper" (23). Hence, in these sections of *Udolpho* and *Ulysses* we encounter two versions of the female Gothic's primal scene: a confined and feminized character frets over the loss of inheritance and of autonomy.

To the casual observer this might appear as little more than a literary coincidence. After all, Joyce's novel alludes to and invokes so many genres that one might easily identify references to several different popular fictional forms on any of its pages. But both Joyce's *Ulysses* and the female Gothic tradition initiated by Radcliffe's *Udolpho* share an overwhelming obsession with the social, political, and gendered problems that accompany structural dispossession. In other words, both *Udolpho* and *Ulysses* inveigh against usurpers and the effect that usurpation has on identity, inheritance, and culture. In chapter 1, I claimed that the female Gothic confronts the problem of structural dispossession—the active, historical dispossession and disenfranchisement of political subjects by cultural, legal, linguistic, and economic systems—more directly than any other form of nineteenth-century domestic fiction. In fact, we find the anxieties concerning structural dispossession secreted in the basic narrative framework of the female Gothic, which moves from female confinement through marital reproduction and toward the autonomy promised by the birth of a male heir who supposedly heals the schism between the masculine and feminine spheres. By actively repossessing the figural body of the mother via her landed inheritance, the Gothic's male heir acts as a hybrid, synthesizing rational, masculine control and corporeal, feminine bodies.

As a strictly allegorical figure, the male heir appears to reconcile the male mind with the female matter of history. He acts as the figure for resolution in the female Gothic, then, and his birth signifies a reconciliation of opposites. At the same time that this masculine inheritor points to the need to ameliorate the structural dispossession that comes with woman's position as object in the marriage contract, his very presence as an inheriting male also reasserts the male/female social binary that his birth intends to heal. Even in the Radcliffean female Gothic, the male heir already seems like a failed allegory, a figure who can never truly resolve the problem of the mother's structural dispossession, a figure who continually reaffirms the very dispossession that he seeks to negate. The son of Mina and Jonathon Harker, whose birth concludes Bram Stoker's *Dracula,* provides another fine example. As the narrator tells us, Mina's son will supposedly grow up to know that some men so loved his mother "that they did dare much for her sake" (400). In this passage, Mina seems as much like a nation as an individual maternal subject. Logically speaking, the inheriting male of the Gothic can never really be fully reconciled to a maternal body that he must both overmaster and reject.[1] The impossible double logic that follows from the birth of this extraordinarily allegorical male heir tends to mark the conclusion of nearly every novel in the female-Gothic tradition.[2]

In the simplest terms, allegory is an extended metaphor in which a character or an object is equated with some singular moral, religious, or social meaning. In John Bunyan's *Pilgrim's Progress,* one of the more obviously allegorical texts in the English canon, a character can emblematize envy or lust or wrath in a very overt way. The English-language Gothic is an inveterately allegorical genre where, for instance, we nearly always encounter feudal Italian counts who are overt emblems of a supposedly backwards, unenlightened, and superstitious Catholic political system.[3] As Kate Ferguson Ellis's *The Contested Castle* asserts, the entire female-Gothic tradition itself allegorizes the struggles for women's autonomy in bourgeois modernity.[4] But the Gothic's essentially allegorical structure becomes more complicated in the Irish tradition. When we find the basic female Gothic narrative framework repeated in gender-disorienting ways in the novels of Charles Robert Maturin, Joseph Sheridan Le Fanu, and even Bram Stoker, we uncover a great deal of the anxiety about masculinity and structural dispossession that succeeded the Acts of Union in Ireland. Following the Acts of Union, the Gaelo-Catholics found themselves thoroughly disinherited and disenfranchised, and the Anglo-Irish ascendancy class lost its parliamentary powers and its sense of sovereignty over Ireland. The Anglo-Irish writers Maturin, Le Fanu, and Stoker deploy the female-Gothic narrative as they retrofit its allegorical emblems to the political problematics and gender anxieties triggered by nineteenth-century British imperialism in Ireland. We find in their Gothic writings male characters who become confined and who react with violence whenever they are identified with the feminine or the maternal.[5]

As the fears of Stephen Dedalus mirror those of Emily St. Aubert, the fears of the male hero in the Unionist Gothic tend to mirror those of the female heroine in the female Gothic. But the male figure in the Unionist Gothic actively longs for the lost power and autonomy of the paternal at the same time that he flees from the limitations associated with the maternal lineage. These male figures do not suffer trauma simply because they have lost mothers. Rather, they signal a traumatic and troubled desire to be saved and differentiated from a maternal background that has become codified as weak, regressive, devolutionary, or parasitic. As male figures caught in female narratives, Unionist Gothic characters like Maturin's Orazio di Montorio of *Fatal Revenge* are torn asunder by the impossible logic of their desires. They long to reclaim the maternal land only as they must reject the maternal identity itself as disempowering and disunified. Hence, a persistent nostalgia for the empowered father and a rejection of the disempowering mother characterizes the fiction of the Unionist Gothic that we have surveyed thus far. The Gothic's allegory of the inheriting son signals a desire to repossess the father's power and an accompanying abjection of the maternal identity. Much like the theory of abjection offered by French psychoanalytic theorist Julia Kristeva in *Powers of Horror,* the Unionist Gothic identifies the maternal—and the feminine itself—with the failure of autonomy. Simply put, male characters who cannot free themselves from a maternal lineage or identity, characters who cannot break away from what Kristeva calls "the hold of the *maternal* entity," can never become sovereign or autonomous subjects in the Irish Gothic tradition (16). They are doomed to end their lives in the throes of an excessively vulnerable sentimentality or in a paroxysm of self-destructive of madness.

As we have already seen, with the rise of Parnellism in the 1870s, the raison d'etre of the Unionist Gothic evaporated, as the "wrong marriage" metaphors imagined during the Union developed into more modern concerns about individuality and national sovereignty. The Anglo-Irish politician Charles Stewart Parnell and his Irish Land League provoked the agrarian agitations of the 1870s and 1880s that eventually led the English prime minister, William Gladstone, to begin work on the Irish Land Acts.[6] Although the Land Acts of 1870 and 1881 were meant to appease the disenfranchised Catholics and to bring a slow end to landlordism in Ireland, they were challenged by the rise of Parnellism and the home rule movement in Ireland. The wrong-marriage crisis of the Union era evolved into the home rule crisis of the fin de siècle. Home rule bills that were intended to reverse the 1800 Acts of Union and allow Ireland some limited form of sovereignty were defeated in the English Parliament in 1886 and 1893, but the question of home rule continued to dominate the political terrain in Ireland for a generation.[7] During this period, the fall and eventual death of Parnell, whose adulterous affair with Kitty O'Shea had weakened the home rule movement, became a symbol of Ireland's own failure and self-betrayal for writers like W. B. Yeats and James Joyce.[8] In a sense, the Gothic genre's emphasis on gender disorientation persists, but it takes a more reflective and subtle form in the post-Parnell period. As Fredric Jameson claims in *The Political Unconscious,* in analyzing a given genre we discover "the formal persistence of such archaic structures—and the signs systems specific to them—beneath the overlay of all the more recent and historically specific types of alienation" (100). The Irish modernist take on the home rule crisis codes an analogous historical problem to the one that troubled the Unionist Gothic. Simply put, as the nineteenth century drew to a close Ireland appeared incapable of achieving the autonomy of home rule, and the literature of the period betrayed a good deal of anxiety concerning this sociopolitical problem.

In *The Picture of Dorian Gray* (1890), written in the midst of the home rule crisis, Wilde borrows from the confinement structures of both the female and the Unionist Gothic in order to imagine how the canny aesthete-*Ubermensch* might accept and manipulate confining social conventions and, so, repossess a limited yet highly stylized form of autonomy. Though it begins with effeminacy and confinement, *Dorian Gray* generates a proto-modernist aesthetic of rewriting, or, that is, of revision. It self-consciously deploys old forms like the Gothic and old texts like *Melmoth the Wanderer* precisely to revise and move beyond the limitations of these forms and texts. Wilde deems the very anxiety surrounding the feminine and the confined as a locus of social power. The formal structure of *Dorian Gray* deploys this power by offering us a protagonist who cannot manipulate conventions and a novel that can. Dorian is destroyed by his fear of social conventions, while the novel uses Gothic conventions in order to push, and finally to extend, the limits of the form itself. Where the Unionist Gothic writers allegorize sociopolitical anxieties, Wilde undercuts them by accepting, understanding, and, finally, reworking social discourse from within. As Lady Bracknell says in *The Importance of Being Earnest,* Wilde's method assures us that one should "never speak disrespectfully of Society. [. . .] Only people who can't get into it do that" (act 3).

As I demonstrated in the last chapter, Wilde's only novel suggests a way to win by conceding, a way to synthesize autonomous power with an identity that has historically appeared feminized. Wilde's solution—to imagine a counterintuitive style that synthesizes oppositions—remains at the level of form. In fact, one of the most Gothic features of *The Picture of Dorian Gray* is the novel's capacity to imagine characters like Dorian Gray and Sybil Vane as allegorical figures intended to represent and embody specific ideas or meanings. In *Dorian Gray,* Wilde relies on the Gothic's heavy-handed use of the emblematic and the allegorical in order to make his own arguments about effeminacy, imitation, and artistic autonomy. In a sense, Wilde's Gothic actively realizes as it allegorizes the historical binary of a modern Irish masculinity. That Irish masculinity had continually been characterized, on one hand, as feminine and weak and, on the other, as terrifying and aggressive. Dorian Gray the character embodies both of these forces, and the double bind destroys him. *Dorian Gray* the novel manages to balance these opposing forces and to embrace both its effeminacy and its aggression. In the end, even though Wilde's allegorical figures are far more complicated than those employed by the Unionist Gothic, both Wilde and the Unionist Gothic deploy allegory in order to represent and to work through the structural disinheritance instigated by British colonial ideology.

So, when we return to the Martello tower sequence that begins *Ulysses* we seem to encounter yet another recasting of the female Gothic's allegory of structural dispossession. Stephen feels feminized, confined, and usurped, and he seeks to flee from his supposed captor and from the Martello tower in order to repossess his birthright. He feels dispossessed and feminized by the structures of a colonial world. So far, he doesn't seem all that different from the allegorical male protagonists and heirs of the Unionist Gothic. In fact, Stephen obviously thinks of himself in allegorical terms. But throughout *Ulysses,* Joyce's stylistic experimentation actively recommends a vast multiplicity of forms and perspectives over the singularity of allegory. *Ulysses* does not deploy the structures of the female or the Unionist Gothic merely in order to reproduce an allegory that transcends the crises of Irish masculinity, then. Rather, among its many styles and innovations, *Ulysses* also works as a mock Gothic.[9] When the Gothic occurs after a second crisis in modern Irish sociopolitical identity, it does so as farce. By imagining Stephen Dedalus as a male heir who fears any association with the mother or any collectivizing association with an Ireland defined in *A Portrait of the Artist as a Young Man* as a vampiric "sow who eats her own farrow," the Gaelo-Catholic Joyce confronts the problem of structural dispossession in a much more self-conscious and overt manner than either the Unionist Gothic writers or Wilde. Like the protagonists of the Unionist Gothic, Stephen hopes to repossess his paternal inheritance. Like Wilde, Stephen imagines that personality, genius, and style can resolve the male subject's conflict with his social world. This first similarity signifies a desire to repossess the historical past while the second indicates a desire to manipulate the social present via the genius of formal style. One of the key differences between *Ulysses* and texts like *Melmoth* or *Dorian Gray,* here, resides in the fact that by merging the two desires (the historical and the formal) in the single figure of Stephen Dedalus, Joyce actually supplies us with a fictive artist who very consciously hopes to use allegory to solve real-world dilemmas. With Joyce's *Ulysses,* the Gothic's use of allegory becomes both self-aware and an actual element of the novel's plot.

As a self-proclaimed artist, Stephen's solution to the particular dilemma of structural dispossession, his attempt to repossess the past by giving birth to himself in art, by becoming his own father-creator, constitutes yet another version of the Gothic's "male heir as resolution" narrative. He craves the paternal power at the same time that he flees the incapacitating history associated with his "beastly dead" mother. Stephen himself is a male heir haunted by the formal framework of the female Gothic, haunted by a dispossessed and derogated maternal history. He hopes to rewrite history through the innovative genius of his personal, aesthetic style. In a sense, Irish sociopolitical and literary history becomes the Kristevan "*maternal* entity" that Stephen must render abject in order to imagine his own autonomy and to reconnect with his paternal power. Although Stephen faces structural dispossession directly, his vision of himself as an aesthetic paterfamilias attempts to escape from the gender disorientation that attends the Irish version of this political and social problem. Where Wilde and the Unionist Gothic allegorize historical conditions, Joyce actually supplies us with an artist-character who seeks to allegorize historical conditions.

In making Stephen an artist who wants to deploy allegory to overcome history, Joyce allows us to see how the Unionist Gothic's allegory of the inheriting male—and, in a larger sense, allegorical thinking *tout court*—actually limits our capacity to understand the multiform complexities of the social world. While allegory can carry political meanings, it also tends to be selective and exclusive. Ever since the advent of Romantic-era criticism, allegory, defined simply as a mode of extended metaphor that allows for a character to represent an idea, has almost always been portrayed as too overt, too vulgar, and too unpoetic.[10] Let's admit that artworks in which characters simply and unambiguously emblematize lust or honesty always seem a bit clumsy or awkward. But the early–twentieth-century German literary critic Walter Benjamin found allegory fascinating precisely because of its ham-handed, unpoetic vulgarity.[11] In fact, in his *Ursprung des deutschen Trauerspiel* [Origin of the German Mourning Play], Benjamin argues that allegory actually helps us to see the material world's failings and limitations.[12]

In a famous passage from his *Trauerspiel* book, Benjamin explains that "allegories are in the realm of thoughts, what ruins are in the realm of things" (178). Allegory demonstrates just how transient and inept are our emblematic modes of making narrative sense of the world. In the end, a character made to emblematize lust tells us far more about our own historical and cultural prejudices regarding sexuality, courtship, and desire than it tells us about the ontological or deep-structure truths of lustfulness. Allegories are intellectual ruins, signs of the limitations of our thinking. In another sense, however, as literal ruins slowly begin to blend into the landscape of a countryside or a city, allegories begin to blend into our intellectual landscapes.[13] They become part of our thinking. For Benjamin our human need to personify a multifaceted idea as a singular allegory points to our inability to comprehend that idea in all of its social, material, economic, and philosophical complexity. We want to compress complex histories into simple narratives and intricate ideas into singular characters.[14] In so doing, we choose the signification of allegory over the multiplicity of historical context. Allegory never really seems up to the task it sets for itself, because naming an idea in allegorical terms finally strips away that idea's historical specificity. As Benjamin claims, critics must occasionally remind us that allegory's clumsiness, its overt attempt to represent an unrepresentable idea points to the limits of human sense making and to our own failure to pay attention to the specific, to the historical detail, and to the material world itself.[15] This is all to say that for Benjamin, allegory is certainly reductive, but if we acknowledge it as reductive and admit that it underscores our limitations, then we can begin to recognize the limits of our own ahistorical truth claims. By noting the limits of allegorical modes of figuration, we become more conscious of the ruins that have blended into our various intellectual, political, and social landscapes. We bring into bold relief what was only background. Perhaps more importantly, we can also begin to construct histories that acknowledge how multiple meanings or competing interpretations of complex historical events and conditions can accrue over time.[16]

Joyce strikes a similar tone on allegory to the one we find in Benjamin. While characters throughout *Ulysses* certainly flirt with appearing strictly allegorical, Joyce is always quick to mock this maneuver, to interrupt it, and to suggest several alternate identities for each potentially allegorical figure who arises in the pages of his novel.[17] By introducing Stephen as a character who consciously hopes to use allegory, a character who wants to make himself into the ultimate allegorical inheriting son, Joyce actually thinks through the static and singular model of identity implicit in allegorical form. That is to say, he mediates allegory. When Hegel discusses the various forms of dynamic, philosophical thinking in the *Science of Logic,* he uses the term *Aufhebung* [overcoming] to describe the structure of dialectical mediation. The term *Aufheben,* sometimes translated as "to sublate," refers to the intricate and subtle procedures of vigorously dialectical thought. As Hegel explains in the *Logic, Aufhebung* has two opposing meanings. He claims that "on the one hand it means to preserve, to maintain, and equally it also means to cause to cease, to put an end to. Even 'to preserve' includes a negative element, namely, that something is removed from its immediacy

[. . .]. Thus what is overcome is at the same time preserved; it has only lost its immediacy" (107).[18] In providing us with Stephen, an artist figure who consciously invokes allegory, Joyce's own literary technique in *Ulysses* removes allegory from its immediacy. He negates allegory as an immediate political procedure at the same time that he preserves it as a mediated historical, literary, and even philosophical phenomenon. Joyce's style allows us to see the very limited and limiting perspective of an artist (Stephen) who wants to imagine himself as the allegorical figure who inherits the past and rights its various wrongs. In this maneuver, as in Hegel's conception of the contradictory nature of overcoming, that which is negated is not destroyed, but, rather, lifted to a more critical and organic level. We see both the limitations and the problems that provoked them, and, hopefully we move beyond them to a new and more reflective point of view.

The point of all this is to say that while both the Unionist Gothic in general and Stephen Dedalus in particular merely use allegory, Joyce's literary technique both deploys and satirizes it. In the following sections we will observe how Stephen's theory of art—embodied most consummately in the lecture on Shakespeare that he delivers in Dublin's National Library—deploys precisely the singularity of the Gothic's allegory of structural dispossession. In the simplest sense, as the Gothic's final inheriting son, Stephen must abject maternal identity and reify paternal power. He reads selectively and exclusively in order to figure himself as the ultimate heir. In contrast, we will see how Joyce offers in the appearance and wanderings of Leopold Bloom an aesthetic that disrupts singularity and accumulates multiple identities. In the figure of Bloom, Joyce draws on and actively embraces the compound stereotypes and diverse meanings inherited from the past in order to establish an alternate way of facing structural dispossession. This is to say that in Bloom, Joyce offers the accumulation of meanings as a mediation of the singularity of Gothic allegory. In a sense, then, taken as a whole, *Ulysses* comes to signify Irish literary modernism's overcoming of the Irish Gothic's allegory of structural dispossession.

II. ABJECTION AND THE MATERNAL GHOST

In such English Gothic novels as Matthew Lewis's *The Monk* or Horace Walpole's *The Castle of Otranto,* the allegory of structural dispossession revolves around the figure of the murdered ghost. In *Gothic Pathologies,* David Punter explains that for the Gothic novel, ghosts nearly always arise on the "site of vanished cultural territory" (1). After all, even in *Hamlet,* that most-discussed of all literary ghost stories, the shade of Hamlet's father rises up in order to point out usurpation, to tell us that all is not right in the state of Denmark. In a sense, Gothic shades are revenants. They are the betrayed dead returning to see that justice is done, returning to inscribe their names in the margins of the textual histories from which they have been erased. Like the inheriting male whose appearance concludes the Gothic narrative, the ghost points back to the problem of dispossession, to the cycle of terror stirred up by usurpation. The Gothic revenant makes an insistent claim on the living characters: recall the past and set it right. Of course, the text of *Ulysses* is full of ghosts. For each of the main characters, specters haunt the paths they take and block off still other paths. Throughout the novel we find Stephen haunted by his mother's ghost. Bloom sees the spectral form of his son, Rudy, and talk of spirits winds a course throughout the novel. Some of these ghosts appear to be exorcised through the course of the novel, while others cast spectral shadows that remain despite the actions of the living characters. In a sense, neither the biological mother nor the biological father allows Stephen to feel as though he will inherit the past, so he develops a theory of ghosts, of spirits from the past who might teach him why he has been disinherited and how he can come into the fullness of his true inheritance. I want to evaluate the claims made by two of the interrelated ghosts that haunt Stephen: the abject Irish maternal ghost signified by Stephen's mother and the powerful paternal revenant signified by Hamlet's father in Stephen's Shakespeare lecture. As Stephen rejects the former, he actively identifies with and embraces the latter.

The maternal ghost appears quite early in the novel. As Stephen defends and recommends himself by turns in the midst of the mock-Gothic Martello tower sequence that initiates the novel's first episode, "Telemachus," we get occasional glimpses of the inner workings of his mind. In the midst of his mock-Gothic scene, Stephen ruminates rather obsessively on his mother's death, on his feeling of indebtedness to her, and on his refusal to pray with her as she lay dying of cancer. In his dreams, her "wasted body within its loose graveclothes" appears to him (9). As he explains in his internal monologue, "Her glaring eyes, staring out of death, to shake and bend my soul. On me alone. The ghostcandle to light her agony. Ghostly light on the tortured face. Her hoarse loud breath rattling in horror, while all prayed on their knees"(9). Predictably, then, Stephen always tends to imagine that May Dedalus's condemning eyes fall on him "alone." Stephen's refusal of his mother in the name of his commitment to personal integrity and autonomy circumscribes nearly all of his activity in the novel. He can never escape from the fact that he wants to escape from his mother. That this ghost first appears in the midst of Stephen's mock-Gothic scene with Mulligan helps to frame the lost mother's centrality to the Gothic allegory of structural dispossession.

Stephen's refusal of his mother signals an attempt to break the hold of the maternal entity, to become a subject, and, finally, to claim his birthright as an artist-creator. In "Telemachus," Stephen thinks of his mother as a "ghoul," a "corpsechewer," who must be rejected in the name of life, and he refuses her ghostly presence with an emphatic, "No, mother! Let me be and let me live." (9). In a very Gothic sense, for Stephen, as for Julia Kristeva, the abjection of the mother is a "*necessary precondition of narcissism*" (13). But Kristeva is also quick to point out that abjection secretes itself into the subject's narcissism as well. As she says in *Powers of Horror,* abjection ends up coexisting with narcissism and "causes it to be permanently brittle" (13). In a sense, then, the narcissistic subject can never truly rid him or herself of the maternal entity. The ghost remains. Hence, Stephen—whose narcissism is, to say the least, brittle—sees his mother's ghost again during the "Circe" episode in Bella Cohen's brothel. When he encounters the maternal entity a second time, however, she seems even more horrifying. Shouting his autonomous credos, the "*non serviam*" of Satan and the "Nothung" of Siegfried's heroic sword—both arch-models of a kind of Romantic solipsism—Stephen seeks to reject his mother's ghost and the religious, historical, and psychological burdens that attend her once and for all (475). In uttering words derived from the *Bible,* from Milton's *Paradise Lost,* and from Wagner's *Der Ring des Nibelungen,* Stephen imagines himself as a self-creating rebel-artist, as a writer who can invoke literary and aesthetic history and posit his own world and his own subjectivity. He wants to use the force of imagination to eschew biology and the debt to the past. Another way of putting it would be to agree with Kristeva herself, who indicates in *Powers of Horror* that in *Ulysses* "the Word alone purifies from the abject," for it is through the power of the literary and allegorical "word" that Stephen Dedalus, the would-be poet, hopes to purify himself (23). As an artist, he will embody the inheriting son who overcomes structural dispossession through an act of creative imagination. But as the opening sequence in the Martello tower demonstrates, Stephen can never seem to shake the feeling that he remains, somehow, the confined and feminized victim of history. This anxiety is further compounded by Mulligan's mock-homoerotic invocation of Wilde's aesthetic "Hellenism," which also serves to feminize Stephen. Stephen appears to recall the weakness that comes from the mother and the feminine throughout the novel. In a sense, the Gothic allegory of the dispossessed mother and the inheriting son has blended into the conceptual landscape of modern Ireland. In attempting to deploy this allegory to liberate himself, Stephen merely hypostatizes it. From a critical perspective, we can see how Stephen invokes an allegory that points out—and even begins to embody—his limitations as a thinker and an artist. He compresses the complex sociopolitical history of colonialism, gender disorientation, and structural dispossession into a singular, emblematic narrative, the narrative of the parasitic mother.

In abjecting the mother, he frees himself from the overwhelming historical and genetic past and discovers a way to inherit a spiritual, literary, and paternal tradition.

Needless to say, when the literary and spiritual problem of ghostliness appears in an overt fashion in his *Hamlet* lecture in the National Library, Stephen inevitably thinks about his mother, about maternity, and, subsequently, about the problem of artistic generation. He ponders the problem of his own origin as the son of May Dedalus, and of his personal aspiration to forge a wholly new self in the smithy of his soul, to imagine—and then to embody—"the uncreated conscience" of his race. If the presence of the mother-ghost implies, for Stephen, that one is trapped in the past, that one remains indebted to or confined by the weaknesses of history, then his *Hamlet* lecture attempts to think of how an allegorical father-ghost might liberate one from that past. As Karen Lawrence explains, Stephen's theory of artistic paternity, of creating oneself in art, "frees him from biology" (89). This theory also frees Stephen from the suffocating implications of *Amor Matris,* from the mother love that he fears may be "the only true thing in life" (207). In fact, when the term *Amor Matris* first appears in the novel, in the "Nestor" episode, Stephen reminds us that the mother's lineage always implies "weak blood and wheysour milk" (28).

In *Ulysses,* Stephen confronts the fear associated with the weakness of the maternal lineage. He confronts the figure who embodies isolation, confinement, and a kind of suffocating *Amor Matris* by evoking his own contrasting notion of literary paternity. The weakness of the disabling mother will be met by the power of the self-creating father. In a very direct sense, for Stephen, breaking with the mother and with biology also constitutes the means of getting shut of the haunting problem of structural dispossession. The mother becomes a memory of limitations, and from her Stephen, the son, inherits weak blood, dispossession, and confinement. By moving from biology to fiction, from history to fabulation, he hopes to write an identity for himself that is cleansed of the debt to and the homology with the maternal entity. Stephen very consciously wants to overcome the burden of his association with the weak-blooded maternal entity, but, of course, he cannot seem to break away entirely. In this way, for Stephen the maternal revenant harks back to the one that confronts Laura in Joseph Sheridan Le Fanu's "Carmilla." Like the vampiric Carmilla, May Dedalus signifies a stifled and stifling history, a confined and weakened genetic inheritance. Like Carmilla, she is a "ghoul" and "corpsechewer," who appears to prey on her living descendants and drain them of their autonomy.

By breaking the bonds of identification with his mother and with a mythic motherland, Stephen hopes to gain his inheritance through a paradoxical act of denunciation. He invokes the Gothic allegory of structural dispossession and, like Oscar Wilde, Stephen hopes that his conscious, unwavering understanding of this narrative will give him power over it. He imagines his personal liberation as an act of recovery, as an act that entirely sidesteps the problem of structural dispossession. He wants to become an allegorical all-father in order to abject the allegorical mother. But his narcissism remains brittle precisely because it remains so wrapped up in the task of ridding itself of—of abjecting—the maternal past. He remains inextricably linked to and obsessed with that which he seeks to overcome. Like the heroes of the Unionist Gothic, then, Stephen longs to reclaim the maternal land of Ireland only as he must reject the maternal identity itself as disempowering and disunified.

III. NOSTALGIA FOR PATERNAL REPOSSESSION

During his Shakespeare lecture in the "Scylla and Charybdis" episode, Stephen offers a theory of literary paternity that he hopes will cleanse him of the historical, social, psychic, and biological connection to maternity. Hence, his aesthetic theory remains bound to his abjection of the mother. Much like the aesthetic that characterizes Wilde's *Dorian Gray,* Stephen's is an aesthetic of revision, and he sees himself as a rebel son, reclaiming his birthright by rewriting an older form. "They List," he tells us during his *Hamlet* lecture "and in the Porches of their ears I pour" (196). With what seems a quintessence of allusive irony, Stephen revises the haunting words of the ghost of Hamlet's father in order to predict the potential effects that his own interpretation of Shakespeare may have on the Anglo-Irish intellectuals who listen to his lecture in the Dublin National Library. The critic of a Derridean frame of mind might inquire as to whether this seemingly lethal reinterpretation of the great poet of the Empire is a poison or a cure, or, perhaps more importantly, both poison and cure.[19] Stephen's version of *Hamlet* links together the themes of paternity and artistic generation, but it also remains haunted by the maternal entity. As his variant of the words of King Hamlet imply, Stephen hopes that his rereading will underscore the work of revision and of the revolutionary power wielded by those who consciously manipulate allegorical figuration. As Stephen begins his commentary on Shakespeare in "Scylla and Charybdis," John Eglinton (William Kirkpatrick Magee), the Anglo-Irish essay writer and marginal participant in the Irish Literary Revival, mockingly claims that Stephen "will have it that *Hamlet* is a ghoststory. . . . Like the fat boy in Pickwick he wants to make our flesh creep" (187–88).[20] Stephen invokes *Hamlet* in order to conjure a phantasm who works to revise and control rather than to merely renarrate a familiar story. But before we evaluate Stephen's discussion of *Hamlet,* let's explore the context of both his lecture and the text it dissects.

As L. H. Platt has argued, Stephen speaks to an audience made up for the most part of members of the Anglo-Irish Literary Revival (738). These figures—primarily the mystic/poet A.E.(George Russell), editor of *The Irish Homestead,* a paper that published and rejected several of Joyce's short stories—also represent an attempt to recover Ireland's usurped history. Revivalists like A.E. and W. B. Yeats worked to recover Ireland's past by establishing a mythos upon which to construct a new History. Hence, Joyce has Stephen engage in a retelling of history in the presence of and in contention with Revivalists, whose express aim, as William Patrick Ryan states in his 1894 manifesto-style biography of the movement, *The Irish Literary Revival: Its History, Pioneers, and Possibilities,* was "to promote in new quarters that enlightened nationality which studies the past, prizes the best in it, keeps it as meet background to lives of noble action in the present" (183). Joyce himself was clearly no great lover of the movement, and in his letter of 8 February 1903 to Stanislaus, he pits the writing of the Revivalists against his own style. "I will write," he argues, "only those things that approve themselves to me and I will write the best way I can . . . So Damn Russell, damn Yeats, damn Skeffington, damn Darlington, damn editors, damn free-thinkers, damn vegetable verse and double damn vegetable philosophy" (2:28).[21] A.E. receives particularly harsh treatment throughout *Ulysses* for his theosophist views and for his pose as a poet-mystic. As a member of the Dublin Lodge of the Theosophical Society, A.E. shared many of his positions with Yeats, the leading figure of the Revival.

Like the Revivalists, Stephen longs for a reconstructed paternal power, but he does not only prize what is best in the past. In fact, as a great cataloger of injustice, he views history as a nightmare and himself as its victim. That the encounter between Stephen and the Revivalists takes place within the space of the library, a sort of holy forum of Irish textual history, demonstrates both Stephen's commitment to revising history and his opposition to the Revivalist version of just such a task. Stephen's lecture, though it does revolve around a curious conception of ghosts, never retreats into mere mythic history. The father he seeks is not the mythic Cuchulain of Yeats's poetry and drama, a figure who resides only in the realm of eternal legend but, rather, an artist-creator who can live in and inherit the present. Stephen wants to replace myth with allegory precisely in order to make a point about the losses and failures of history and to avoid the ahistoricality of Revivalist idealism. In Stephen's version of *Hamlet,* specters take on a more material meaning, then. They must point back to structural dispossession. As in Gothic fiction, for Stephen the ghost requires, in fact insists upon, altering the relationships that exist in the material world.

Thus, in the Scylla and Charybdis dialectic set up in the text, the Revivalists come to represent the whirlpool of Charybdis—call it

Platonic—thinking. They attempt to construct a mythic or ideal past as a model for the kind of approach to history that Ireland should take in the present. However, this takes the form of the colonization of the mythic past, and, as Platt argues, is a "means by which a declining class [the Anglo-Irish ascendancy] attempted to preserve for itself a cultural and intellectual position" (739). This mystical immateriality works to discern, and where it cannot discern, to imagine, a coherent pattern in history. Such techniques find their apotheosis in W. B. Yeats's *A Vision*. As A.E. tells us in "Scylla and Charybdis," "Art has to reveal to us ideas, formless spiritual essences. . . . The deepest poetry of Shelley, the words of Hamlet bring our mind into contact with the eternal wisdom, Plato's world of ideas" (185). It is important to note here, that for Joyce's A.E., "our mind" is a universal and collective one, an inheritance at once fully gathered together and thoroughly ideal.

Stephen is a member of the Catholic petit bourgeois, a group on the rise in late nineteenth- and early–twentieth-century Ireland. Against the ahistorical formlessness of A.E.'s idealism, the Gaelo-Catholic Stephen will propose a concept of the betrayed and murdered Form's salvific potential. His Gothic allegory leads him to look for the betrayals and lost inheritances of history and not simply for eternal, ahistorical wisdom. Near the beginning of Stephen's discussion, Eglinton claims that "it makes my blood boil to hear anyone compare Aristotle to Plato" (186). Stephen has always demonstrated a proclivity for the more materialist Aristotle, a tendency that not only subtends how his approach to life, literature, and writing in general differs from that of his interlocutors, but also underscores his position as a Catholic, influenced by Aristotelian and Scholastic thinking. The Revivalists long for the mythic power of a Cuchulain. As a Catholic, Stephen thinks in somewhat more material terms, and he longs for a narrative about usurpation and about the son's desire to recover the inheritance he was denied. In a sense, he is not moved to emulate mythic models, but, rather, appears to be injured by the stories that have come to us from the past. In the confrontation between Stephen and the Revivalists that takes place in "Scylla and Charybdis," then, we encounter competing modes of nostalgia. Stephen's historical nostalgia collides with the Revivalist mythic nostalgia. Throughout the lecture, Stephen seems quite anxious to demonstrate the differences between his own method and that of the Revivalists. He seems anxious, that is, to connect *Hamlet,* the work of art, to the actual material conditions in which it was produced. Where the Revivalists embrace a legendary and unearthly paternal power, Stephen develops an allegory of historical victimization and structural dispossession.

For Stephen, the past must be countered by allegory not myth. Unlike the Revivalists, Stephen actively struggles to avoid thinking in terms of myth. His Shakespeare commentary starts by thinking not so much of mythification, but rather of the interaction between literature and the real-world conditions in which it is produced. But in the end, he also thinks in terms of ghosts and of the dead spirit transfigured into real, physical communion. His characters may be reductive and emblematic, but they are emblems derived from the material world. As we will come to see, in this reinterpretation of *Hamlet* the battle between materialism and idealism is joined, but Stephen attempts to negotiate between the two by allowing his Scholastic, Catholic-inflected thinking about transubstantiality and consubstantiality to invade his theorizing about Shakespeare. In the Catholic ceremony, the spiritual and the material join in the act of communion. Thus, it is his Catholicism, that Jesuit strain, which Mulligan reminds us is "injected the wrong way" in Stephen, that marks him as different, that separates him in both learning and custom from the English and the Anglo-Irish ascendancy with their accompanying narratives of the civilizing process (8). In a sense, Stephen can claim a more victimized status because as a Gaelo-Catholic he can construe himself as more authentically Irish and more authentically disempowered than the ascendancy class.

Joyce's approach to these passages allows us to see how the Anglo-Irish effort to appropriate a mythic past simply mirrors the colonization of Ireland by England. Joyce reveals the Revivalists' emphasis on mythic history as an attempt to construct a Grand Myth of State in a manner similar to the British Empire. Hence the nationalism of the Revivalists, like that of the Citizen in the "Cyclops" episode, is a mimic-discourse, an approach that still bears the marks and characteristics of the oppressor. Here *Ulysses* announces the crisis of a nation whose approach to history dooms it to live in an immaterial "artifice of eternity" and to reside forever in the shadow of the colonial usurper. Stephen's Gothic allegory records injustice at the same time that it hopes to inherit that which has been lost.

As Seamus Deane explains in "The Provincial Intellectual," Stephen's interest is in "the creation of himself" (81). He wants to extricate himself from an unsatisfactory history, so he creates through the act of fabulation. He goes back to the most lauded work in English literary history, invokes its ghost, and then compels the specter to reveal the fissures in the narrative it has helped to construct. In fact, Shakespeare seems to haunt the entire first half of *Ulysses,* and Stephen's lecture is an attempt to exorcise this ghost through confrontation and commentary. Mulligan informs us at the outset of the novel of Dedalus's creative interpretation of *Hamlet* while Stephen himself, clad in black, yearns guiltily for his mother. Meanwhile, the Martello tower, as the Englishman Haines tells us, takes on the aspect "somehow of Elsinore" (18). Stephen's confrontation with the ghosts of history seems to enact the desire for a Gothic form of justice, an attempt to find hope for the present through the repossession of the past. To some extent, then, he can imagine his lecture in the National Library as the speech of the outside of history, or the speech of the history of the outside—that is—the voices outside, inscribed in the margins of, the textual speeches of *Hamlet* and English history. Here we begin to see the problem with Stephen's theory as well. If the father and the son must become one in the Gothic in order for the son to repossess the mother's land (her figural body), then the allegory of the inheriting son does not really heal but merely points back to the mother's structural disinheritance. Stephen betrays a nostalgic longing to repossess the father's power, but he also figures the father as a vulnerable victim. His narcissism, as Kristeva would doubtless point out, seems quite brittle here. Far from abjecting the maternal entity and establishing an autonomy founded on paternal inheritance, Stephen has imagined a father whose confinements and weaknesses actually appear homologous to the mother's. The father-creator becomes another instance of the Gothic double bind of Irish masculinity that haunts nineteenth-century fiction. As a persistent double character, the potentially powerful victimizer is always already a victim, and Stephen's Shakespeare lecture operates by realizing, by manipulating, and, finally, by surrendering to this binary.

If Shakespeare is the great poet of the British Empire, then he is also a figure for the usurper, a figure for the interpellating narrative constructed by British imperialism, a narrative that haunts Irish history. However, in Stephen's commentary, Shakespeare is also, perhaps paradoxically, the ghost of King Hamlet, the ghost who seeks a voice. Stephen sets the scene:

> A player comes on under the shadow, made up in the castoff mail of a court buck, a wellset man with a bass voice. It is the ghost, a king and no king, and the player is Shakespeare who has studied *Hamlet* all the years of his life which were not vanity in order to play the part of the spectre. He speaks the words to Burbage, the young player who stands before him beyond the rack of cerecloth calling him by name:
>
> *Hamlet, I am thy father's spirit*
>
> bidding him list. To a son he speaks, the son of his soul, the prince, young Hamlet and to the son of his body, Hamnet Shakespeare, who has died in Stratford that his namesake may live forever. . . . Is it possible that that player Shakespeare, a ghost by absence, and in the vesture of buried Denmark, a ghost by death, speaking his own words to his son's name. (188–89)

In establishing that Shakespeare must have played King Hamlet in the first production of the play, Stephen argues that Shakespeare is both a figure for the English usurper and the shade of the usurped and murdered king. Stephen also associates himself with the bard by claiming that Shakespeare wears the castoff suit of "a court buck." Stephen, as we remember from "Telemachus," wears one of Buck Mulligan's suits throughout the day. In addition the son-Hamlet becomes identical with the son-Hamnet. So we get the image of specters, of their other selves in the real world, and of players, and indeed authors, filling the roles of specters. And all of this is framed by the figure of the lost or dispossessed son. In the passage, we witness a collision of the fictive and the actual, the spiritual and the material. But how does this curious haunting of textual history work in *Ulysses*?

Stephen interprets King Hamlet as a creative sublimation, a metaphor of Shakespeare's own betrayal by his wife, Ann Hathaway, who, so Stephen argues, committed adultery with Shakespeare's brothers Richard and Edmund. Through the figure of Ann Hathaway, we catch another glimpse of Stephen's fear of the feminine. The feminine figure, the mother of Shakespeare's son, Hamnet, receives blame as the weak-blooded betrayer whose son dies. Though the usurpers here are all men, for Stephen it is the weak or parasitic maternal entity that allows the male usurper in the door. By focusing on being "overborne" by woman, Stephen hopes to find a way to overcome the weaknesses of the past and to establish a steadfast, patriarchal identity for the future. Many of the so-called facts for Stephen's commentary are drawn largely from *William Shakespeare* by George Brandes, *The Man Shakespeare and His Tragic Life-Story* by Frank Harris, and *A Life of William Shakespeare* by Sidney Lee, texts widely dismissed today, but Stephen's biographical study attempts to disrupt *Hamlet* by allowing the ghosts of the material world that surrounded the text to disfigure the text itself, to show the text of *Hamlet* as a story of structural dispossession and paternal repossession.

Stephen explains that King Hamlet's speech "is always turned elsewhere, backward. Ravisher and Ravished. . . . he is a ghost, a shadow now, the wind by Elsinore's rocks or what you will"(197). As he does so often throughout the chapter, Stephen uses the term "will" here to suggest Shakespeare as the punning player within the ghost. "Who is the ghost from *limbo patrum,* returning to the world that has forgotten him? Who is King Hamlet?" Stephen asks (188). As both usurper and usurped, ravisher and ravished, Shakespeare, the creator, is reinterpreted by the historical circumstances that surround and give birth to his creation. The ravisher ravished is the victimizer victimized, and in this case the victim appears as the usurped father rather than as the confined mother. Importantly, this is also where Stephen suggests that the specter's voice is heard "only in the heart of him who is the substance of his shadow, the son consubstantial with the father" (197). He suggests, then, a linking up or a joining together between the father and son that mirrors the consubstantiality of Jehovah and Jesus. In rejecting the mother, Stephen has rejected biology entirely, choosing instead to focus on literary and spiritual paternity rather than on the messiness of a genetic reproduction that is weakened by its relationship to the maternal entity. In *Hamlet,* as in the Gospels, the son must act out and embody the narrative set up by the father. The son enacts justice as, and in the name of, the father. As Stephen paraphrases, "You are the dispossessed son: I am the murdered father" (189). But the description of King Hamlet as ravisher ravished as "King and no King" is where the ghost of Shakespeare becomes the analogue for yet another shade. We have the figure of a usurped leader under the shadow of adultery, betrayal, and death. Shakespeare's Ghost finds its other in the "shade" of Parnell.

A specter is haunting both *Ulysses* and Irish history: the specter of Charles Stewart Parnell, a figure whose name never even receives mention in "Scylla and Charybdis." In an essay written during the period of his greatest commitment to socialism and printed in the Triestine Irrendentist paper, *il Piccolo della Sera,* Joyce refers to Parnell as "the ghost of the 'uncrowned king'" (*The Critical Writings* 228). If Shakespeare is a figure for the interpellative narrative of British imperialism in *Ulysses,* then Parnell shares the stage as the usurped though "uncrowned" king, a "King and no King." It is obvious to almost any reader of *A Portrait* and *Dubliners* that Joyce found something despicable about Ireland's betrayal of Parnell. In an oft-quoted passage from *A Portrait,* Stephen complains of the fact that no honorable revolutionary "has given up his life to you [Ireland] and his youth and his affections from the days of Tone to the days of Parnell but you sold him to the enemy" (220). For Stephen, the authority of the Church, interpellation by the colonizers, and Ireland's self-betrayal all seem to congeal in a rather grotesque form around the Parnell split. In this refigured Gothic allegory, the betrayed Parnell becomes the arch-father who can appear both as a victim and as a powerful revolutionary spirit.

But is the Parnell split somehow encoded in Stephen's gloss on Shakespeare? After all, in Stephen's lecture, it is Shakespeare who is more sinned against than sinning, and, of course, it was Parnell's adulterous affair with Kitty O'Shea that undermined his position both in Ireland and in the English Parliament. If Stephen's Shakespeare, as King Hamlet, is both usurper and usurped, then in *Ulysses* he serves as textual double for Parnell, Ireland's "uncrowned king." In both cases the betrayer is a brother. Where Shakespeare is betrayed by Richard and Edmund, his filial brothers, Parnell is betrayed by Irishmen, his figurative brothers (and by churchmen, or monkish, "brothers"). We see in the Parnell story, then, what we see in the Shakespeare commentary: "the theme of the false or the usurping or the adulterous brother" (*Ulysses*

212). But this comparison folds back on itself as well. Parnell also figures as the adulterer, so he remains Shakespeare's other. As a ghost, he enacts the role of ravisher of English imperial history, a ravisher who was betrayed and, as Joyce tells us, torn to pieces by the Irish who did not wait to "throw him to the English wolves" (*The Critical Writings* 228). A ghostly Parnell who can appear both as powerful and as victimized is the perfect allegorical father for Stephen Dedalus. Parnell appears in *Ulysses* as the other of the ghost of Shakespeare, as the thoroughly concealed shade of the shade.

IV. AESTHETIC PATRIMONY

In his *Parnell and His Party 1880–1890,* Conor Cruise O'Brien claims that Parnell's presence on the stage of Irish history suggested that Ireland's problems could be resolved by "personality" (350). Likewise, in his seminal biography, *Parnell,* F. S. L. Lyons claims that Parnell offered the nation "self-respect."[22] Parnell clearly allowed the Irish imaginary the idea that history could be countered by personality. The shade of Parnell in Joyce's *Ulysses* presents questions that bear the same resonances as those suggested by Stephen's Shakespeare. How do we deal with betrayal? How does one escape a suffocating history and give birth to a new one? Stephen's answer is clear: aesthetic patrimony. For him, one must repossess through the act of self-creation. Here, the suggestive double valence of this consubstantial ghost allows Stephen to rethink the nightmarish history of colonization.[23] Stephen's invocation of ghosts implies that all is not right, that something has gone awry. In the ensuing commentary, the shade of Parnell, the ravisher ravished, punctures the overblown aspirations of both Revivalist nationalism and British parliamentary democracy. In the National Library, Stephen suggests through his Shakespeare lecture that both systems have failed to liberate Ireland in any meaningful sense. What Stephen adds to all this is a singularly compelling, though unequivocally egocentric, question: who is the inheriting son consubstantial with the revolutionary father? He sees in the figure of the son who can inherit or repossess the land, the solution to the betrayals and structural dispossessions that attend the colonial system.

Stephen's lecture on Shakespeare, precisely because it is a lecture, bears with it certain historical implications about the time in which it is evoked. Think of the National Library episode as an event that is both a reflection on and deflection of the past. Stephen presents a counternarrative, one that appears piecemeal and demythologizing. Nonetheless, he attempts to write for modern Ireland in the margins of *Hamlet.* This event provides us with an image of adultery and betrayal, an image that might well disfigure the master narrative of British colonialism that lends a coherent structure to both English epic history and to what *Ulysses* refers to as the Anglo-Irish desire for a national epic "yet to be written" (192). Stephen provides us with an important critical insight, a moment in which the economy of textuality in *Hamlet* and the material facts of colonization meet to rework history. Much of the criticism of *Ulysses* that focuses on nationalism explores Stephen's struggle to forge the "uncreated conscience of his race."[24] But, does Stephen's counterhistory interrupt stories of progress or suggest that we should seek out all of the traces of Ireland's lost past in the narrative of British imperialism? Stephen clearly has a notion of the totality against which he launches his concealed critique. Without a notion of this colonizing whole and its accompanying narratives of complicity, against which to inveigh, without some theory about this totalizing system that eliminates, when it cannot subordinate, difference, Stephen's lecture would have little significance beyond aesthetic posturing.

Stephen's counterhistory remains limited, however, and in many ways he fails to see the fuller implications of his commentary. His allegorical mode of reading finally replaces one nationalism with another. He certainly seems willing to listen for all of the polyvalent implications of the paternal ghost because such a ghostly figure allows him to focus on his own rights and on what he might take from the past. Through the notion of the artist-creator, Stephen delivers a demythologized Shakespeare, a new critique of colonialism and a skillfully concealed revision of the Parnell story. However, all of this also provokes Stephen's thinking about the Trinity. "He who Himself begot," he tells us, "middler the Holy Ghost, and Himself sent Himself" (197). His musings on the consubstantiality of the Father and the Son lead to his famous theory of art in which the artist becomes "the father of all his race"—the father of himself (208). The appearance of the Catholic doctrines of transubstantiation and consubstantiation, holdovers from Stephen's Jesuit education, play central roles in his notion of the artist as creator. In addition, they underscore a kind of Gothic element to Stephen's notion of spirits. As in much Gothic fiction, the ghost seems to get invoked by an apostate Catholic and within the context of Catholic ritual and ceremony. Not only are the Son and the Father one in the Catholic catechism, but the transubstantiation of the bread and wine enacts an *anamnesis,* a memorial that signifies the "literal presence" of Christ in the Eucharist. In the Vatican's *Catechism of the Catholic Church,* we discover that the moment of *anamnesis*, the instance of memory, presents "to the Father, the offering of his Son which reconciles us with him" (341). Hence, not only are the Father and Son one, as are Hamlet *pere* and Hamlet *fils,* but, as with Stephen's theory of art, the Father is reconciled to all material creation. Stephen figures himself as the consubstantial son enacting the narrative prepared by Parnell, the revolutionary father, and, in so doing, Stephen reincarnates the revolutionary father in art. Stephen has, thus, joined the spiritual Charybdis to the material Scylla by finding an avatar of the Father-creator's wishes in the materiality of the Son's (textual) body and of the real physical communion (the work of art) that finds its home in the bodies and souls of the believers. Through aesthetic metempsychosis, the artist becomes both the creator and reconciler, the Father and the Son. The "weakblooded," "wheysour" milk of the mother appears to have been thoroughly rejected.

This notion of art allows Stephen to awake from the nightmare of history by giving birth to himself. It seems as though he has erased the maternal entity entirely. In Stephen's aesthetics, the artist comes to embody both Father and Son, and as an analogue to the paradox of the Christian Triune God, the Artist/Father gives birth to himself in art. Finally, however, Stephen's attempt at Romantic self-creation reads as yet another reductive narrative, and a particularly patriarchal one at that. Following the structure of the Anglo-Irish Gothic, Stephen suffers confinement and feminization, and he responds by wishing to become the inheriting son. His theory of art allows him to imagine himself as both the revolutionary father and the Gothic's inheriting son. Following Wilde's example, Stephen's weapon of choice is art, the realm of aesthetic autonomy. He renders a kind of counterhistory only as he opts for what is to him an even more attractive meta-narrative: the Romantic self. He figures himself as "entelechy, form of forms" (189). Later, he goes on to quote Maeterlinck in order to say "*if Socrates leave his house today he will find the sage seated on his doorstep. If Judas go forth tonight it is to Judas his steps will tend.* Every life is many days, day after day. We walk through ourselves . . . but always meeting ourselves" (213). For Stephen what persists through history is, finally, not structure or materiality, but typology and identity, not a series of earthly ghosts but the *Geist.* He embraces the Romantic ideal of the autotelic or self-determining, purposive subject. That is to say, in the end his thinking remains as bound to idealism as A.E.'s.

The problem with Stephen's thinking is precisely that patriarchal, Catholic context of thought that also underwrites his most revolutionary moments. His theory of the creator draws on Catholic doctrine and, thus, remains confined by the teleological and purposive schema of messianism that sanctions Christian notions of salvation. For Stephen redemption must always provide a conclusion, a way out. Inevitably, this canny gloss on Shakespeare risks being reinserted into the arc of Stephen's own thoroughly theorized, but no less entrapping, mimic-discourse. Following the genealogy that I laid out in chapter 1, we can see that despite his overt attempt to deal with structural dispossession, Stephen has been assimilated wholesale into the Gothic double bind that characterized Irish writing since Edmund Burke and William Sampson. Stephen's

Parnellite Shakespeare—the ravisher ravished—becomes another version of that doubly-bound allegory. Stephen's adaptation is certainly a more erudite and self-conscious allegory, but it is an allegory nonetheless. His fear of being identified with a confined, singular, weak-blooded femininity allows him to imagine masculine inheritance—the paternal lineage—as the messianic answer to history's betrayals and failures. But if we read Stephen's narrative carefully, we find that the mother's abjection is reinscribed in the father's insistent vulnerability. The powerful ravisher, in other words, must also be the disempowered and ravished figure as well.

Despite the fact that Stephen's lecture emphasizes paternity, usurpation, and a murdered king, he fails to realize that one of Hamlet's most profound miscalculations is his inability to recognize his connection to his mother, Gertrude, until it is too late. Both Stephen and Hamlet obsess about how to recover the father's power, but they also overlook the implications of the mother and of "*Amor Matris,* subjective and objective genitive" (207). Although both Stephen and Hamlet introduce overtly revolutionary elements into their own stories, they both finally fail to overcome the structural dispossession entailed by those stories. They both tell stories that exclude rather than include. In reading Stephen's aesthetic theory, then, we must bear in mind that his attempt to deal with structural dispossession listens for potentially revolutionary and disruptive voices while, at the same time, failing to hear much of the ghostly, garbled, double speech uttered by many of those voices.

Perhaps Stephen's failing speaks of an even larger failure. When we read Stephen's deficiencies as a reflection of the larger failure of allegory to come up with a liberatory political criticism, then we begin to engage more dialectically with the problem of thinking historically. For critic Theodor Adorno, the artwork's failure is essential to its critical character. As he explains in *Aesthetic Theory,* "History is the content of artworks. To analyze artworks means no less than to become conscious of the history immanently sedimented in them" (85). History, we might argue, remains concealed in the cracks of the work, in the spaces in which an artwork that strives for some formal wholeness fails to account for its own discontinuities, its own logical inconsistencies, its own oversights. The truth comes out negatively. For Adorno, works of art allow something to appear that does not exist in empirical memory or understanding. Hence, Adorno explains, "the nonexistent is mediated to them [artworks] through fragments of the existing, which they assemble into an *apparition*" (83). The repressed or the abject, that which could not be thought or admitted, comes into reality in art in the form of a ghost, the spectral image of the forgotten. The failure of Stephen's mode of allegory lies in its desire to abject the mother and reduce a complex history to a narrative of inheritance and paternal power. This failure underscores the fact that Stephen's real debt to the Irish Gothic subsists in his inability to resolve the problem of structural dispossession by simply repossessing the past. To do so, he must cut away the elements that don't fit within the framework of his narrow self-conception.

The problem with Stephen's own "aesthetic theory" seems to be that he believes in a reified paternal "artist" who makes no mistakes rather than in a work of art that does. He wants to awake from history rather than to it, and hence he opts for a rather solipsistic and, despite his intentions, regressive notion of the self. His allegorical thinking provides us with a conscious theory of history at the same time that it reveals an unconscious and reductive theory of value. For Benjamin, allegory produces a language in which "detail is of no great importance" (*The Origin of German Tragic Drama* 175). Stephen refuses to question certain alienating meta-narratives about patriarchy, economy, and identity, at the same time that he longs to challenge the dispossession implied by imperialism and structural dispossession. Though Stephen's thinking demonstrates his literate and satiric ingenuity, he seems unwilling to admit precisely how attached his own theory is to the literary and historical forms that preceded it. In his schema, autonomous artists do not engage critically with history, so much as they work their way free of it. At issue here is the fact that Joyce's mocking of mythical thinking through Stephen also takes the form of a subtle mockery of Stephen's own limited position. Stephen attempts to negotiate between the Aristotelian Scylla of materialism and the Charybdis of Platonic mysticism with his theory of transconsubstantiality. In the end he lapses into a Romantic myth that appears far more transcendental than material. Finally, for Stephen the detail is of little importance. Accumulating details or different identities and acknowledging the pesky problems that accompany complex material relations do not seem to matter to him precisely because he wants to imagine himself as the emblematic Gothic heir. In so doing, he cannot look at the specific, historical conditions that complicate his theory. To paraphrase Marx's words from the *Grundrisse*, Stephen's theory—like commodity capitalism—erases "natural specificity" and chooses, instead, to suggest a universal, ahistorical value or identity (165). Stephen locates himself outside of history. At this point in the episode, however, Bloom, the text's Wandering Jew and "new-womanly man" appears to interrupt Stephen's allegorical narrative and to suggest other ways of facing and dealing with structural dispossession and with the identity problems that it generates. What Stephen has missed that Joyce has not is the trace of this other Other who haunts the extratextual margins of his own narrative. Stephen has already failed to recognize the sociohistorical and psychic implications of the mother-ghost. When Bloom passes between Mulligan and Stephen, the young aesthete bent on recovering the lost powers of the father fails to recognize the material implications of a real-world father as well. As Bloom appears, we must ask whether this encounter, which marks the conclusion of both the National Library episode and of the final chapter of the novel in which Stephen fills the role of main character, offers us a dialectical overcoming of the Gothic allegory of dispossession.

V. THE ACCUMULATION OF THE PAST

The Gothic primal scene that begins the novel is repeated near the conclusion of the National Library episode. Buck Mulligan has appeared once again to tease and feminize Stephen, and Stephen, having completed his allegorical tale of structural repossession, thinks to himself, "Part. The Moment is now" (217). Upon delivering his theory of aesthetic patrimony, he hopes to break with the so-called usurper and with the entire history of disinheritance. He wants to end the Gothic story that is Irish history. He remains nostalgic for paternal power and quite anxious to move forward into a future that promises a reconstructed version of that power. But as Stephen and Mulligan prepare to leave the National Library, and we observe the moment in which they will supposedly part company, we are told, "a dark back went before them" (218). The "dark back" that steps before Stephen and Mulligan belongs to Leopold Bloom. The adjective, "dark," in this context refers to Stephen's exchange with Garret Deasy in the "Nestor" episode, where Mr. Deasy calls the Jews a "Dark People" a people who "sinned against the light" (34). As he exits the National Library, Bloom is also characterized as walking like a "pard," a medieval term for a black panther.[25] But the phrase "a dark back went before them" has wider resonance than simply allowing for yet another instance in which Bloom's and Stephen's paths nearly intersect. It measures out a symbolic relationship that bears both on Christianity's relationship to Judaism and on the notion of inheritance that subtends the entire text of *Ulysses*. This notion is far more complex and inclusive than the Gothic allegory of the inheriting son. That this moment at the end of "Scylla and Charybdis" also repeats and complicates the power dynamic of the novel's opening mock-Gothic sequence indicates that history cannot merely conclude—as Stephen wants it to-because time does not move, in linear fashion, into the past. Instead, it accumulates and sediments in the now.

The passage contains the obvious parallels to the *Odyssey*. Bloom passes, Odysseus-like, between Mulligan and Stephen, but the phrase "a dark back went before them" also marks Bloom's passing out of the library doors "before" either Stephen or Mulligan. Bloom, unlike Stephen, actually appears capable of negotiating between a Scylla and a Charybdis. The fact that we see only Bloom's back implies that the two Irishmen who have been discussing *Hamlet*, ghosts, and patriarchy follow him. Bloom's Judaism, emphasized here by reference to his darkness, reveals the text's attempts to thematize the dialectical tension in the relationship of this Semitic Odysseus to Christianity. Christian notions of redemption and messianism claim to follow, inherit, and otherwise subsume the trail mapped out by Judaism. But here we see only the Jew's back. The gentiles who follow have no access to the face of this other, and his intentions remain dark and unknown to them. He is not safely and temporally behind but, rather, in front of and "before" them. Christianity's inheriting of Judaism's path to redemption puts the Catholic Church in the position of son and heir to the Judaic father, but, as with most Western conceptions of patrilineal succession, the father must be dead, obsolete, in order for the son to inherit. Judaism becomes an object structurally dispossessed by Catholic and Christian theories of history. In order to instantiate this inheritance, Christological history must involve a notion of *chronos* or chronological time and, subsequently, of progress, of events receding into the past as they fail to fit within the futural movement of either a strictly linear narrative or a teleological schema. If inheritance implies a nostalgia for the father's time, then this nostalgia can only occur in the father's absence.

Stephen operates within this schema, an ontology of linear time, and, despite his pointing to the need for critical engagement with the past, he simply relocates history within the self-fathering, individual subject. He takes Idealist and Cartesian histories to their ultimate, and ultimately aesthetic, extremes by allowing only for a subjectively constructed history, a human creator incarnating himself in art. That Bloom remains shaded, unknown, and partly unseen to the gentiles who succeed him implies that their inheritance itself is partial, perhaps even parasitic, and that his obsolescence is illusory.

We first encounter the problem that Judaism provides for chronological notions of history and inheritance in "Nestor," the novel's "History" episode according to Joyce's Lenati schema. There, as I've already noted, we see the anti-Semitic Anglo-Irishman, Mr. Deasy, define the Jews as "wanderers" who "sinned against the light" (34). For Deasy, the Jewish people remain dark, alien, the other par excellence. To Deasy, the supposedly deicidal Jews have been, and will continue to be, punished by history, which, he claims, "moves towards one great goal, the manifestation of God" (34). For Deasy's thinking, all that has occurred or can occur is a demonstration of God's will. He stands in for the most reactionary fin de siècle historians, many of whom, following the lead of the infamous Russian invective, *Protocols of the Elders of Zion,* pitted the idea of an international Jewish banking conspiracy against the inevitability of Christian teleology.[26] "Nestor" enunciates the figurative appearance of Bloom at the point where the National Library episode, the "Dialectic" chapter according to the Lenati schema, enacts his literal presence. As Neil Davison indicates in *Ulysses and the Construction of Jewish Identity,* in the text Bloom himself finally comes to represent the assimilated Jew's double binds: "the struggle to straddle both a Jewish and a nationalist identity, to believe oneself a Jew while often rejecting organized Judaism, . . . to occupy mercantile roles and not be condemned by the left as a paradigm of bourgeois greed" (10). Most importantly in *Ulysses,* Judaic historiography, symbolized by the disruptive appearance of Bloom at the end of the National Library episode, operates in a way that negates Stephen's Christological, teleological mode of thinking history.

Zakhor is the Hebrew word signifying God's command: "Remember." As Yosef Yershalmi explains, the Torah unconditionally enjoins the tribes of Israel to cultivate memory (5). The verb, *Zakhor,* is complemented by its lowercase obverse, *zakhor,* or forgetting; thus, Yershalmi asserts, "as Israel is enjoined to remember, so is it adjured not to forget" (5). Initially, this collective memory was translated through ritual and recital, much as were early versions of the Homeric epics. Hence, the events of Passover became commemorated in Passover rituals and festivals, many of which have survived in present-day Judaism. This provided the Hebrew people and the rabbinic tradition with a curiously fluid sense of history. As Yershalmi goes on to explain, in the rabbinic universe of early Judaism, "ordinary barriers of time can be ignored and all ages placed in an ever-fluid dialogue with one another" (17). If people were not there to witness the carving of the Commandments and the events at Sinai, then, Yershalmi claims, "Sinai must be borne along the conduits of memory to those who were not there that day" (10).

This Judaic notion of memory signifies the presence of the past. The Hebrew people experience the past through collective remembering, an act that occurs in the now rather than through chronological record. The experience of memory finds its apotheosis in the study of the Torah, the matter of memory, and as Gershom Scholem explains, "The Torah is a living organism, a tapestry woven from the ineffable Name of God . . . The Torah is therefore not a dead or calcified thing. Rather, in each of its 'limbs', in each and every word, there shine forth an infinite number of lights and secrets" (*On the Possibilities of Jewish Mysticism and Other Essays* 141). If the Torah is living, Scholem goes on to explain, then "talk about the past is false, for the past was never completely past" (158). It lives in relationship to the now. It affixes itself dialectically to any present context or practice. Hence, for rabbinic Judaism, and, as Scholem's studies of the Kabbalah have demonstrated, up through the Middle Ages and even into the early phases of the Enlightenment, thinking about the past relied on an ontology of the incomplete, a dialectic of fragmented, concealed, and accumulated histories that ran antithetical to the Catholic calendar and its ontology of linear time. In the "Hermeneutics of

Midrash," Gerald Bruns explains that the Torah "is always contemporary with its readers or listeners . . . always oriented toward the time and circumstances of the interpreter" (106). In Hebrew culture, new ideas came in the form of a radical reinterpretation of the past, which was not so much taken as past, but rather as part of the ever-living, redeemable present. As Bloom says in "Circe," "Past was is today." Interactive remembering, the act of memory, becomes the trope of such a historiography, and, as Scholem explains, a notion of "metempsychosis" becomes its medium.[27]

The very term *Torah* has multiple meanings in the Jewish tradition. When we refer to the Torah, we invoke both the written Torah (the Scripture) and the oral Torah (a diffuse body of written teachings and commentaries by rabbis, teachings that include Midrash [exegetical investigations of written Torah] and the Mishnah [an interrogation of Scripture that works to establish the boundaries of the *Law* or the *Halakhah*]).[28] In *Classical Judaism: Torah, Learning, Virtue,* Jacob Neusner explains,

> The Holy Scriptures were transformed by the Judaic sages. And . . . through the workings of Midrash the Hebrew Bible became the written half of one whole Torah, oral and written, revealed by God to Moses our Rabbi at Mount Sinai. Thus, Midrash works in three dimensions, first, as explanation of meaning imputed to particular verses of Scripture, second, as a mode of stating important propositions, syllogisms of thought, in conversation with verses or sustained passages of Scripture, and, third, as a way of retelling Scriptural stories in such a way as to impart to those stories new immediacy. (36)

Thus, Midrash is a form of hermeneutics that enters into conversation with its subject-object of study. Midrashic commentators such as Rashi (Rabbi Izchaki), Rambam (Moses Maimonides), Ralbag (Levi ben Gershin), and Hirsch (Samson Raphael Hirsch) interpreted Scripture by relating the written Torah to their own generations. But these commentaries actually constitute part of the oral Torah. They constitute a marginalia to the written Torah that is also part and parcel of the whole Torah. Subsequently, these commentaries were often written in poetic forms that made them easy to recite and remember. They work as part of Judaic collective memory. Many of the Midrashic commentaries argue with a previous Midrash.[29] The Midrashim of the oral Torah become part of the overall text, Torah. Hence, the rabbinic tradition offers a text that is opened up by glosses that interpret, question, and, to some extent, even criticize the Scripture. This form of historical thinking expands the possibilities of the Torah. Torah is not just the Scripture but also the glosses, marginalia, and disputes. In a sense, history and time do not pass but, rather, accumulate.[30] That is to say that meaning works through accumulation rather than singularity, exclusion, or even evolution.

In the various encounters between Stephen and Bloom in *Ulysses,* Joyce presents the tension between linear, reductive, allegorical approaches to meaning and the more expansive ones implied by Midrashic conceptions of memory. In fact, during the "Ithaca" episode, as Stephen listens to Bloom chanting the opening lines of "Hatikvah," the eventual anthem of Israel, the narrative voice asks: "What was Stephen's auditive sensation? He heard in a profound ancient male unfamiliar melody the accumulation of the past" (689). That Bloom's song signifies both the accumulation of the past and an unfamiliar melody signals how his identity addresses many of the problems suggested by Stephen's allegory at the same time that it overcomes those problems by introducing elements unheard of or misrecognized by the narrow scope of Stephen's allegory. In a sense, Bloom's oft-derogated, heterogeneous persona preserves the critique of power relations implicit in Stephen's thinking while also negating that critique by suggesting a way to endure and work through disempowered identities. He includes where Stephen excludes. He accumulates where Stephen reduces. As we'll come to see, this notion of accumulation overcomes as it preserves Stephen's allegory of structural dispossession. Stephen's allegory has a projected teleology, and his inheritance ends the narrative of dispossession. The accumulating method evoked by Bloom, however, offers a critique of master narratives without devolving to a singular story that must either conclude or replace all previous stories.

When Judaism entered into modernity, the approach to history that worked through *Zakhor* and historiographic metempsychosis often served to further highlight the individual Jew's difference from and liminal position to European culture. Western historiography had taken on a particularly "scientific" character. Of course, in the nineteenth century, this "Science" of history eventually lead to Leopold Von Ranke's famous and influential dictum that historians record "*wie es eigentlicht gewesen ist*" [what really happened] (x). Such strictures are, by now, a familiar part of the limitations inherent in Enlightenment thought, which, as Theodor Adorno and Max Horkheimer convincingly argue, sought to "disenchant" the world and render it subject to the laws of "calculability."[31] So their argument goes, "man imagines himself free from fear when there is no longer anything *unknown,*" when there are no shadows or ghosts (16). Instrumental reason, coupled with the ontology of linear time, renders a progress-driven notion (or even a means-ends conception) of history, and anything that lies outside of such a notion, anything contradictory to its means or *unknown* within its scheme becomes a source of fear (much like Deasy's fear of the Jews). Historical memory becomes subsumed wholesale by an allegorical narrative of progressive, inheritable, linear time.

Beginning in the early nineteenth century, modern Jewish studies began to adopt many of the characteristics of Enlightenment thought. In the face of growing anti-Semitism and anti-Jewish riots, Jewish students formed a kind of antidefamation league, which lead to *Wissenschaft des Judentums,* the "Science of Judaism." In 1822 Immanuel Wohlwill (pseudonym: Immanuel Wolf) published an essay entitled "On the Concept of a Science of Judaism" in the journal of *The Society for the Culture and Science of the Jews.*[32] Arguing that the Jewish people had been alienated from the rest of European culture in part by the Judaic approach to history, Wohlwill claimed that the Jews

> must raise themselves and their principle to the level of science, for this is the attitude of the European world. On this level the relationship of strangeness in which Jews and Judaism have hitherto stood to the outside world must vanish. And if one day a bond is to join the whole of humanity, then it is *the bond of science, the bond of pure rationality, the bond of truth.* (220)

Ironically, Wohlwill's words underscore the predicament of the assimilated Jew in modernity. To fit into modern Europe and to avoid anti-Semitism is to give up precisely that living, collective approach to memory and history that formulates Judaism's historiographic identity. Paradoxically, then, assimilation in some sense erases precisely those differences that act as the very condition of possibility for cumulative Jewish memory in the first place. As noted Jewish philosopher and historian Franz Rosensweig indicates in "Jewish Learning and the Return to Judaism," without a home country Jews attempted to assimilate to European life, but this only increased their alienation. Like Bloom, they are both assimilated and alien. "It is to a book," Rosensweig reminds the Jews, "the *Book,* that we owe our survival" (282). Hence, in Joyce's typological use of Judaism, modern Jews become wanderers, a dispersed nation of the text rather than merely members of a geographically imagined community. As Rosensweig claims, "We hail from the periphery. The oneness of the center is not something that we possess clearly and unambiguously, not something we can be articulate about" (283).[33] From this perspective, the Judaic people owe their identity not only to a text, and a rather fragmented one at that, but also to their position on the periphery of Western culture. In light of this, God is often referred to in Hebrew as *Ha-Makom,* which means "the Place itself." According to the geography of postrabbinic monotheism, the Jewish people were in God's country anywhere. Hence Judaic monotheism becomes a strategy for being-at-home even in the condition of exile. As Joyce translates this in *Ulysses,* wandering is home and home is wandering.

The paradox of this nation of the text resides in the fact that Christian teleology, with the addition of a "New" testament, works to inherit the riches of the past and to disinherit Judaism itself. The Jew who inherits the Torah and its sense of memory is simultaneously disinherited of his or her memory through the subsumptive logic of Christian doctrine, a doctrine that renders the fragmentary and accretive text, Torah, as the finished narrative, the Bible. The Torah implies an inheritance that is open-ended, a text that, in some sense, accumulates different and conflicting meanings. But, the Judaic memory, unlike the teleological narrative inherited by the Christian, operates through the functioning of *Zakhor,* through the being-in-the-moment of memory. As opposed to Christological narrative-*chronos,* this notion of time and memory allows for an inheritance that remains dispersed rather than fully gathered together, dialogic rather than monologic, social rather than solipsistic. In the rabbinic tradition of Torah, memory works as an open-ended dialogue with the living past.

Joyce plays upon this notion of an open-ended dialogue with a living past by representing Bloom as the textual embodiment of the Wandering Jew, a seemingly allegorical character whose nomadic, fragmentary appearance in literary history actually signifies a protean, accretive identity. The Wandering Jew appears in the Gothic in both Matthew Lewis's *The Monk* and C. R. Maturin's *Melmoth the Wanderer.* In both texts, the Wandering Jew pops up, apparently out of nowhere, and disrupts the tightly structured generic logic of the Gothic narrative. Hans Ulrich-Mohr traces the lineage of the various and sundry literary incarnations of the Wandering Jew through such early texts as *Beowulf* (in the figure of Grendel) and Chaucer's *The Pardoner's Tale* to its later manifestations in Gothic fiction and Romantic poetry (249–50). The Gospels of Matthew and John speak of a Roman officer who strikes Jesus before the Crucifixion. The stories derived from the Gospels, Ulrich-Mohr explains, "depict this man either as a boundless violator of God's majesty, or as a poor sinner, or as a wicked heathen, or even as a Jew. His name is 'Cartiphilus' or 'Buttadeus/Botadeo' i.e. the God-striker" (249). In the Gospel of Matthew, Jesus says, "There are some standing here who shall not taste death till they see the Son of Man coming in His kingdom" (16:28). In Christian legends, these words announce the punishment of the God-striker. He must wander the earth till the return of Christ. In German literature, he is referred to as *der ewige Jude* [the Eternal Jew], and is called Ahasherus, a generic name for Jews. In his 1783 song, "*Der ewige Jude,*" Christian Schaubert paints the Wandering Jew as a homeless, intellectual refugee, a sort of proto-Romantic hero.

In Lewis's *The Monk,* the Wandering Jew helps to exorcise a ghost and to tell the story of Beatrice de Las Cisternas, a woman who was betrayed and murdered by her lover. In Maturin's *Melmoth,* the Wandering Jew figure acts as a collector of stories about the novel's demonic victimizer, John Melmoth. In both cases, then, the Wandering Jew tells stories that interrupt and add to the overarching narrative. Throughout his various textual odysseys, the Wandering Jew seems eternally occult, despised, and, in a sense, forever expunged from, or rather blasted out of, Christological history. He exists on the periphery, expelled from a tale that has disinherited him. The life of the Wandering Jew, as depicted in *The Monk,* in *Melmoth,* and in many of the other literary texts that evoke his image, works in a rather discontinuous fashion. Never at home, never at rest, he becomes an analogue for Jewish diaspora, and strangely enough, for the enigmatically unfinished nature of Judaic historiography. His story, unlike that of Jesus and Christianity, remains as picaresque and incomplete as it is phantasmagoric. The Wandering Jew constitutes a figure eternally refigured, but unlike Christ, never fully transfigured. His narrative does not end. Rather, it accumulates more experience. It generates more and more textual variants.

The issues facing Judaic historiography play out in powerful ways in *Ulysses.* Many of these problems revolve around Bloom as the text's symbolic "Eternal Jew," the dark back who goes "before." The motif of the Wandering Jew remains one of those provocative elements of the novel that many have acknowledged and few have bothered to work through. Joyce's familiarity and sympathetic identification with the exile consciousness of Judaism is well-documented.[34] In addition to the evidence in the catalogues from his Trieste library, which included such books as Theodor Herzl's *Der Judenstaat,* Salomon Funk's *Die Entstehung des Talmuds,* and Harry Sacher's *Zionism and the Jewish Future,* a spate of recent critical studies has uncovered many references to Judaica concealed in both *Ulysses* and *Finnegans Wake.* Bloom's role as a symbolic Wandering Jew plays into most of these studies. In fact, Marilyn Reizbaum's exemplary *James Joyce's Judaic Other* claims that Joyce's most significant attraction to the modern Jew and to "the wanderer" lies in the fact that these figures allowed him to explore the condition of always being "the 'other' regardless of locale, and by that position to foreground the question of the relationship between the category of identity and cultural construction" (33–34). But Bloom's wandering also bears on the novel's approach to thinking about inheritance and structural dispossession.

When Bloom enters the National Library, Stephen has already been interrupted by the entry of Mulligan and an iteration of the novel's mock-Gothic opening. Despite the fact that Bloom never speaks in the episode, he is much spoken of. As soon as he is out of earshot, Mulligan cries out, "The sheeny ! . . . O, I fear me, he is Greeker than Greeks" (200). Thus, Mulligan identifies the wandering Bloom as an accursed Jew. In addition, Mulligan attempts to feminize Judaism by calling Bloom "Greeker than Greek," a reference to the Greek practice of older men initiating young boys into the world of sexuality by taking youths as lovers. Bloom will go on to become the text's "new- womanly man" as well. In essence, nearly all of Stephen's various neuroses and identity fixations are displaced onto Bloom in this passage. Later, when Stephen begins ruminating on debt, he reminds his audience that Shakespeare "drew Shylock out of his own long pocket" (204). An offended Eglinton chimes in by challenging Stephen to "prove that he [Shakespeare] was a jew" (205). The text rehearses and interrogates nearly all of the anti-Semitic myths that have been the peculiar province of Christian history. But Stephen's criticism of Shylockian greed also operates as a criticism of Christianity's notion of linear time. "Jews," he reminds us, are those whom "christians tax with avarice" (205). Here, the text offers a quick, associative pattern that unites anti-Semitism to Bloom and to Shakespeare. We have already encountered Stephen's attempts to identify with a Parnellite Shakespeare, but here, the text deflects the comparison away from Stephen and toward Bloom. Bloom's resemblance to a Shakespeare who lost a son, ceases to have intercourse with his wife, is cuckolded, and, perhaps a tad too early on, loses his father is a profound one. But the comparison does not end there.

Through his Shakespeare lecture, Stephen links his theory of art to the idea of the son consubstantial with the revolutionary father, the son who, as identical and nonidentical with the father, enacts a revolutionary interrogation of the past. In "Circe," when Lynch states, "The mirror up to nature," the stage directions explain,

> *Stephen and Bloom gaze in the mirror. The face of William Shakespeare, beardless, appears there, Rigid in facial paralysis, crowned by the reflection of the reindeer antlered hatrack in the hall.* (567)

When both Bloom and Stephen look into the mirror, they transform into a single, painfully portrayed, cuckolded figure. Together they are the betrayed Bard. Earlier on in "Circe," Bloom is criticized as being "as bad as Parnell was" (492). If Parnell is the other of Shakespeare in Scylla and Charybdis, then the moment when Stephen and Bloom transform into Shakespeare presents us with a nearly perfect moment of accumulation. Stephen becomes Shakespeare becomes Parnell becomes Bloom, the Wandering Jew. And let us not forget that before Parnell was voted out of office, he appealed to the Irish people by claiming that it was only fair "to ask—that I should come within sight of this 'promised land'" (Callahan 41). Hence, Parnell links himself to Moses, the Judaic messiah who does not enter the Promised Land, the messiah whose life remains somehow incomplete. Identities are compound rather than singular here. Moreover, the Shakespeare figure's cuckolded status refers us back to the fact that though paternity might always remain, as Stephen explains, "a legal fiction," the connection between child and mother might end up being "the one true thing in life." Here, the lived similarities, the suggestive alternatives, display the truly stunning stylistic possibilities of Joyce's polyvalent prose.

Bloom, the father, is linked to Stephen, the consubstantial son, and the Holy (literary) Ghost, Shakespeare, finds materiality reflected in this union. Bloom who subsists as the wanderer, a representative of the fragmented ontology of an eternally refigured history, merges with Stephen, an allegorist who, himself, works through totalization. The text presents in the juxtaposition of Bloom and Stephen an overcoming or Hegelian *Aufhebung* of the problem of allegory. Bloom, refigured as Stephen, Shakespeare, Parnell, the new-womanly man, and the Wandering Jew, offers a character who can point to and work through multiple narratives of dispossession without sacrificing or abjecting any one of them. Bloom can identify with the feminine, with the rejected, and with the disinherited, and, so, he can face up to and imagine himself in any number of narratives. Moreover, he can connect disparate narratives together. The determinate critique of structural dispossession offered by allegory is realized in a character who can embrace competing and accumulating identities. In Volume 3 of *Capital,* Marx claims that the excessive accumulation of capital will invariably trigger the crisis of overproduction, a crisis that will bring out the contradictions inherent in industrial capitalism. While excessive accumulation certainly triggers the overproduction of narrative in Joyce's *Ulysses,* the overproduction of narrative actually allows us to apprehend and acknowledge the complex, interrelated, competing, and contradictory elements that comprise historical discourse.

Hence, although the direction of Stephen's Shakespeare commentary may be reinscribed within a nostalgic, patriarchal pattern, the larger, dialectical pattern of *Ulysses* complicates this strategy. Joyce's reflexive technique forms a constellation of thought that brings the past in the form of accumulated meanings into a present that actively disfigures an overarching master History. The disruptive though seemingly nonchalant appearance of Bloom affords us an opportunity for mediation. In foregrounding the contradictions within several of the text's teleological schemas, Bloom's appearance at the end of the National Library episode embodies the Judaic notion of memory and exile, and so, acts as a gloss on Stephen's gloss—one that negates the reductive elements of the Gothic's allegory of dispossession. Bloom's cumulative identity comes into conflict with Stephen's allegorical one. Bloom certainly appears attacked and victimized throughout the text, but rather than merely repeating identities, he learns to work through them. At any moment in the text, he can embody Parnell, Shakespeare, the Wandering Jew, and the new-womanly man. Where Stephen's musings attempt to exit from history via self-realization, Bloom's wanderings inevitably lead us back into history via more micrologically structured notions of accumulating and competing histories. Bloom encounters the Gothic phenomenon of apparitions, but for him they provide images of a different history, they offer moments of messianism but no messiah.

The dialectical relationship between Stephen and Bloom remains only a potential one within the text. At the end, Stephen and Bloom do not reunite in some utopian otherworld as do Christ and Jehovah. When such moments appear as possible in "Ithaca," Stephen, who holds on to his allegorical notion of the inheriting son very tenaciously, simply withdraws and walks off into the Dublin night. Hence, precisely by missing out on a potential father in Bloom, Stephen is also necessarily absent when Molly Bloom, the text's arch-mother, begins to speak in "Penelope." Having refused the mother's speech in "Telemachus" and again in "Circe," he cannot stay at 7 Eccles Street to hear the maternal entity speak in a fashion that subverts and revises patriarchal conceptions of order, linearity, and inheritance itself. Despite his narrative of allegorical repossession, then, Stephen finally rejects both a mother and a father. The novel, on the other hand, offers us a series of possibilities. If we can imagine Bloom and Stephen in consubstantial terms—"Ithaca's" "Stoom" and "Blephen"—then we might also be able to make the further leap to imagining a world in which the feminine voice, the voice of the structurally dispossessed mother-ghost, speaks against reductive formulations of history. In some sense, rather than fully realizing that conclusion, the text offers us only its utopian possibility.

VI. LITERARY HISTORY AND THE JOYCEAN GOTHIC

In Stephen Dedalus, Joyce provides us with an artist-character who consciously longs to deploy allegory in order to represent and aestheticize a sociopolitical struggle. Stephen, the first saint, meets Dedalus, the artist-wanderer. In so doing, Joyce produces both a literary analogue for Wilde's Sebastian Melmoth persona and a character who attempts to embody, and finally to resolve, the tensions of the post-1798 Irish national and Gothic imaginary. Wilde's *The Picture of Dorian Gray* invokes and revises the narrative tropes of the Unionist Gothic in an effort to place the social structures that preexist the aesthete/subject under the control of that very aesthete/subject. For Wilde, however, to alter a convention is to admit that one is to some degree confined by that convention. Stephen Dedalus plays a similar role in *Ulysses,* which begins with the mock-Gothic sequence in the Martello tower. Stephen frets about as he acknowledges his confinement, but he also seeks a way out, a way to inherit paternal power and, so, to bring the allegory of Gothic Ireland to an end. As is implicit in his notions of Parnell and Shakespeare, Stephen hopes to use the force of personality to triumph over the failings of history. Joyce challenges and finally overcomes Stephen's Gothic allegory by introducing the disruptive and accretive character of Leopold Bloom. Where Stephen hopes to abject and escape certain identities, Bloom inhabits them.

When we first encounter the mock-Gothic structure in "Telemachus," Stephen appears burdened by both the usurper, Mulligan, and the maternal ghost, May Dedalus. In true Gothic form, he generates a theory of reconstructed paternal power that will deliver him from the hands of the usurper and from the weakness of the maternal entity. Stephen's lecture in the National Library lays out his aesthetic theory and, so he hopes, liberates him from his confining history. But Bloom's appearance in the National Library introduces the possibility that the past accumulates, that history is never a single narrative, but, rather, a series of complexly-related, interlocking contexts, economies, conflicts, and tropes. Hence, when *Ulysses* invokes the Gothic narrative of dispossession later in the "Oxen of the Sun" episode, the Gothic itself has transformed into a thoroughly parodied genre, a mode of narrative representation that is merely to be set next to any number of other modes of representation. In the "Oxen of the Sun" mock-Gothic section, we begin, yet again, with the figures of Mulligan and Stephen, who sit in the lobby of the National Maternity Hospital. "Malichias' tale began to freeze them with horror," we are told (412). Haines, Mulligan's English friend, appears from behind a secret panel with a volume of Celtic literature in one hand and a vial of poison in the other. This supposedly chilling tale goes on to repeat the basic outline of Stephen's *Hamlet* lecture as well. Now, however, the lecture appears utterly ridiculous and ends with the revelation that "the Black Panther was himself the ghost of his own father" (412). As we recall, when he left the National Library, Bloom was described as stepping like a pard or, that is, a black panther. This parodic Gothic sequence, which appears near the conclusion to the "Oxen of the Sun" episode, marks Joyce's relationship to the Unionist Gothic and to the allegory of structural disinheritance that it generated.

Joyce responds to and invokes the allegory because it is part of Ireland's national imaginary, but he also ironizes that allegory and introduces us to both a character (Bloom) and an explosively allusive writing style (the text of *Ulysses*) that accumulate many different textual identities and forms at once. Joyce notes the allegory that had become part of Ireland's intellectual, political, and social landscapes. But, he deploys a method of writing that willfully embraces the polyphony of literary and textual history in order to both represent and overcome the narrow confines of Ireland's Gothic conventions. In so doing, he suggests a way to move beyond the confines of a singular and allegorical narrative of nation and toward a more transnational and fluid conception of identity. In mocking the Gothic's primal scene of confinement, Joyce's novel invokes the critique of dispossession offered by the Unionist Gothic, only to suggest alternate ways of imagining the narratives that come to us from the past. Joyce's dialectic works to overcome the limitations of the Gothic, and, so, his dialectics, like the optimistic "yes" that concludes the chorus of voices in *Ulysses,* remains affirmative and utopian. His Gothic does not attempt to resolve the political dilemma, but, rather, to present different ways to imagine and rethink that dilemma. As we will see in the next chapter, in his own prose fictions, Samuel Beckett picks up on Joyce's experiments with Gothic confinement. Where Joyce produces a mode of writing that attempts to move beyond the Gothic allegory, however, Beckett goes in a very different direction. Beckett emphasizes and hypostatizes the Gothic's female-confinement narrative, converting it into the ontological condition of the modern subject.

CHAPTER 5

Engendering a Cartesian Gothic

Generic Form as History in Beckett's Fiction

> I am in my mother's room. It's I who live there now. I don't know how I got there.
>
> —Samuel Beckett, *Molloy*

POLITICAL BECKETT

A curious footnote interrupts the thorough summary of Beckett criticism recounted by Richard Begam in *Samuel Beckett and the End of Modernity.* "Because they have exerted little influence," Begam explains in the footnote, "I have omitted from my account of Beckett criticism the Marxist discussions of his work" (192, n. 13). Of course, Begam's insight seems quite correct, and despite the fact that such major Marxist literary critics as Georg Lukács and Theodor Adorno wrote essays that engaged with Beckett's writing, the modern critical tradition has had a difficult time mapping the left-political implications of Beckett's work.[1] Begam's account, which traces the evolution of Beckett criticism roughly from Hugh Kenner to Jacques Derrida, remains illuminating nearly a decade after it was written precisely for its assessment of the apparent void that Beckett occupies within the Marxist tradition or, rather, that the Marxist tradition occupies within Beckett criticism.[2] Marxism, simply put, has counted for little more than a footnote in Beckett scholarship. Likewise, most contemporary critical evaluations of modernism, as perhaps best demonstrated by *Semicolonial Joyce,* the volume of essays edited by Derek Attridge and Marjorie Howes, have cautiously acknowledged

James Joyce's work as part of the overall matrix of twentieth-century postcolonial writing. The same cannot honestly be said for the work of Beckett, Ireland's heir-apparent modernist. Like a host of others, Lois Gordon has claimed that Joyce's ambivalence "toward Ireland touched a responsive chord in Beckett," and that this shared ambivalence was at the heart of the Joyce-Beckett relationship (60–61).[3] That traumatic and troubled memories of Ireland provided the raw material for both Joyce's polyphonic imagination and Beckett's muted literary utterances may be undeniable, but any subsequent suggestion that the aporias of Irish experience—particularly the colonial experience—are as central to Beckett's work as they are to Joyce's remains subject to debate. Furthermore, despite the impact of such studies as David Lloyd's *Anomalous States,* John Harrington's *The Irish Beckett,* Seamus Deane's *Celtic Revivals,* and Eoin O'Brien's *The Beckett Country,* Beckett's texts are less often seen as exemplars of post or metro-colonial writing than as extensions of, or perhaps bookends to, the basic metaphysical problematics of Western thought.[4]

So, why does Beckett appear to remain on the sidelines of political critique, particularly during the last thirty years, during an age of political literary criticism that spawned Fredric Jameson's *The Political Unconscious,* Edward Said's *Orientalism,* and a host of identity-political and cultural studies texts that read modernists ranging from Virginia Woolf and E. M. Forster to Joseph Conrad and T. S. Eliot strictly in terms of their admitted or concealed political commitments? We seem to have jumped directly from the expansively allusive, humanist readings of Beckett offered by the likes of Kenner, Richard Ellman, David Hesla, and Vivian Mercier to the kinds of poststructuralist interpretations fostered by Derrida's revision of Saussure and recommended to us by Begam, Anthony Uhlmann, et al.[5] To put it another way, why did we move from a Beckett figured as a Dublin Descartes to a Beckett refigured as a deterritorialized Derrida without ever generating a New Left Beckett to mediate between the two? In what follows, I want to suggest that when we begin to look at Beckett's fiction in terms of the literary genres that it invokes, we should be able to generate a political Beckett.

As Vivien Mercier's by now classic study, *Beckett/Beckett,* demonstrated as early as 1979, the scholarly study of Beckett's work appears to be obsessed with the antinomies that structure his various novels and plays. In fact, Mercier's book organizes its interrogation of Beckett's oeuvre precisely in terms of these antinomies. So we encounter in the pages of *Beckett/Beckett* a writer who obsesses about the Mind/Body, Man/Woman, World/Ireland distinctions. In each case, we have a first term (Mind, Man, World) that attempts to claim universal status and a second term (Body, Woman, Ireland) that embarrasses a universal claim through its trenchant, irrevocable particularity. In 1961 Kenner himself had called Beckett "the comedian of the impasse," so it appears that the formal obsession of Beckett's novels and plays, the inability to adjudicate between binary oppositions that freezes Vladimir, Estragon, Watt, and the Unnamable in their respective tracks, finds an analogue in critical approaches predicated upon the "language of paradox" fetishized by erudite readers like Kenner and Messier or the paradox of language discussed by philosophers like Derrida, Maurice Blanchot, Julia Kristeva, and Gilles Deleuze. In these approaches, Beckett's art subsists as a clever balancing of irreducible, mutually exclusive oppositions. In what has become one of his most cited comments, Beckett once wrote that modern writing reflects the fact that "there is nothing to express, nothing with which to express, nothing from which to express, no power to express, no desire to express, together with the obligation to express."[6] Of course, Marxists and postcolonial theorists have something rather emphatic to say, so, at least at first glance, it seems unsurprising that Marxists seeking practical ways to interrogate capitalism's considerable excesses or postcolonial theorists searching for "authentic" representations of Irish or nationalist experience would find little of interest in Beckett's minimalist, carefully distilled rethinking of philosophical and metaphysical binaries.

Most of the politically oriented critics who have engaged with Beckett, critics like Tyrus Miller, David Lloyd, and David Weisberg to name only a few, have followed the path cut by Adorno's seminal 1963 essay, "Trying to Understand *Endgame.*"[7] Adorno's argument, reduced to its most basic premises, represents Beckett's oeuvre in general, and *Endgame* in particular, as a negative allegory of modern capitalist society.[8] Beckett's work represents precisely what happens when the theory of constitutive subjectivity that Enlightenment thinkers had hoped would free individual humans from any kind of master/slave dialectic miscarries, and individuality itself becomes a kind of prison that limits the possibility of human community and collectivity. Miller, Weisberg, and a host of others restate Adorno's argument while also demonstrating the various ways through which Beckett's work challenges and exceeds the limits of Adorno's markedly reflective and ingenious method of "negative critique." But even when we concede that Adorno's reading of Beckett is correct, we still have to admit that the Adornian line of reasoning may never have fully caught on in the academy because political critique itself tends to seek out practical answers to social problems. Political literary critics often tend to look for a specific author or work to provide practical insights that lead to tangible goals, or else these critics look for a work of art to make overt and specific criticisms of the social world, criticisms that lead to generalizable codes of action. Simply put, then, Beckett's stark aporetic style seems difficult to politicize in any very overt fashion. Perhaps if we take a look at Lukács's thoughts on Beckett, we might get a clearer picture of the implications of this problem for Beckett criticism and, conversely, the implications of Beckett's work for interrogating and rethinking the politics of generalizability itself.

Lukács's argument about Beckett, published in the essay "The Ideology of Modernism," holds that Beckett's work follows the modernist pattern of "escape into neurosis as a protest against the evils of society" (198). In fact, for Lukács, Beckett's work carries this pattern to the furthest reaches, the "*ne plus ultra*" of degradation, the point at which "perversity" and "idiocy" become glorified (198). The problem with modernism, for Lukács, subsists in its inability to move from individual detail to general significance without devolving into rank abstraction. Beckett's modernism, then, bears overtly reactionary implications by shoring up the immediate particularity of bourgeois and petit bourgeois isolation, by offering isolation as an escape from the "evils of society" without ever bothering to spell out precisely what those evils might be.[9] In these terms, modernism becomes an obsession with the symptom rather than with the disease or its possible cures. Because Lukács's arguments appear at best irresponsibly reductive and at worst absurdly programmatic, they have never had much currency in the academic study of Beckett's work. But it makes some sense to take the dialectic that Lukács's work recommends—the dialectic of the general and the particular—seriously, especially in light of the academic obsession with Beckett's use of binaries. In Lukács's thinking, the possibility for a politically engaged literature resides in its capacity to move from the specific or individual detail to an overarching problem of general or universal significance. We must move dialectically from the particular to the general in order to have political critique, then. From a Lukácsian perspective, by emphasizing the form of individual consciousness, a modernist author like Beckett simply cannot seem to move to the more generalizable level of content-based and concrete situations offered by more traditional, and hence more accessible and politically efficacious, literary forms like realism. Though Lukács's arguments amount to a reductio ad absurdum reading of modernism, his emphasis on the generalizable implications of the work of art hold some insight. If we juxtapose this basic claim about generalizability as the foundation of political critique against what I have referred to as the expansively allusive, humanist reading of Beckett offered by someone like Hugh Kenner, we might find a way to uncover a New Left Beckett who can mediate between the binarist obsessions of the humanists on the one hand and the poststructuralists on the other. We might begin to uncover the general "evils of society" against which Beckett's work inveighs.

In the essay, "The Man in the Room," which begins his 1961 book, *Samuel Beckett: A Critical Study,* Kenner works hard to place Beckett in the tradition of literate interpreter-parodists of the grand European conversation about consciousness that succeeded the Cartesian revolution in skepticism. Near the end of the essay, Kenner concludes that Beckett's novels, most particularly the *Trilogy* of *Molloy, Malone Dies,* and *The Unnamable,* are "a compendious abstract of all the novels that have ever been written, reduced to their most general terms" (63). In Kenner's scrupulously cogent and capacious reading, Beckett moves to generalize not so much about material or political history—the kinds of topics for which Kenner's criticism has no real use—but rather about literary history and, more specifically, the history of that most Cartesian and bourgeois of forms, the modern novel. Following Kenner, we might be led to ask how Beckett's work interrogates and repeats the limits and sterile boundaries of the bourgeois novel itself. We might even ask if Beckett's fiction takes the basic question of Kantian liberalism (can this maneuver, action, set of principles be universalized or generalized?) and hypostatizes it by pushing it to the furthest reaches of generality, the space where generality and concrete reality turn back into a pure and finally inhuman order. We might certainly conclude that by enacting a dialectic where one element invariably transforms into its other, Beckett's work suggests that thinking and action themselves have become synonymous with inertia, being has collapsed into not-being.

It occurs to me, however, that of the various critical approaches that we have had to Beckett's work, few have actually followed Kenner's lead in attempting to place Beckett himself as a critic of the general, or, for want of a better term, "generic" forms of the novel. But Beckett's own critical writing nearly always announces his interest in generic forms. In "The Essential and the Incidental," his 1934 review of Sean O'Casey's work, Beckett reminds us that "a proper estimate of Molière as master of prose dialogue depends largely on a proper estimate of him as a very humdrum practitioner of the alexandrine" (82). Only through a close analysis of the flat and often failed forms that a writer like Molière invokes, Beckett warns, can one even begin to place a Molière in literary history. The aim of this chapter will be to elaborate on the political implications of Beckett's early to mid-fiction by reading it in terms of the generic tropes that it most often evokes. One might set Beckett in the history of the novel of ideas. His novels, replete with references to the philosophies of Augustine, Schopenhauer, and Leibniz, certainly fit into just such a category. Or, we could see Beckett as the end point of the bildungsroman because, after all, his novels and novellas certainly parody the progress-driven teleology of that form. All that being said, however, the formal features that appear most frequently in Beckett, the generic tropes that he plays with most often, seem to be those of the Gothic, more specifically, of the female Gothic.

With Eyal Amiran, most critics tend to read Beckett's fiction in terms of a metaphysical journey motif charted by the philosophical binaries of

"Wandering and Home," and this motif allows us to read Beckett's writing as the *Fin de Partie* of the entire Western intellectual tradition that begins with Plato.[10] Such a reading unpacks the extraordinarily abstract nature of Beckett's markedly reflective, philosophical speculation. In this version of things, Beckett's fiction is read as mapping the terrain of signification, erased subjectivity, metaphysical torpor, and death while simultaneously engaging in the Stephen Dedalus–like meta-aesthetic concerns about art. On the one hand, this reading provides us with Beckett the philosopher of art and, on the other, with Beckett the artist who philosophizes. As a result, critics tend to interpret Beckett's novels as philosophy or, at best, as art objects that illustrate certain claims about the problem of art in modernity. In contrast to the wandering-and-home motif of this mostly metaphysical approach, the Gothic literary tradition, the dark double of British domestic fiction, is determined by the male-exile and female-confinement structure. Moreover, as we've seen, following the Unionist Gothic, the Anglo-Irish version of this structure nearly always converts male exile into female confinement. The males in the novels of Matruin, Le Fanu, Stoker, and Wilde appear as confined by the logic of domesticity as do the females of Radcliffe, Brontë, or Austen. When we read Beckett in this tradition, then the abstract wandering-and-home motif transforms into the more concrete Gothic exile-and-confinement motif in which male wanderers appear in the same carceral terms as their female counterparts. Even Beckett's wanderers, even his exiles, seem peculiarly confined and thoroughly isolated. If the twin issues of confinement and gender anxiety act as the political unconscious of the female Gothic, might Beckett's early fiction work to hypostatize these problems, to represent the literary tropes of the female Gothic as the concrete political reality of an Enlightened modernity whose children have either miscarried or been born sterile? [11]

This may, in fact, be the element of Beckett's work that allows Linda Ben-Zvi to claim that it is possible to think of all of Beckett's "characters, as fundamentally feminine, no pun intended. At the same time that Beckett delineates roles that fix people in place, he also tends to subsume both men and women under categories culturally assigned to females, and theoretically assumed to delimit their world" (57).[12] Furthermore, in *Gothic Pathologies,* David Punter, a critic concerned primarily with the Gothic, claims that there is "more to be said about Beckett as a Gothic writer, and perhaps more to be said in general about the minimalist, reductive component of Gothic which stands over against its manic, self-justifying, self-doubting proliferations" (18). A proper estimate of Beckett as one of the more socially astute and historically reflective readers of modern fictional forms, then, depends largely on a proper estimate of him as a practitioner of certain Gothic tropes. Beckett's early to mid-fiction reworks the dialectic of the general and the particular—while asserting the basic political critique that this dialectic recommends—precisely by reading literary genres themselves as the indices of historical macroproblems, and this seems like a very Lukácsian thing to do. The specific characters in Beckett, the Murphys, Watts, Molloys, and Malones, all point back, as Kenner rightly indicates, to the history of the novel, but they also point to the novelistic form's inability to make good on its Cartesian promise of freeing the "life of the mind" from the materiality, confinement, privation, and anxiety to which the body is inevitably subjected. From a political perspective, then, Beckett's art does not subsist only as a clever balancing of irreducible, mutually exclusive oppositions, but rather as a subtle method of dialectical reversal, a conversion of one form into its other.

In joining Lukács's notion of generalizability to Kenner's insight about the compendious literary history invoked by Beckett's novels, then, I am making the basic claim that the fiction that Beckett wrote between 1939 and 1951—beginning with *Murphy* and ending with *Malone Dies*—works to ontologize the basic tropes of the female Gothic, and so, to represent a modernity circumscribed by capitalism and imperialism as engendering precisely those kinds of disempowered, suffocating subjects who find themselves trapped within the structures laid out by novels like Anne Radcliffe's *The Mysteries of Udolpho,* and reinscribed in the gender-disoriented Irish Gothic tradition by writers like C. R. Maturin, Joseph Sheridan Le Fanu, and Bram Stoker. Beckett constructs his critique of modern conceptions of autonomy within the very architecture of the literary forms that preceded him.

When he is read in light of the history of the Irish Gothic that I have constructed thus far, Beckett offers a political—and so generalizable—critique of the ways through which capitalism's instrumental reason and colonialism's ideological violence have created subjects without autonomy who, nonetheless, seek after that autonomy as desperately as do the women trapped in the attics, castles, and monasteries of the Gothic and the gender-disoriented men trapped in the big houses of its Anglo-Irish equivalent. Hence, Irish modernism's particular obsession with autonomous art, which we have already seen in the writings of Wilde and Joyce, finds its ultimate, and ultimately Gothic, realization in the prose fiction Beckett published in, roughly, the years between 1939 and 1951. Gothic tropes continue to find their way into Beckett's later works like *Ghost Trio, Eh Joe, Not I,* and *Ill Seen, Ill Said,* but, beginning with the *Trilogy*'s finale, *The Unnamable,* Beckett's writing focuses more often on the aesthetic problem of mimesis itself and less often on evoking and criticizing the structural dispossessions signified by the domestic and colonialist histories of British prose fiction.[13]

Up to the *Trilogy,* Beckett uses generic form to invoke historical problematics. With *Molloy* and *Malone Dies,* as we will come to see, the text's own situatedness becomes the point of Beckett's prose fiction. After the *Nouvelles* and *First Love,* his work moves from thinking about form to thinking about the text's historicity itself. Roughly speaking, then, after World War II, Beckett's work allegorizes the limitations of modernist conceptions of artistic autonomy. Approaching Beckett in terms of his appropriations and re-visions of the Gothic form will allow us to read Beckett in two coextensive ways. First off, we will see how his pre- and postwar fiction responded to and parodied the formal conventions of the female Gothic. In so doing, we will also interpret the movement that begins with the *Trilogy* as the continuation and apotheosis of—rather than as a break with—Beckett's prewar interests in modernist revisions of form. In reading the beginnings of his postwar *Trilogy* as founded upon the generic Gothic framework parodied by the earlier fiction, we will begin to see the political implications of Beckett's work more clearly. Beckett's postwar work is certainly not apolitical, but after the war, Beckett's work begins to problematize the notion of politics itself.[14]

By imagining autonomy itself in the same terms that the female Gothic deploys to describe the structures that delimit female subjectivity, much of Beckett's prewar fiction anticipates and extends the boundaries of feminist political critique to include all of the subjects constructed in and by modernity. Beckett reimagines the crisis of modern politics by making the experience of the feminine into the universal category, and any Marxist or postcolonial reading of his work should begin by acknowledging this. In the sections that follow, I will demonstrate how several of the fictions written by Beckett during these years, particularly *Murphy, First Love,* and the first two texts of the *Trilogy,* evoke, concretize, and finally disarticulate the basic cyclical structure—the movement from confinement to reproduction to autonomy—of the female and Anglo-Irish Gothic forms. Situating Beckett in relation to the Anglo-Irish Gothic tradition allows us to read his work as a response to the political problems of national identity and bourgeois autonomy, or, that is, to bourgeois nationalism, without, subsequently, making Beckett into either an Irish nationalist thinker like W. B. Yeats or a committed socialist like Sean O'Casey. Like Joyce, Beckett is not a Gothic writer in the same way that Maturin or Le Fanu is. Rather, Beckett's work constitutes a response to Ireland's Gothic cultural imaginary. We will come to see how Beckett deploys literary tropes from the Gothic that appear as worn-out and moribund as his aging characters in order to represent autonomy itself—the final object of desire for Stephen Dedalus, the self-creating raison d'etre of Wildean aestheticism, and the subject position par excellence of capitalist and patriarchal social formations—as impossible in a modern and dualistic world that renders all subjectivity, to appropriate Linda Ben-Zvi's words, "fundamentally feminine."

II. CONFINEMENT: BECKETT'S CARTESIAN GOTHIC AND MURPHY'S MIND

Murphy is a novel about an Irish expatriate male who lives in London, works in an asylum, obsesses about his own consciousness, and eschews the demands of his body, so it might at first seem odd to read such an overtly philosophical novel as embodying the basic tropes of the female Gothic. As we have already seen in chapter 1 and in the Joyce chapter (chap. 4), however, from an ideological perspective, the female Gothic works to resolve the anxiety of gender and imperial dispossession through the birth of an acknowledgeable male heir who must be allowed to inherit the ancestral land and, if only figuratively, to repossess the body of the mother. The fruit of the maternal womb palliates the fear of structural dispossession that a woman experiences in light of her status as object in the marriage contract. Likewise, the thought of regeneration and reclamation implicit in the idea of an Union of kingdoms seems to allow the colonized people to hope for a future that will eventually afford them some kind of sovereignty, however limited that may be. In both cases, a fruitful marriage with a more masculine other gets represented as productive of new forms while residual anxieties about the loss of autonomy remain implicit, if often concealed, in the marriage metaphor itself.

Despite all indicators to the contrary, however, by deploying the narrative cycle of confinement and reproduction, the female Gothic finally reasserts the validity of a male epistemology. The women of the female Gothic novel might desire autonomy, but the social and psychic structures of a dualistic worldview keep the feminine associated very firmly with weakness and reproduction, with, that is, the body. Underlying the Gothic form, then, is an epistemological worldview in which man remains akin to the *res cogitans* of the soul and woman with the *res extensa* of nature and the body.[15] Beckett's Murphy imagines himself as *res cogitans* only as he eschews all facets of *res extensa*. The women of the female Gothic remain subject to those bodily and corporeal weaknesses that can never really be brought under full conscious control. Regardless of whether the woman is the overly sensitive, swooning Emily St. Aubert or the self-assured Jane Eyre, she invariably experiences the corporeal fragility of the body in a way that sets her apart from the male figures in the novel. The female Gothic might signify an unconscious critique of the patriarchal epistemology that attends a mind/body dualism where man is associated with the organizing and conceptual realm of the mind and woman with the inert, controllable, and frail realm of the body, but those same Gothic novels end by imagining a natural and transhistorical order that affirms the Cartesian dualism that they seems to rail against. This is all to say that the male heir who is born at the end of the Gothic novel might at first appear to reconcile these opposites, but he invariably signifies a false reconciliation and, so, the very reassertion of the opposition. The masculine remains as the organizing and unifying principle while the feminine fades into the space of corporeal weakness.

In the fiction of Maturin and Le Fanu, the issue of structural dispossession takes the form of a gender disorientation where male or male-identified characters appear in narratives that had generally been coded as feminine. Despite the gendered anxiety that provides much of the tension in Maturin and Le Fanu, the identity formulations in their texts tend to fetishize masculine autonomy while also depicting it as a subject position that the contradictory or double self developed under colonialism can never fully maintain. The male characters in these novels never desire a rethinking of the mind/body dualism of a patriarchal worldview. Instead, they just want to be treated like men. Hence, Maturin and Le Fanu inveigh against certain sociopolitical problems by suggesting that a nostalgic return to an originary, paternalistic identity will supply all of the answers. In Stoker, the gendered anxiety caused by confinement finds a most overt realization in the character of Jonathan Harker. In a very direct way, Stoker asks us what happens to the social world when men's minds are as confined as women's bodies. In Wilde's dazzlingly counterintuitive mode of writing, confinement and gender anxiety are paradoxically converted into a decadent mode of autonomy. In each representation of this problem, however, the solution is finally imagined as a form of control that either reasserts or rethinks the privileges of a masculine autonomy and its attendant patriarchal epistemology. In *Ulysses* Joyce thematizes this nonsolution in the character of Stephen Dedalus, who wants to escape a material history by giving birth to an ideal form of himself. To balance Stephen, *Ulysses* also offers in the figure of Leopold Bloom a "new-womanly man" and *homme moyen sensuel* who can act as both a body and a mind. To some extent Beckett's work takes up where Joyce's leaves off, but Beckett's rearticulation of this problem never seems quite as hopeful as Joyce's. In Beckett, a new-womanly man doesn't overcome the failings of a mind/body dualism so much as he inhabits them.

The humanist-philosophical interpretations of Beckett, as perhaps best exemplified by David Hesla's markedly learned 1971 study, *The Shape of Chaos*, and the poststructuralist theoretical approaches summed up in Begam's *Samuel Beckett and the End of Modernity* tend to agree on a singular insight. As Hesla explains, "The influence of Descartes on Beckett is obvious and pervasive" (14).[16] For the humanists, then, reading Beckett necessarily includes the task of rereading Descartes and other dualistic thinkers like Arnold Geulincx and Nicolas Malebranche. Kenner himself reads Beckett as a kind of latter-day, melancholic Cartesian comedian. For the poststructuralists, Beckett pushes Cartesian rationality, and the mind/body problem upon which it is predicated, to such insane extremes that the basic Cartesian unit of thought, the rationalist *Cogito ergo sum,* can be reread as *Cogito ergo demens.*[17] Let's take this locus of agreement between the humanist Beckett and the poststructuralist Beckett seriously. If Beckett's prose fiction does in fact provide us with a collection of moribund bodies trapped within the confines of their own, personal rationality, then Beckett undoubtedly draws upon Descartes's mind/body dualism in order to allegorize the philosophical condition of modern consciousness. The third maxim of Descartes's *Discourse on Method* presents us with the primal scene of the mind/body problem. Here, Descartes explains that he always seeks "to conquer myself rather than fortune, to change my desires rather than the established order, and generally to believe that nothing except our thoughts is fully under our control" (20). Thus, for Descartes, when we make "a virtue of necessity" and seek out the truth only in the space of our own minds, we never desire freedom while imprisoned, health while sick, nor riches while impoverished (20). The body only gets in the way of rationality, and the Cartesian "method" hopes to liberate the mind from the failings and untruths of the material body. The innovative genius of Cartesian rationality lies in its capacity to enfold objectivity into subjectivity. Objective truth can be reached only through an extreme form of subjectivity, or, that is, truth can only be established upon the orienting foundation of the individual's disembodied, nondesiring *Cogito.* Truth, then, remains outside of the material world and within the framework of an incorporeal rationality.

For a philosopher like Elizabeth Grosz, the problems with Descartes's thinking seem apparent. In *Volatile Bodies,* Grosz explains that Cartesian dualism positions consciousness outside of the world, "outside its body, outside of nature; it is also removed from direct contact with other minds and a socio-cultural community" (7). Cartesian dualism, then, articulates a method through which bodily sensations, which are connected with lower-order, animal phenomena, can be transcended, understood, and, hopefully, controlled by the mind. The mind is to control the body, so it follows that a masculinist or misogynist culture codes the feminine as corporeal and vulnerable and the masculine as metaphysical and transcendent.[18] As Grosz indicates, from the feminist perspective, masculinist culture finds

> convenient self-justification for women's secondary social positions by containing them within bodies that are represented, even constructed, as frail, imperfect, unruly, and unreliable, subject to various intrusions which are not under conscious control. Female sexuality and women's power of reproduction are the defining (cultural) characteristics of women, and, at the same time, these very

> functions render women vulnerable, in need of protection or special treatment. (13–14)

Following up on Grosz's point, we might say that woman's reproductive capacity marks her as embodied, but it also marks her life as a prolonged period of confinement. Woman must be a body while man, subsequently, remains free to live the life of the mind, the life of pure conceptual organization. We can conclude from all of this that Cartesian mind/body dualism clearly results in—even necessitates—the social regulation of female bodies. To a large extent, then, the distinction between a private sphere, where the intimate family resides, and a public sphere, where rational-critical work might take place, replicates the basic divide of Cartesian dualism on a massive socioeconomic and cultural scale.[19] As this dualism renders the male mind autonomous, however, it also renders it isolated. If one follows the logic of mind/body dualism carefully, the autonomy attributed to the male "mind" seems as confining and isolating as is the frail and imperfect body of the female. What remains concealed by Descartes method and revealed by Beckett's fiction is the fact that a male mind positioned outside of the corporeal and the communal finally seems as disphoric and, more importantly, as contained as the female body. The humanists and the poststructuralists are of course correct in claiming that Beckett's work remains shot through with references to Descartes, but Beckett's Descartes is also a very Gothic Descartes. Beckett's fiction often represents the tropes of confinement and gender anxiety that characterize the female Gothic as the concrete reality of the Cartesian "male mind," and we glimpse an early version of this representation very clearly in Beckett's first novel, *Murphy.*

Adhering to the basic pattern set up by Joyce's depiction of Stephen Dedalus in *A Portrait of the Artist as a Young Man,* Beckett's *Murphy* traces the experiences of an Irish expatriate who attempts to escape the confines of Ireland via the Cartesian mind, but Murphy fails not only because of the mind's imbrication with concrete reality but also because the autonomy for which the mind longs invariably devolves into vacuity.

The ultimate desire for Beckett's Murphy is to transcend the body and enter a zone where consciousness itself partakes of a "flux of forms, a perpetual coming together and falling assunder of forms" (112). Moreover, Murphy seeks to realize the perfect "will-lessness" implied by a Cartesian method that separates truth from either desire or material need (113). In chapter 6 of *Murphy,* the narrator attempts to articulate the boundaries of "Murphy's mind" (107). This brief, hermetic chapter enacts in miniature nearly all of the thematic conflicts of the larger novel.[20] Hence, it acts not only as a content-based description of the inner workings of Murphy's mind, but also as a formal simulation of

Murphy's hermetic relationship to the other characters who inhabit the larger world imagined by the novel. This dialectical technique of using form as the realization of content characterizes nearly all of Beckett's mature work. The trick is, however, that in the earlier pieces like *Murphy,* the characters themselves don't recognize this. The "Murphy's mind" chapter finally provides a perfect summation of all that Murphy comes to represent in the text. Hence, even though Murphy wants to remain at the hermetic level of mind—or reflective content—the chapter itself, in embodying content through its formal maneuvers, reminds us that Murphy is always already a material body as well. As we look more closely at the "Murphy's mind" chapter, I want to draw particular attention to the way that Beckett engages mind/body dualism by translating it into a literary content/form dialectic.

As we're told in the chapter, "Murphy felt himself split in two, a body and a mind," and though he knows that the two factions must have some intercourse, he sees his mind as "bodytight" (109). From the opening of the text, we've learned that in order to escape from the vicissitudes of the social world and the desires of the body, Murphy sits "naked in his rocking-chair of undressed teak" in the darkest corner of his room while seven scarves hold him in place (1–2). Like most of Beckett's male protagonists, Murphy continually flees from the feminine and from the desires of the body. Murphy clearly fears the bodily desire that his fiancée, Celia, represents, and his wish to make his mind "bodytight" signifies his attendant fear of being as unfree and as dependent as are the desiring women of the novel. Naked on the undressed teak, Murphy's body simulates the mute objecthood of the furniture in his room. The rocking chair moves, certainly, but its slow, repetitive motion actually moves Murphy beyond the needs of the body. Only by enacting this ritual and silencing the body's needs does Murphy "come alive in his mind" (2). When his mind is "hermetically closed" to the world without, it becomes alive within and free to enjoy the pleasures of what he calls the "three zones" of "light, half light, and dark" that circumscribe his thought.

The first zone, "forms with parallel," however, remains somehow attached to the material world, even if only by the force of imaginative reworking. In this first zone, Murphy experiences the pleasure of "reprisal" and can imagine the homosexual Ticklepenny forced to rape Miss Carridge, the possessive prostitute who seeks after Murphy throughout the novel. The second zone, "forms without parallel," allows for the purer pleasure of contemplation where nothing needs to be reimagined or corrected. These two zones provide Murphy with a great deal of freedom. Here, he can choose to gaze at a malleable simulacrum of the real world or move through the half-light of "unparalleled beatitude" (112). But the third, or "dark," zone transcends the first two by providing

Murphy with "nothing but commotion" (112). In this zone, surrounded by the infinite "flux of forms," Murphy is not free but, rather, "a mote in the dark of absolute freedom" (112). Though he finds it pleasant to rearrange the world in the first zone, and blissful to escape it through contemplation in the second, Murphy discovers in the "will-lessness" of his third zone something that requires less real-world effort than either pleasure or bliss. At the novel's ironic conclusion, Murphy dies of "shock following burns" while sitting in his rocking chair and devolving into the truth of his mind's three zones (261). The word "shock" here should draw our special attention, since it acquires its force in the novel as the antithesis of the blissful pleasure of nonexistence that Murphy seeks in his room and in the infinite regress of rooms in his mind. Despite his Cartesian attempts to separate mind from body and to reside in the various recesses of the mind's truth, shock—and, as the coroner explains, "burns always shock"—finally brings Murphy back to the humiliations and anxieties of the body (261). He has not lost himself in the transcendence of the three zones but, rather, has been torn from those zones by the overriding, shocking truth of his own embodiment.

Murphy's inevitable move back to the material truth of the body resonates with the critical essays about modernism that Beckett had been writing during the late twenties and early thirties. In his 1929 essay, "Dante . . . Bruno. Vico . . Joyce," Beckett praises Joyce's *Work in Progress,* claiming that the text "is not to be read—or rather it is not only to be read. It is to be looked at and listened to. [Joyce's] writing is not *about* something; *it is that something itself* . . . When the sense is sleep, the words go to sleep . . . when the sense is dancing, the words dance" (14). Beckett suggests that Joyce has written in such a way as to reconcile form with content. Present throughout Beckett's essay, hidden behind his unconcealed adoration of Joyce's prose, is a vague belief in the capacity of art to do, or, rather, to *be* something that affects experience in the real world. For Beckett art impacts the thinking subject, that same individual that he so often parodies in his drama and fiction, and even a cursory reading of Beckett's work underscores what he learned from Joyce. Watt's obsessive calculating actually works to create a sense of the tedium and isolation that follows from the idea of calculation itself. The slow, desperate, apparently meaningless waiting present in so many of Beckett's texts enacts at the level of form the very boredom that seems to be the pronounced content of a text like *Waiting for Godot.* Beckett's work situates its characters and its readers in a lonely and seemingly inaccessible space by embodying, only as it endlessly ponders, the conditions of boredom and tedium. Following Joyce, he attempts to fuse form and content, to create art that is not *about* something but rather *is that something.* In the work of art, then, Beckett imagines an *Aufhebung* or Hegelian overcoming of the antitheses of form and content. Like the

Hegelian conception of *Aufhebung,* Beckett imagines this overcoming as containing or realizing that which it negates. In the dialectic a first term is only negated when it is absorbed into and fully realized by a second. Beckett's emphasis on form as the realization of content works to overcome the antitheses of material corporeality and immaterial consciousness. Form becomes the corollary of the body while content becomes the corollary of the mind. A content/form distinction that is overcome by a literature that is not *about* something but rather *is something* correlates to a mind/body distinction that is overcome when consciousness recognizes that it is always already a body. Beckett's writing criticizes and kicks against the boundaries of a Cartesian dualism by rethinking the mind/body distinction through the literary dialectic of content/form.

Subsequently, in his brief 1931 volume, *Proust,* Beckett explains:

> the old ego dies hard. Such as it was, a minister of dulness [*sic*], it was also an agent of security. When it ceases to perform that second function, when it is opposed by a phenomenon that it cannot reduce to the condition of a comfortable and familiar concept, when, in a word, it betrays its trust as a screen to spare its victim the spectacle of reality, it disappears, and the victim, now an ex-victim, for a moment free, is exposed to that reality—an exposure that has its advantages and its disadvantages. It disappears—with wailing and gnashing of teeth. (10)

Beckett goes on to explain that for Proust, the sources of this "sacred" moment are found in the "physical world" (23). For Beckett, then, the encounter with "new phenomena" results in a reversal of consciousness. Although in referring to the subject as an "ex-victim" this passage betrays the kind of optimism that the mature Beckett would regret, from a certain perspective, his entire literary output might be framed by this aesthetic theory. As the old Cartesian ego appears confined and anxious, Beckett articulates its resistance, its disappearance with "wailing and gnashing of teeth," as it collides with that which cannot be conceptualized, with the corporeal reality of a world full of uncontrollable, vulgar, and very real bodies (3).

If, for Descartes, the body humiliates the purer rationality of the mind, for Beckett the pretentious mind humiliates the more concrete and material truths of the body. When the mind seeks to become its own place in Beckett, that place always appears as confining as the body. So, we conclude Beckett's first novel with Murphy, tied to a chair in his room, dying of burns in a curious parallel of the fate of Charlotte Brontë's Bertha, the proverbial madwoman trapped in the attic of Thornfield in *Jane Eyre* who also perishes in flames and confinement. Pure rationality has followed its way in to the deepest Cartesian recesses of the mind and come out the other side as virtually identical to a very vulnerable and embodied madness.[21] When Murphy's isolation devolves into a self-immolating madness, the escape that the mind had promised becomes as corporeal and feminizing as the confinement it had fled.

Just as we've seen in other Anglo-Irish Gothic novels, in *Murphy* the male-exile narrative transforms into a version of the female-confinement narrative. For *Murphy* the fear of the feminine is fully realized as female confinement transforms into male confinement. Beckett's achievement is not only to demonstrate that consciousness can never really be elevated over the corporeal, but also to break with a Western tradition of thought that sees consciousness as controlling the body, or to negate the structural dualism that imagines psychical autonomy and mastery as possible in the first place. If the male model of the individual subject, as set up by Cartesian thought, becomes the model par excellence of the bourgeois private self, then Beckett's writing is never content simply to criticize that model as too exclusive. He does not offer us a politics of sympathetic identification. If he did, then Beckett's works would fit squarely into a tradition of liberal political thought that, since John Locke's rewriting of Thomas Hobbes, has simply sought to extend the rights of the privileged to at least a few of the disempowered individuals in society. Rather, Beckett renders the private, masculinized self impossible by demonstrating how it is always already the incarcerated, feminized body that it wants to master, deny, or escape. In fact, any model of human interaction that relies on the idea of mastery appears horribly and resolutely hollow in Beckett's writing. The concept of mastery, whether it takes the form of self-mastery or of the mastery of the other, always appears in Beckett's prose in such negative, parodied, dehumanizing terms as to cancel it as a subject for serious discussion. Both metaphysical self-control (the mastery of the mind over the body) and, subsequently, political control (the political mastermind commanding the body politic) get converted into self-immolating blindness in Beckett's Cartesian Gothic.

III. REPRODUCTION: NOSTALGIC NATIONALISM AND DOMESTIC FICTION IN REVERSE IN *FIRST LOVE*

I believe that the concretizing and rethinking of philosophical dualism has a fixedly sociohistorical genesis and formulation in Beckett's novels. Beckett's Cartesian Gothic can hypostatize female confinement as the truth of the male mind and, so, imagine the failure of the Cartesian method in part because the social world of Ireland in the twenties and thirties—a world preoccupied with the notion of bourgeois nationalism—can be seen as embodying a markedly similar set of gender anxieties and political paradoxes. If we trace the sociopolitical precedence for the confines of Murphy's mind to the problems that engaged the attention of the Irish intellectuals in the thirties, then we begin to see how Beckett's writing often deploys generic conventions in order to articulate the historical problems fostered and symptomatically embodied by Cartesian thought.

By the time that Beckett came to write *Murphy,* Ireland was entering the Free State [*Saorstát Éireann*] era overseen in part by Eamon de Valera's *Fianna Fail* [Soldiers of Destiny] government. After the Articles of Association between Ireland and the British Empire were finally signed on 6 December 1921, W. T. Cosgrave eventually became president of the Free State. De Valera and his republican group had never desired a treaty with the British, and upon taking office in 1932 de Valera's Free State government had already been working hard to rewrite the laws and the constitution of Ireland to reflect the central values of "Faith and Fatherland" that would re-establish Irish autonomy by staking a claim for a masculinity founded upon Gaelo-Catholic traditions rather than on British notions of common law. Like the fiction of Maturin and Le Fanu, then, the Free State deployed a nostalgic rhetoric that attempted to reclaim and reassert the privileges of a lost masculine autonomy. By 1937, de Valera had replaced the original constitution, put together by Michael Collins, with a "Faith and Fatherland" version that attempted to assert Ireland as a fully autonomous state. To some extent, then, Free State nationalism follows the pattern of nostalgic, bourgeois nationalism that we first encountered in Edmund Burke's *Reflections on the Revolution in France,* in which he argues that a benevolent citizenry can only secure liberty by looking backward to patrilineal ancestry in order to look forward to posterity (29). During the Irish Free State period, Beckett took particular issue with what he saw as the inevitable failures and oversights of this basically dualistic approach to decolonization.

As I also noted in chapter 1, the term *an t-athardha* was used up through the seventeenth century in Irish-language poetry to denote Ireland as the "Fatherland." Following the colonial efforts of the British in Ireland during that century, this locution disappears only to be replaced by the ideal of Ireland as mythic "Motherland." This figure receives a most powerful realization in W. B. Yeats's *Cathleen Ni Hoolihan,* in which the Mythic Mother, avatar of the Nation, calls her sons to make the ultimate blood sacrifice in order to redeem and restore her verdant lands to their original, untouched condition. Richard Kearney has argued that after the advent of British colonization, particularly in the *Aisling* poems, Ireland came to be identified as "a vulnerable virgin ravished by the aggressive masculine invader from England" (77). In the patriarchal terms set up by British colonization, chiefly in the Victorian period when the paternalistic structural dynamic of the private sphere became linked with Britain's "manly" cultural mission of civilizing the entire world, Ireland's dispossession became encoded in her newly imposed language and in the political unconscious of her literature. The poetic emphasis on colonized Ireland as both ravished female and Virgin Mother reflects the cultural strictures placed upon, or, rather, the impossibility of, woman's self-possession. It also signifies the Irish male's double affiliation to femininity. De Valera's government sought to re-establish the figure of the "Fatherland," *an t-athardha,* and, so, rediscover Ireland as the provenance of a distinctly autonomous masculinity.

In an essay entitled "Censorship in the Saorstat," initially written for *The Bookman* in 1935, Beckett, who was also drafting the novel that would become *Murphy,* inveighs against what John Harrington has come to call the "cultural exclusivism" of early twentieth-century Ireland (23). In the essay, Beckett's ire is turned against the Censorship Act of 1929, which registered the names of books that had been deemed "unwholesome" by a board of five readers. Part 4 of the Censorship Act appears to be of particular interest to Beckett because it prohibits, as he explains, "publications advocating the use of contraceptives" (*Disjecta* 86). "France may commit race suicide," he tells us, "Erin never will. And should she be found at any time deficient in Cuchulains, at least it shall never be said that they were contraceived" (86–87). The Censorship Act operates to purify the mind and to regulate the reproductive body. Moreover, in drawing attention to the desire for more "Cuchulains," Beckett parodies the Free State's retrogressive desire for a vigorous, premodern model of masculinized heroism. The upshot of this registry of prohibited books seems quite clear to Beckett: the Celtic Free State must remain both internally pure, since authors like O'Casey, O'Faolin, Joyce, and even Beckett himself mustn't be read by the Irish peoples, and hermetic, since "foreign" writers like Döblin, Cassanova, and Gorki must never find their way in to Ireland in the first place. With characteristically acidic wit, Beckett goes on to claim that the act finally embodies the nation's paradoxical "sterilization of the mind and apotheosis of the litter" in such a fashion as to imagine a "paradise peopled with virgins" (87). For Beckett this model almost seems like inbreeding—the most extreme and xenophobic version of mimetic reproduction imaginable—the offspring of which is more an excrescence than an heir.

In *The Irish Beckett,* Harrington indicates that Beckett's attacks on cultural exclusivism are also attacks on the basic grammar of an Irish Free State nationalism that worked rather desperately to depict an impenetrable Catholic Ireland as the opposite of an all too flexible British liberal cosmopolitanism (23). The need to establish an Ireland that was at one and the same time essentially Catholic and utterly unaffected by British culture was a move that the Free State attempted to make in order to break more fully with the embattled history of colonialism that had shaped Ireland's political and social landscape at least since Cromwell's military incursions in 1649. Hence, the move to censor and eliminate contraception also works to assert an authentic Catholic identity for Ireland. This move was also, quite clearly, a nostalgic attempt to recapture a premodern Ireland and represent it as a kind of fully dressed, authentic paternal self severed from its modern identity as the sister kingdom and spouse of England. In "Censorship in the Saorstat," Beckett links Irish Catholicism's prohibition against contraception with its overtly paradoxical desire to keep both alien and internal concepts from bearing any fruit in modern Ireland. Although the Irish Free State appears universally opposed to contraception, it readily draws up laws that stand as prophylaxis against the reproduction of ideas and the dissemination of the new. Simply put, prophylaxis becomes forbidden at the same time that it acts as the modus operandi of the state. Regeneration is insisted upon only as it is also rendered impossible. Finally, what the Censorship Act aims at is merely the production of sameness. We see in "Censorship in the Saorstat" an early form of the logical impasse that would become the sine qua non of all of Beckett's literary output. Here, however, the impasse appears to be linked very specifically to the impossible material conditions that follow from an ideology and a legal system that extols singularity, hermeticism, and sterility while simultaneously calling for fruitful generation. In attempting to identify an authentic, non-British or non-European masculine self, Ireland had cut itself off from the developing, cosmopolitan world, confined itself within the precincts of a premodern and finally sterile system of values. Self-confinement becomes a remarkably barren form of provincialism. At the same time, by actively identifying itself as the other of Britishness, Irishness continued to define itself in terms of its imperial identity, even if only negatively. In the end, Ireland does not escape its identification as wife and sister kingdom, so much as it rails against the confines of that very identity in seeking to assert itself in terms of "Faith and Fatherland." The autonomy promised by a supposedly authentic Irish identity, then, collapses into the kind of confinement that characterized both the formal structures of the Unionist Gothic and the Romantic solipsism propagated by Stephen Dedalus throughout *A Portrait of the Artist as a Young Man* and *Ulysses*.

By deploying Gothic modes of confinement in *Murphy*, the novel he was writing in 1935, then, Beckett intervenes into the mythos of Free State hermeticism by representing autonomy and authenticity as fruitless ideological formations. In *Murphy* Beckett had depicted the world of an Irish expatriate who lives by "silence, cunning, and exile" as hermetic, disembodied, and self-immolating. In his subsequent fiction, he would go on to depict the zealous drive to recover an authentic, "othertight" identity—the same drive that underscored Free State nationalism—as unproductive and sterile. Let's not forget that the first-person narrators of *Watt, First Love,* and the *Trilogy* all work to remember and recover an identity that they hope will provide autonomy and self-mastery. If we take the argument that Beckett makes in "Censorship in the Saorstat" seriously, then autonomy and authenticity both appear to leave Irish masculinity in a position where it must act in the world while never really leaving the confines of the womb. So the cycle of confinement and reproduction worked out in the female- and Anglo-Irish Gothic traditions as a palliative metaphor for the problems of structural dispossession takes a different turn in Beckett's fiction. Reproduction transforms into the repetition of a stillborn social order. Reproduction, in Beckett's oeuvre, becomes the very symbol of stagnation and sterility. One cannot help but to be reminded here of Pozzo's claim in *Waiting for Godot:* "They give birth astride a grave." Beckett converts the reproduction metaphor that circumscribes the generic world of the female Gothic into its other, into a world where procreation miscarries because it always aims at the re-creation and reassertion of an "othertight" autonomy. Seven years after publishing *Murphy,* Beckett would begin writing in French, and one of the texts that he composed in 1946, *First Love* [*Premier Amour*], enacts the Gothic's generic cycle of domestic confinement and reproduction while representing both the suffocating social truths at the core of this generic form and the self-destructive implications of the zealous drive for autonomy.[22] In *First Love,* Beckett reverses the basic structures of domestic fiction, including the gendered identities upon which it relies, in order to point to the Gothic implications of domestic ideology and to the stultifying effect that nostalgia has on political and individual action. In fact, as Beckett leaves the English language behind in order to write *First Love* and the other *Nouvelles* (*The End, The Expelled,* and *The Calmative*), he also euthanizes the corpus of English domestic fiction itself in order to perform a postmortem on the nationalist ideologies and identities that it helped to produce.

In "Writing in the Shit: Beckett, Nationalism and the Colonial Subject," David Lloyd provides what amounts to the most dynamic and compelling critical reading of *First Love* and, subsequently, the most influential rendering of a "post-colonial Beckett" to date. Lloyd suggests that if Beckett offers a radical negation of Western metaphysics, he also negates the "objective hegemonic force" of the West's political ethos (41–42). Lloyd's argument rests on the idea that the more cosmopolitan Irish modernist writers like Joyce and Beckett engaged with and invariably rejected the kind of overtly nationalist notion of Irish writing fostered by Daniel Corkery's *Hidden Ireland.* For Lloyd, the strain of nationalist writing recommended by Corkery inaugurates "a subtle but decisive shift from the recognition of the economic and political threat that Gaelic culture faced from British imperialism to the representation of that culture as lost, past, primitive, fragmented and, indeed, feminine. This shift is inseparable from the specific project of bourgeois nationalism in Ireland, namely, the forging of a sense of Irish identity"

(45). Hence, *First Love,* which begins with the first-person narrator claiming, "I associate, rightly or wrongly, my marriage with the death of my father," depicts the ruminations of an Irishman who continually looks back with nostalgic longing to the sense of identity and meaning represented by the past (25). Lloyd demonstrates that Beckett's writing deflates this nostalgia by playing it off against a rigorous critique of the "logic of identity that at every level structures and maintains the postcolonial moment" (56). In Lloyd's reading, the "objective hegemonic force" of Western imperialism always controls the discursive field of identity, and the longing for an authentic identity is, in itself, always already a grand concession to the Western ethos.[23] Beckett's writing realizes the limitations of identity politics, and it goes on to critique the logic of identity itself.

Lloyd's arguments, as convincing and erudite as they are, have been challenged by still other politically oriented Beckett critics who prefer to depict Beckett in conflict with enemies like reification or, in the case of someone like David Weisberg, with the problem of political commitment itself. In fact, Weisberg launches an offhanded, but no less powerful, critique of Lloyd's essay. For Weisberg, Beckett must be separated from writers like Yeats or Joyce because, "Beckett himself (unlike Joyce) had no interest in being an Irish writer and throughout his works he parodies such a notion" (176). Furthermore, Weisberg's book, *Chronicles of Disorder: Samuel Beckett and the Cultural Politics of the Modern Novel,* argues that Beckett never launches an overt political critique, opting instead to parody the contradictions and failures of autonomous art itself. Weisberg asserts that Beckett takes up certain formal maneuvers in order to parody the modernist conception of the great authorial genius embodied by, say, Joyce or Proust. If we join these two apparently contradictory approaches, however, we might arrive at something closer to the truth of Beckett's politics. When we take up Lloyd's arguments about *First Love* as a denunciation of nostalgic nationalism and connect them with Weisberg's claims about Beckett's self-reflexive disarticulation of autonomous art, we end up with a Beckett who parodies certain literary forms in order to reveal the historical and phenomenological conditions that gave birth to and circumscribed the efficacy of those very forms.[24] We read Beckett into both the Irish literary and European modernist traditions rather than extracting him from either. By placing Beckett in the tradition of the Irish Gothic and its generic accoutrements, we politicize Beckett's vague, literary "Irishness"—which readily accommodates the colonial and gender binaries that we have seen in Maturin, Le Fanu, Wilde, and Joyce—precisely by reading this tradition as the historical ground upon which Beckett's larger intervention into the conceptual failings of dualistic thought is built. The Gothic Ireland behind *First Love* provides an exemplary stage upon which to enact the various failures of a dualistic epistemology and to analyze the social set pieces that dualism works to generate.

"I associate, rightly or wrongly, my marriage with the death of my father, in time. That other links exist, on other levels, between these two affairs, is not impossible," the narrator of *First Love* explains (25). The death of the father "in time" becomes the most substantial obsession of the story's narrator. Upon reading these lines we might be led to ask: At what point in time does the father die? Is the father's time recoverable? Like Murphy, the unnamed narrator in *First Love* asks his various questions in hope of establishing an othertight autonomy. From near the beginning of the novella, he tells us that he has "only one thought in my mind, to be back in my room and flat on my back again" (28). Unlike Murphy, however, the narrative voice here associates the longed-for solipsistic autonomy with a lost father, and, so, with the system of paternity that allowed for privacy and autonomy in the first place. *First Love* expands the terrain of Beckett's Cartesian Gothic, then, by interrogating the nostalgic longing for the past engendered by Free State nationalism. The great crisis of the narrator's life comes when he is forced, after his father's death, to leave his paternal refuge. Though the executors of his father's will give him what little money his father had, the narrator reports telling them, "Keep this money and let me live here, in my room, as in Papa's lifetime" (29). If Emily St. Aubert of the Radcliffean female Gothic bemoans the loss of her father, and the Montorio brothers of Maturin's *Fatal Revenge* are finally displaced by the loss of their father, then the narrator of *First Love* readily fits into the schema of lost domestic affection upon which the basic Gothic framework is built. His entire narrative is predicated on the loss of the private, domestic self associated with the paternal ideal. Like Stephen Dedalus, he hopes for a kind of consubstantiality with the father, and, like Stephen, this longing dooms him to obsess about and be contained by a lifeless past.

The narrator goes on to characterize his father as a figure for a "great disembodied wisdom" who stands in opposition to the corporeal love that one feels with the "lips," "hands," and "hearts" (29). In *First Love,* the father comes to represent not only the nostalgia for the lost comforts of youth, but also the longing for a past figured precisely as an isolation from the needs and desires of the body and of the outside world. Again, we see the Gothic framework in Beckett in terms of the Cartesian metanarrative of the male mind. Beckett applies a good deal of pressure to the generic conventions by depicting his narrator from the very outset of the story as more isolated and psychically dissonant than either Maturin's Montorio brothers or Radcliffe's Emily. The narrator appears stuck in a historical and narratival loop, condemned to seek out the comfortable pattern of a moribund, failed bourgeois autonomy. For Beckett, a genre that longs for a return to the past is always already a failed one. By deploying a narrative structure built upon the hope of fecund reproduction and by foregrounding the logical failures of this narrative—including its failure to palliate its character's sense of dispossession—Beckett interrogates the structural, self-collapsing dualism at the heart of modern conceptions of autonomy. Beckett's *First Love* depicts nostalgia as a form of containment that renders all of the subject-centered narratives constructed in and by modernity as female-confinement narratives. As in *Murphy,* then, far from liberating the masculine subject, the longing to evade the vicissitudes of the body and to devolve into the recesses of the mind actually traps the supposedly "male mind," and converts the space of that mind into a metaphor for the structural limitations placed upon the "female body."

The narrator of *First Love* hopes to evade the communal and bodily experience of other people and devolve into a private, disembodied self. In fact, when he does experience bodily desire in the form of a "rigid phallus," he explains, "one is no longer oneself on such occasions, and it is painful to be no longer oneself" (31). Furthermore, he claims that "what goes by the name of love is banishment, with now and then a postcard from the homeland" (31). Banishment from the isolated—and so from the presumably free—self is the price one pays for interaction with others. The autonomous, nondesiring mind remains the figure for the homeland, then, but we seem to be irrevocably exiled from this nostalgically figured homeland by the mere presence of others. Throughout the narrative, we see quite clearly that the historical moment of the dualistically conceived self for which the narrator longs has passed away. The father's time is irretrievably gone. In fact, the narrator's persistent and obsessive need to reassert its virtues seems unambiguously pathetic, almost infantile. The narrator's longing for the dead past remains so strong, however, that he lingers in graveyards, and, as he tells us, "the smell of corpses, distinctly perceptible under those of grass and humus mingled, I do not find unpleasant, a trifle on the sweet side perhaps, a trifle heady, but how infinitely preferable to what the living emit, their feet, teeth, armpits, arses, sticky foreskins and frustrated ovules" (26). Throughout, the narrator clearly prefers a dead past to the living, breathing, embodied present in which he is forced to live. In fact, the experience of "first love" that the narrator has with Lulu—whom he later renames Anna—seeks to re-establish the ideal, disembodied space of the paternal household while eschewing both paternity and generation themselves as limiting. The narrator longs for the privileges of a patriarchal world, including the right to rename the bride, while, at the same time, living out a confined, sterile, solipsistic existence.

After the death of the father in time, the narrator tries to get on as best he can, sleeping in barns and on benches, but he can find neither a room nor the sense of will-less autonomy that he had in his father's house.

In Lulu/Anna he discovers someone who desires his body, and this presents him with a problem. To give in to Lulu/Anna, he must admit to and embrace bodily desire, but he can never truly do this. However, when he hears that she has a room, he is "most agreeably surprised," and goes with her to see the apartment (38). At the apartment, Lulu/Anna hopes to seduce the narrator, but as soon as he arrives, he makes it clear that he desires to re-create the basics of the room in his father's house. As she stands naked in front of him, he goes about putting all of the furniture out of the room and into the hallway. "There were hundreds of pieces," he tells us, "large and small, in the end they blocked the door, making egress impossible, and a fortiriori ingress, to and from the corridor" (40). Having re-created the basic arrangement of the room in his father's house and barred the door, the narrator appears reasonably content. He wants to produce a comfortable sameness, and in a sense, his logic lines up quite precisely with the Free State Ireland of Beckett's "Censorship in the Saorstat" essay. By stopping up the exits and entrances and attempting to re-create his old room, the narrator has imagined the room as his mind and, subsequently, performed a kind of paradoxical act of contraception. In seeking the old he has refused the new, but to do so he must block off all intercourse with the outside world, and, so he thinks, the possibility of new bodies and new forms that might appear, complicate his world, and take him even farther away from himself. As the story unfolds, however, we will come to see that his desire to purify the mind and regulate the body actually proves to be impossible.

We have here, then, a move away from the essentially realistic, though ironic, pattern of action and failed self-discovery of *Murphy* and toward an attempt to represent the very desire for a recognizable narrative pattern itself as the only authentic determiner of identity. The desire for a recognizable pattern drives Beckett's characters. As we've seen in the Unionist Gothic, the Anglo-Irish version of this narrative generally turns on the inability to determine who violates and who is violated. In Beckett, we often find characters who live out established narrative patterns only to discover that their lives are violated by the patterns themselves. The particular trick of this structure in Beckett's fiction remains the fact that the characters compulsively, though almost nonchalantly, accept these patterns. The narrator obsesses about narrative pattern—about form itself, about a formal structure that can contain his anxieties and, indeed, his identity—while simultaneously shutting out the corporeal world. The formal and historical structure of that narrative pattern is already in place, and the narrator of *First Love,* like Vladimir and Estragon in *Waiting for Godot,* chooses to go through the motions of following the pre-established pattern. In Beckett's world, the nostalgia for the formal pattern itself signifies an absolute failure to imagine a world that might work in any other way. The narrator's nostalgia for disembodied paternal time always directs his course inward. Hence, in the end he appears very similar to Murphy, but, in the same sense, he also prefigures the claustrophobic set pieces that will come to characterize Beckett's drama. By choosing a worn-out and virtually lifeless narrative, the narrator of *First Love* seeks an existence that has no intercourse—in all the senses of that word—with contemporary life. In order to maintain such an existence, however, he needs more than just a room. He must also have someone to provide for him, to keep him in the room. Thus, through a dialectical method of writing, Beckett's story works to conceal or repress bodily need and desire and realize the space of the mind at the same time that it continually reveals the inescapable material and historical truths that accompany the fact of embodiment.

Lulu/Anna becomes the figural father for the narrator, providing for his every need, as Beckett offers, in *First Love,* an ironic inversion of the normative, gendered structure of the domestic sphere. In seeking out his autonomy, the narrator continually renders himself in terms of the feminine sphere. He eventually discovers that Lulu/Anna earns her money through prostitution, or, as she tells him: "we live by prostitution" (43). The narrator does not really seem to care about this. In fact, he seems more bothered by the fact that the clients, who meet Lulu/Anna in another room, occasionally make enough noise to disturb his quiet, abject self-reflection. Even though we clearly see in this passage the collapse of Cartesian dualism and the attendant metaphor of the separate spheres as the father figure and provider—now explicitly embodied as a woman—lives via the business of the body, the narrator, stuck in the obsessive narrative pattern that has circumscribed his life and experience, does not seem to take any notice. The nostalgic longing for a disembodied autonomy promised by the room, linked in Beckett's story to the father, invariably turns back to the marriage metaphor. As the narrator eventually admits, he must "use the word marriage, it was a kind of union in spite of all" (45). The nostalgia that leads to the marriage provides the narrator with the financial support to live in his "room," but, by reversing the gender dynamic of the Gothic, Beckett places the male character in the social space generally reserved for the vulnerable female. In so doing Beckett converts the nostalgic longing for the father's time, the longing that characterized Free State nationalism, into a profoundly feminizing mode of autonomy. The tactic of gender reversal that Beckett deploys throughout the text transforms male autonomy into female confinement.

Like most stories in the Gothic mode, *First Love* ends with a birth, and so with a male heir who supposedly signifies reconciliation and repossession. But Beckett's story reveals the boundaries of this narrative structure. In fact, the "union" formed between Lula/Anna and the narrator actually falls apart at the birth of the child. To appropriate Beckett's words from "Censorship in the Saorstat," then, the birth that ends *First Love* represents the nostalgic narrative of the father's time as "the sterilization of the mind and the apotheosis of the litter." When Lulu/Anna tells the narrator that she is pregnant, the narrator denies responsibility and extols the virtues of abortion. Finally, as he tells us, "what finished me was the birth" (44). He leaves the apartment during the child's birth, pursued by the incessant crying of the newborn infant. The cries pursue him "for years," and although his story concludes, he complains that the cries never will. Though it continues to haunt the present, the father's time is irrecoverable, and neither a union nor a sundering can recapture it. So, *First Love* sets up as it parodies the rudimentary confinement and reproduction cycle of the female Gothic. In furthering the basic dynamic of the Cartesian Gothic that began in *Murphy,* Beckett gives us yet another male subject who flees community and corporeality in order to seek the truth of his own internal logic. Even in attempting to be only and solely "himself," however, the narrator of *First Love* finds himself in the same constraints that bind the women of the Gothic to the most secluded sections of the private sphere.

What sets this particular story apart is Beckett's insistence on depicting the nostalgia for the room in the father's house as a debilitating phantasy, an escape into confinement. Beckett's political allegory subsists in his capacity to imagine social identity—in this case, a hermetic masculine autonomy—as adhering to a kind of aesthetic logic.[25] If figural, narrative patterns render an identity, then Beckett's writing suggests that, conversely, literal, political identity remains subject to aesthetic critique. The aesthetic logic that Beckett disarticulates in *First Love* clearly resonates with the logic of identity that David Lloyd finds in Irish bourgeois nationalism. The Beckettian narrative depicts bourgeois nationalism's attempt to establish a sense of Irish identity founded on the Free State cornerstones of "Faith and Fatherland," then, as retrogressive and, finally, provincial and antihumanist. Nationalisms predicated on the recovery of a nostalgic past, as Beckett's "Censorship in the Saorstat" reminds us, also desire a kind of internal, regulated purity that appears as a form of self-mastery. In the aesthetic logic of Beckett's critique, the Irish Free State's desire to isolate the mind and purify the body appears as a feeble attempt to reassert precisely that masculine autonomy that had failed in the first place.

In his groundbreaking study of decolonization and revolution, *The Wretched of the Earth,* Frantz Fanon interrogates the ways in which a Western conception of subjectivity filters into, only as it fragments, the communities of a colonized people. "The colonialist bourgeoisie," Fanon tells us, "hammered into the native's mind the idea of a society of individuals where each person shuts himself up in his own subjectivity, and whose only wealth is individual thought" (47). For Fanon, the colonized individual's supposed wealth turns out to be as personally isolating as it is socially impoverished. Fanon's concern with the idea of shutting the self up in its own subjectivity, of the resolute failure or disappearance of community, seems to be the very province of Beckett's re-vision of the Gothic narrative of structural dispossession. By the time Beckett came to write *First Love,* of course, the Gothic, and the various Gothic revivals that it had inspired in Ireland, seemed fully exhausted as a genre. By deploying the formal and gendered logic of the female Gothic in reverse, *First Love* depicts any model of national identity predicated on recovering a masculine autonomy as equally exhausted. Following David Weisberg's arguments, then, we can see how Beckett launches his political critique precisely by parodying the maneuvers of past literary forms. The narrative structures from the past contain us within the past. Now, when we recall Lukács's conception of a political aesthetic predicated on the move from the examination of the specific social problem to the general socioeconomic cause, we can readily see how Beckett reads early twentieth-century nationalism as one of the stillborn children of centuries of imperialist and capitalist expansion. From the perspective of Beckett's rewriting of the Gothic, the problem of structural dispossession and the hope for a male heir who can repossess the past continue to haunt and frustrate contemporary conceptions of national and political sovereignty. Though his fusing of literary and sociopolitical history might often appear somewhat abstract, in *First Love* Beckett connects philosophical abstraction to the historical circumstances that frame and construct them. As Stephen Connor says in *Samuel Beckett: Repetition, Theory and Text,* Beckett's characters and narrators "struggle to make sense of a world that they are always inextricably in" (45). In order to do this, Beckett deploys a specifically modernist revision of the Gothic genre because modernism's almost painful level of self-reflective writing allows him to depict the confined self of modernity in all of its self-willed incarceration. Finally, in the social world of *First Love,* conformity by isolation is revealed as the condition of possibility for conformity by mass identification.

IV. AUTONOMY: THE WRITING OF A GOTHIC SELF IN *MOLLOY* AND *MALONE DIES*

The typical female Gothic concludes with a marriage and an heir. The women depicted in these novels have escaped the confines of some nefarious count, discovered true love, and recovered something akin to the paternal homes they had lost. We generally find these women enjoying the hope that such autonomy seems to bring. From another perspective, they have simply found themselves liberated into another kind of confinement. Although the threat of imminent bodily harm appears to have been removed, women like Radcliffe's Emily must still learn to subsist solely and wholly within the domestic sphere. The women in these novels are saved from overtly violent incarceration and, occasionally, the threat of the supernatural only to find true bliss concealed with and for them in the private sphere. Femininity, constantly threatened by rape and incarceration, must be protected by the regulated sexual economy that occurs in the most secluded space of the private sphere, that of the "intimate" family. This space also acts as a psychic symbol for woman's confinement. Houses like *Jane Eyre*'s Thornfield mirror the overcrowded minds and innermost fears of their various female inmates. The women in these novels reflect the ideological hierarchy of the mind/body dualism of the separate spheres. Essentially, woman becomes an object acted upon and may be transformed through such action into a subject that culture might eventually deem capable of agency—a dialectic structurally analogous to that of the colonized subject.[26] The fictive conceit of *Jane Eyre,* that the text we read is Jane's own memoir, already indicates a latent desire to break with the male heir formula in favor of self-possession, and, quite obviously, Jane's autobiography acts both as her offspring and as her self-articulation. The ideology of the private that these novels reflect, support, and, to some degree, resist serves a dual purpose. On the one hand it provides objective support for those in power, in this case, those with access to both the public and private spheres, against any collective challenge, while on the other it provides subjective fulfillment for the disempowered in an escapist notion of the individual and an infinitely deferrable belief in future equity.

Up to this point, I have examined how Beckett deploys the structures that we see in female Gothic to allegorize, first, the double bind of masculine identity in modern Ireland and, second, the larger problem of a Western socioeconomic and political structure based on a limiting conception of mind/body duality. These problems are more than mere parallel formations. They reflect a causal relationship. The mind/body duality produces both the condition of possibility and the ideological warrant for the double bind of a colonized masculinity. I have argued that Beckett uses formal tropes borrowed from English and Irish literary history in order to render material and political histories subject to aesthetic critique. He depicts certain identities, and the modern logic of identity politics itself, as coextensive with, and in some cases developed by, formal innovations in the history of narrative. He invokes as he parodies the confinement and reproduction structure that animates the plot of Gothic and domestic fiction. A careful reading of Beckett's fiction reveals characters who are stuck in generic narratives and, subsequently, the ideological ways in which modern narrative itself becomes caught up in national identity. His characters imitate the generic literary forms that have preceded them just as the real world mimetically reproduces and relives the elements of anterior social narratives.

Upon completing the *Nouvelles* in 1946, Beckett began to plan his *Trilogy* of novels, *Molloy, Malone Dies,* and *The Unnamable,* and in the *Trilogy* he moves a step beyond the allegorical and aesthetic speculation of *Murphy* and *First Love.* The prose writing in the pre-*Trilogy* texts seems like a pessimistically distilled and minimalist reconciliation of Joycean stream of consciousness and Proustian conceptions of memory. From its first pages, the *Trilogy* appears more formally inventive, dynamic, and hermetic than any of Beckett's previous writings. In *Murphy* and *First Love* he had deployed dualism against dualism. Hence, the texts tend to reverse the typical gendered binaries one finds in British domestic fiction. Murphy ends his life as confined and as insane as does Bertha in *Jane Eyre.* The narrator of *First Love* longs for the protective confinements of the domestic sphere with all of the impotent melancholy of the heroines of Samuel Richardson's novels. Through this tactic of negative reversal, Beckett reveals the underlying truths of the domestic sphere, of colonialist politics, and of mind/body dualism. This tactic tends to remain at the level of narrative structure, so that Murphy and the narrator of *First Love,* the supposedly Cartesian minds in each story, remain remarkably unaware of their own feminized positions. Essentially, then, both texts remain true to that central facet of modernism: the ironized hero. Though form and content certainly merge in these texts by Beckett, they remain separate in the minds of the protagonists who accede to the demands of Cartesian dualism.

The method of composition we see in the *Trilogy* remains predicated on Beckett's self-consciously dialectical method of fusing form and content. The words still isolate when the sense is isolation; they bore when the sense is boredom; they confuse when the sense is confusion; they alienate when the sense is alienation. In the following section I will demonstrate that in the *Trilogy,* Beckett begins to move from deploying allegory to unpack sociopolitical problems to allegorizing acts of writing and interpretation themselves. He moves to what we might call a level of meta-allegory. Beckett's method reads history genealogically and, unlike many of the modernist writers who precede him, he resists the urge to claim that his approach will escape or eliminate the confines of social discourse. *Molloy* is not a modernist narrative that bears a striking resemblance to the female-confinement narrative, but the story of a modernist writer who recognizes his confinement within the anteriority of narrative form. He knows that his writing merely follows upon and reasserts the themes and tropes of the various texts that have preceded him. Moreover, he begins to realize that the texts he writes will neither liberate nor protect him from structural dispossession. Starting with *Molloy* Beckett's modernist characters have actually realized the autonomy longed for by the heroines of the female Gothic and the gender-disoriented heroes of the Anglo-Irish Gothic. One would think that freedom and wholeness would accompany such levels of autonomy and self-awareness, but having achieved his apparent liberation from others, the Beckettian male character really has nothing to show for it. He writes because he has the power to do so, but this writing only increases his isolation, and any attempt to read his writing only serves to increase the isolation of the reader.

Molloy, Beckett's most written-about, and perhaps most admired, novel seems to have been hastily pieced together between May and November of 1947.[27] The novel's bipartite structure works almost like that of the detective novels Beckett read for pleasure and relaxation.[28] In the first section, we encounter the thoughts and related wanderings of Molloy, an indigent and far from sane writer who claims to write his fragmented yet carefully balanced story from the confines of a bed. The second section offers us the report of Jacques Moran, an inspector who has been sent to discover the whereabouts of Molloy. From this description, *Molloy* does not seem that different from Victorian sensation fiction like Wilkie Collins's *The Woman in White,* which compiles a number of letters and diaries into a suspenseful and mysterious tale of conspiracy. In the end, however, Beckett's Inspector Moran might just turn out to be Molloy, but the text remains ambiguous and canny enough on this point to allow for other interpretations as well. Has Molloy the writer imagined Moran, or has Moran the detective-interpreter imagined the author he seeks? The text refuses to resolve these fundamental ambiguities. But *Molloy*'s pride of place in the Beckett canon may well derive from the fact that from its very first page, even from its first line, the text begins to dismantle the entire gendered history and structural framework of the English novel.

Attempting to leave behind the nostalgic phantasies of *First Love,* the narrative voice that initiates *Molloy* actually begins by admitting, "I am in my mother's room. It's I who live there now. I don't know how I got there" (7). We have moved, then, from the longing for the father's time to the narrator's admitted identification with the mother. This reads like an ironic instance of self-realization because, as the narrator goes on to confess, from within the space of his room, the Cartesian paradigms of male epistemology and transcendence seem to have collapsed. Even when Molloy wanders in the world outside of his room, he remains confined and isolated, and the entire convoluted story that he tells remains circumscribed by the framing narrative of the mother's room. In the *Trilogy,* Beckett no longer seems preoccupied with the specifically nostalgic social world of the Irish Free State, but rather with the larger material and philosophical problems that brought it into being. "The truth is," Molloy explains, "I don't know much. For example my mother's death. Was she already dead when I came? Or did she die only later? I mean enough to bury. I don't know. Perhaps they haven't buried her yet. In any case I have her room. I sleep in her bed. I piss and shit in her pot. I have taken her place. I must resemble her more and more. All I need now is a son" (7). Molloy begins to establish a Cartesian pattern of skeptical questioning by admitting what he does not know, but in the end he cannot establish truth on the foundational site of the ego but, rather, only on that ego's similarity to the dispossessed mother. He has "taken her place." Molloy, obsessed with his own physicality, is as much body as *Cogito*. And in this case, as the ego fails to be incorporeal and autonomous, it is also revealed to be fully mimetic. What appeared as modernist modes of irony in the previous texts, has transformed into a self-conscious critique of that irony. Simply put, even a character or narrator who recognizes his limitations cannot exceed them. Beckett's work moves from allegorizing historical problematics to rethinking the problem of mimesis itself, then. In Beckett's fiction mimesis displaces allegory. Mimetic knowledge derives from the material world rather than from psychic rationality. The skeptical, knowing man of *Murphy* and *First Love* has finally recognized his mimetic resemblance to the confined, corporeal woman. In Beckett, however, self-recognition never liberates the self.

From a psychoanalytic perspective, this passage appears magnificently overdetermined. The critic of a Freudian or even a Lacanian bent might pause here to ask why Molloy has failed to transition away from identification with the mother.[29] But, we encounter in the first lines of *Molloy* not only an Irish male subject's inability to transition away from the mother, but also his collision with and confinement within narratives that he has not originated. "Was mother's name Molloy? Very likely. Her name must have been Molloy too," he explains (23). Throughout the first section of the novel, we witness a subject struggling, rather impotently, with the very anteriority of generic structure as he also attempts to add to and alter that structure. What if the Gothic's male heir, the figure who would palliate the mother's structural dispossession, actually comes to mirror and embody her dispossession? What if the mother's name, then, the name signifying loss and dispossession, is also the son's name, is also the name of the "I" who attempts to speak? Another way of approaching this might be to say that we encounter from the opening pages of *Molloy* the overt collision of novelistic forms. As Molloy recounts his sense of identity with existential torpor, stylistic experimentation, and a cautiously staccato voice, we witness modernist technique—in the form of a painfully solipsistic, fragmentary stream-of-consciousness narration—collide with the basic narrative framework of English domestic fiction. If the narrative desire of domestic fiction, and, indeed, of the entire ideology of the separate spheres, moves toward the realization of a domestic space where the woman can find a safe haven for herself—and the female Gothic signifies the fear that this safe haven might turn out to be a type of prison—then *Molloy* begins by identifying a male subject who finds himself trapped precisely in the "mother's room," cut off from history, community, and the encounter with any kind of public. Disrupting the basic Gothic narrative with this gender reversal does not, however, bring that narrative to a conclusion. Rather, it extends this narrative on into infinity. Beckett ontologizes Gothic structures of confinement. Starting with *Molloy*, Beckett's narratives on page and stage never really conclude, nor, I might add, do they ever really begin. They certainly start and they certainly cease, but the reader has the sense of having walked in on a story already in progress and of having departed, exhausted, but never the less too early, from a story that has no conclusion in sight. What's more, by foregrounding the act of writing, *Molloy* represents this conundrum, very self-consciously, as a problem that might be understood in terms of literary language and generic structure.

Soon after admitting that he is in his mother's room, then, Molloy goes on to explain that he lives by writing, and despite everything else that he comes to symbolize in the novel, Molloy remains a writer who receives money for the pages he writes (7). Thus, we have in *Molloy* a novel about novel writing that is also a novel consciously obsessed by and trapped within the formal conventions of English Gothic fiction itself. Although *Murphy* and *First Love* deploy a Gothic structure, their protagonists seem blissfully unaware of this fact. *Molloy* raises the stakes by suggesting that even the writer who seems aware of the sociopolitical and literary narratives set up for him, even the autonomous artist—for whom modernity seems to reserve the power to create ex nihilo, to bend and rewrite discourse and its various constructions at will—remains trapped within the confines of systematic, ideological, and narrative history. Avoiding the nostalgia for the father's time does not liberate the subject. In Wilde and Joyce, we get versions of the autonomous artist that still hold out some hope for liberation. In Wilde's plays, the nearly Nietzschean will of the aesthete helps him to rewrite the world around him. Wilde always imagines a playwright within the play, a character who, like Lord Goring in *An Ideal Husband,* can rewrite and redirect the action and events and, so, manipulate the social order through sheer acts of genius and wit. While Joyce parodies Wildean aesthetics in the figure of Stephen Dedalus, he also holds on to some hope that the careful and capacious reader will discover in the dialectic of Stephen and Bloom precisely that fusion of the spiritual and material, of self and community that Stephen has missed. Taking a note from Joyce, Beckett's *Molloy* places as much pressure on the interpreter—the careful reader—as it does on writing and aesthetic autonomy.[30]

In his particular *Aufhebung* of modernist speculation on the artist and the confinement structure of the female Gothic, however, Beckett introduces into the dialectic of form and content the third category of mediation. By developing the bipartite structure of the first novel in his *Trilogy,* Beckett allows us to glimpse the artist at work in the figure of Molloy, a character who seems to perceive that aesthetic form is the medium in which he lives and moves. Though he fails, the author attempts to construct autonomous meaning in the pages he writes. What's more important, Molloy seems to realize, even from the very opening of his text, that the field of identity remains the province of historical, political, social, and psychic forces beyond his control. He knows he will fail, and he tells us, "What I'd like now is to speak of things that are left" (7). But, in providing us with the interpreter/literary critic at work in the figure of Moran, Beckett observes how the reader who goes in search of an author's meaning also gets caught up in a narrative that mimetically reproduces the ideological and systematic confinements of the past. The work of modern art, itself, becomes a structure of confinements, a system so immanent that it provides a photonegative of the immanent, interiority of the bourgeois home and of the private individuals who reside therein. The first set of texts that we explored reflects on this structure allegorically; the *Trilogy* and the later texts start to mime it, to replicate it, or, more directly, to literalize it. More and more in Beckett's work, confinement comes to be the controlling and, for lack of a better term, literal metaphor.[31] Furthermore, this confinement attempts to affirm the Cartesian conception of an objective truth that can be reached only through an extreme form of subjectivity. In Beckett, the novel's form has come to imitate the social hermeticism of modern subjectivity itself. If the modernist author has moved into the space of his own autonomy, he has also invited the reader to do likewise. Later, we'll see Beckett take this problem a step further by imagining in the space of the theater, and on the circumscribed space of the stage, an even more literal room in which to confine his performers and his audiences.

Molloy's formal dynamism, which provoked George Bataille to refer to the novel as "repellent splendor incarnate" and Lukács to call it the *ne plus ultra* of decadent modernism, relies precisely on the stylistic innovation of a modernist autonomous artist who can use language to bend perception and the world to his will (131, 198). But this formal dynamism finally and resolutely undercuts itself by converting autonomy into confinement and formal innovation into the obsession with form. Molloy himself tries to understand and deploy forms in order to escape from both his literal and figural confinement, and Moran attempts to understand and deploy formalism in order to discover meaning and conclude his odyssey. In both cases, the obsession with form transforms into its own rather obsessive narrative prison. The modernist forms invoked and parodied within the text not only fail to liberate the authorial subject, they actively reify his isolation and social quietism. As a novel, *Molloy* foregrounds the collision of modernism and Gothic fiction by imagining the act of writing itself as the staging area for the autonomous self, but the escape and resistance signified by autonomous art, and therefore by the written self, always turns out to be an escape back into confinement. As much as he has modernized the Gothic, then, Beckett has also begun to Gothicize modernism. The obsession with form, the artist's capacity to rework action and the world through the structural dynamism of aesthetic balance and symmetry, comes to embody this problem in *Molloy*. For Molloy the escape provided by rewriting the self always leads back to the confines of form, and, moreover, to the ur-confinement of the mother's room. By enlarging the dialectic of form and content (and so, of body and mind) to include the act of interpretation, Beckett interrogates not only the structural dualism of modern Western thought, but also the very real ways in which this dualism circumscribes our ability to inhabit, imagine, or criticize our social world. By pushing the Gothic to its Cartesian limits in a novel like *Murphy* or a novella like *First Love,* Beckett articulates modern fiction's failure to offer any real way of thinking either the body or collectivity. What seems to be left to the artist is form itself, then, and Molloy inhabits form as intensely as the characters in Maturin, Le Fanu, and Stoker inhabit castles and as fully as the characters in Wilde and Joyce inhabit the space of their own autonomy. Form provides him with both comfort and focus.

Section 1 of the novel, written by Molloy, continually rehearses as it revolves around the obsession with form. In the most famous example, Molloy obsesses about the formal methods for sucking stones. In attempting to find some symmetrical, balanced, and aesthetically pleasurable method for sucking stones, Molloy explains:

> I took advantage of being at the seaside to lay in a store of sucking stones. They were pebbles but I call them stones. I distributed them equally among my four pockets, and sucked them turn and about. This raised a problem which I first solved in the following way. I had sixteen stones, four in each of my four pockets these being the two pockets of my trousers and the two pockets of my greatcoat. Taking a stone from the right pocket of my greatcoat, and putting it in my mouth, I replaced it in the right pocket of my greatcoat by a stone from the right pocket of my trousers, which I replaced by a stone from the left pocket of my trousers, which I replaced by a stone from the left pocket of my greatcoat, which I replaced by the stone which was in my mouth as soon as I was sucking it. Thus there were still four stones in each of my four pockets, but not quite the same stones [. . .] But this solution did not satisfy me fully. For it did not escape me that, by an extraordinary hazard, the four stones circulating thus might always be the same four. In which case, far from sucking

> sixteen stones turn and about, I was really sucking four, always the same, turn and about. (69)

Molloy goes on to problematize, rethink, and rework his method for sucking stones for an additional five pages before claiming that, "however imperfect my own solution was , I was pleased at having found it all alone, yes, quite pleased" (74). Throughout the passages, he appears to seek diversity. He wants to assure himself that he will get through all of his stones, that his formal practice will yield a multitude of possibilities. Although this section might be taken as merely a critique of a hyperrational Cartesianism, it also clearly mocks the escapism of modernist aesthetic symmetry. Modernism, even in its more revolutionary moments, acts as its own immanent escape from an oppressive, instrumental, and limiting rationality, but it also invariably ends up emulating the structural confines and metaphors of that very rationality. Weisberg correctly argues that in *Molloy,* "the 'mania' for an artful order, for a principle of distinction, is always contrasted with the condition of poverty and privation" (84). But it is important to add that these conditions are not only social problems in Beckett's mid- to late work. For Beckett, even the artist's power becomes poverty, and even private thought becomes privation. Finally, the artist ends up embodying the failures of a socioeconomic world predicated upon instrumental rationality and Cartesian dualism. As we have already seen, in Beckett's writing we almost always start with a self-referential or autonomous self, but the qualities of community and propriety that the bourgeois novel—from Richardson through Austen, Dickens, George Eliot, and E. M. Forster—had sought to negotiate as the criteria for polite society, have been thoroughly drained away. We still have a confined, autotelic self who, merely through the act of writing down his thoughts, seems to desire to communicate with an outside world, but this self's immanent, self-collapsing, compulsive, uncivilized behavior prohibits any real communion. In a figure like Molloy, we have a writer who appears to have become so himself, so pleased at having found and constructed his solutions all alone, that all intercourse with the outside world must either conform to the formal structures that he manipulates or else be eliminated, forgotten, or rejected.

In part 2 of the novel, we discover a voice that, at least at first, appears more sane, controlled, and socially adept than Molloy's. As the inspector sent to find Molloy and to "grasp the Molloy affair," Moran promises to shed some light on section 1 of the novel (98). As such, we pick up his "report" on Molloy with the same kind of interest that we might have had when picking up the earliest critical road maps to Joyce's *Ulysses* (92). But Moran does not really seem to be able to clarify either Molloy's meaning or the meanings of *Molloy.* He cannot fully decode the Molloy story. He follows Molloy, anxiously and carefully, so carefully, in fact, that he begins to emulate the formal dynamic of Molloy's writing and the formal obsessions of the Molloy section of the novel. He obsesses about his son and his mother, notes the similarities between his own name and the name of his descendant, and he begins constructing long lists of questions that offer possible solutions to the problems he seeks. Finally, he tells us, "I have spoken of a voice telling me things. I was getting to know it better now, to understand what it wanted. It did not use the words that Moran had been taught when he was little, [. . .] but in the end I understood this language" (175–76). As an agent reading and attempting to grasp the form of Molloy, Moran begins to follow along and understand that form, but he certainly does not clarify its meanings. This might be why Maurice Blanchot's 1959 review of the novel claimed that *Molloy* leads the reader on a "path of endless error" (142).

In *Aesthetic Theory,* Adorno recounts the experience of careful reading in his theory of mimesis. For Adorno, "truth content cannot be something made" (131). The work of art does not create truth; rather, truth is sedimented in it, or, as he explains, what has been repressed is "drawn into the dynamic of history" through art (131). For Adorno, art is mimetic in that it reflects the history into which it is drawn and from which it springs. "Under patient contemplation," Adorno explains, "artworks begin to move. To this extent they are truly afterimages of the primordial shudder in the age of reification" (79). In "patiently contemplating" the art object, the interpreting agent follows the inner dynamics of the work. Hence, the mimetic function of art is imitated by the interpreter, or, as Adorno says, "only those who imitate them understand them (125). The subject becomes dialectically enfolded into the artwork's mimesis of the historical moment. The result is an experience with history. The artwork has the character of a moment, and the experiencing subject encounters that moment through patiently contemplating the work. The work remembers the moment; art is an *anamnesis,* a mnemosyne, a type of communion that measures out both the appearance and disappearance of a specific historical point in time. But, Adorno further explains that artworks are ghosts of the moment, apparitions, rather than simply copies. In them the shudder [*erschüttertung*] of the moment is reenacted. To analyze the work is to become aware of the history sedimented in it, but in encountering the object and imitating it through patient contemplation, the subject shudders as well.

The whole of *Aesthetic Theory* builds toward Adorno's discussion of the "aesthetic shudder." As he explains:

> The experiencing subject, from which aesthetic experience distances itself, returns in aesthetic experience as a transaesthetic subject. The aesthetic shudder once again cancels the distance held by the subject.

> Although artworks offer themselves to observation, they at the same time disorient the observer who is held at the distance of a mere spectator; to him is revealed the truth of the work as if it must also be his own. The instant of this transition is art's highest. It rescues subjectivity, even subjective aesthetics, by negation of subjectivity. The subject, convulsed by art, has real experiences [*reale Erfahrungen*]; by strength of insight into the artwork as artwork, these experiences are those in which the subject's petrification in his own subjectivity dissolves and the narrowness of his self-positedness is revealed. (269)

This participation in the work's mimesis of the moment causes the subject to shudder. But if bourgeois experience is as profoundly interiorized and isolating as Adorno had argued it was in his 1933 *Kierkegaard: Construction of the Aesthetic,* then the experience that the reader of modernist autonomous art imitates is, precisely, the experience of immanence and isolation. By following the formal structure of a confined self, the reader experiences the truth of bourgeois interiority negatively. The interpreter experiences the limitations and confinements of autonomy, and this is precisely what happens to Moran. As his anxiety about his own textuality and his understanding of Molloy reach a zenith, Moran's story folds back on itself. He began by telling us, "It is midnight. The rain is beating on the windows. I am calm." (92). Having followed after Molloy, Moran concludes by returning to his initial words. He explains that "I went back to the house and wrote, It is midnight. The rain is beating on the windows. It was not midnight. It was not raining"(176). As an interpreter, Moran follows Molloy in earnest, but in so doing, he also begins to emulate Molloy's cyclic, repetitive, and formally obsessive writing. In writing his own journey in the form of a report to be presented to the authorities, Moran has begun to worry about the aesthetics and the physicality of the text itself, and about how that physicality mirrors his own vulnerability. Like Molloy, then, Moran the reader has become aware of his own textuality, of his integral relationship to the anterior narratives that have confined and produced his identity. What's more, he realizes that in converting consciousness into text, he has joined mind to body and, subsequently, rendered legible the vulnerabilities and interdependencies of both. When mind and body join in a vulnerable text, *Molloy* draws to a conclusion, but Moran's narrative leads us directly to the next volume in the *Trilogy, Malone Dies,* a text obsessed with its own physicality.

As a trope, the threatened notebook, dubbed by H. Porter Abbott the *Topoi* of the "intercalated narrative," has remained a central component of the temporal schema of the English novel since its inception in *Pamela* and Richardson's concept of "writing to the moment." For Abbott, as a mode of storytelling, "intercalated narrative" requires that the story we read is written by at least one of the characters and that the "time of the writing is contained by the time of the events recorded" (71). In Stoker's *Dracula* this trope underscores the novel's anxiety about its own truth claims. As casebooks of evidence filled with letters, journal entries, newspaper clippings, and the like, Gothic texts like *Dracula* dedicate a great deal of their stylistic dynamism to proving their documentary and empirical character. The text must be considered not only as a story, but as a material object that plays a role within that story. Jürgen Habermas touches on this singularly modern social phenomenon in *The Structural Transformation of the Public Sphere* by arguing that letter writing itself was a sort of precursor to the subjectivity fostered and reflected by the bourgeois novel. For Habermas, through letter writing the enlightened individual, capable of entering into "purely human relations" with those in his or her intimate sphere, unfolds his or herself in his or her subjectivity, the "innermost core of the private" (48–49). The letter becomes a physical imprint, or, if you will, the proof, of the metaphysical soul, and, likewise, the diary acted as "a letter addressed to the sender, and the first-person narrative became a conversation with one's self addressed to another person" (49). In some sense, then, any novel that betrays anxiety about its own physicality and truth claims attempts to connect the mind to the body. As a conversation with the self addressed to an audience, the intercalated narrative forms a kind of archeological record of that which cannot be seen, of the most intimate thoughts, of the solitary self. It converts the unseen mind into the textual body. Nonetheless, writing, the body, and the mind are all juxtaposed with solitude here, or, in more resolute terminology, with confinement. The material presence of the manuscript gets linked to and proves the existence of the private self—the immaterial soul—of its fictive writer, and anything that threatens the existence of the documents likewise threatens the interiority of the writer. Hence, Dracula, who is coded as premodern, never speaks for himself in Stoker's novel because he does not count, so to speak, as a private self, but rather as an inchoate, threatening other.

As we have already noted, for someone like Fanon, the social paradox of liberation as confinement finds ideological resolution when the subject realizes that his or her only wealth resides in the capacity to remain hermetic, shut up in the self. The private, Cartesian soul comes to form a protected space that seeks to escape temporality and to write itself onto infinity, and onto the objects in its sphere, only as it also stigmatizes corporeality as untrue and vulgar. In the end, the written self, whether it be Stoker's Jonathan Harker, Maturin's Ippolitto di Montorio, or even Richardson's Clarissa Harlow, marks out precisely the territory in which bourgeois subjectivity enacts its own reification. Subjectivity as the inner core of privacy becomes mythologized and the dualism of the permanent written subject, the static prison of the ever-same, gets packaged as perpetual internal freedom. The fictive written self comes to mirror the limitations of bourgeois subjectivity. Up to this point, we have seen how Beckett uses the Gothic forms implicit in the domestic novel to demonstrate that the supposedly Cartesian male mind remains as confined as the corporeal, feminized body, or, that is, that the hierarchical logic of a mind/body dualism always works to isolate the bourgeois subject and to leave that subject with an authentic sense of powerlessness. Politically speaking, then, Beckett's work represents the social stasis of the ever-same. Unlike many of the writers before him, however, Beckett's writing refuses to repackage the ever-same as liberating or, for that matter, as qualitatively different from the incarceration that characterized the female Gothic. If the individual's only wealth is his or her interiority, then alienation from the social acts as the a priori condition of what modern culture calls the "human condition."

Like Molloy, however, Malone recognizes and admits to the gender identity problems that come with the narrative tradition he inherits. In fact, he reminds us on several occasions that he is actually unable to locate his own genitalia. He explains, "I do not expect to see my sex again" (235). In *Anomalous States,* David Lloyd claims that, under a masculine imperial economy "possession of the phallus becomes the index of authenticity, of control over identity," but Beckett's Malone does not evince any real nostalgia for the power or time of the father (54). He writes because he has the power to do so, but in recognizing that his exercise book demarcates the boundaries of his identity, he also recognizes that writing will not provide the escape from social confinement that modernist writers had hoped. The central conceit of *Malone Dies,* that a dying writer inscribes his tales in a notebook in order to pass the time while he dies, allows us to fit the novel in with the intercalated narrative structure discussed by Abbott. The stories Malone plans to write will be, as he explains, "almost lifeless, like the teller" (180). He plans to tell four stories and, time permitting, to speak of those things that remain in his possession. He never really finishes his stories. In fact each one tends to slide into another, and Malone has a hard time keeping all of the characters and plot details separate.

Near the beginning of the novel, Malone, trapped in his sparse, antiseptic room, writes in his exercise book, "What am I doing now, I wonder, losing time or gaining it?" (182). Here, he invokes one of the most significant paradoxes of the intercalated narrative. He contemplates whether the individual who inscribes memories, thoughts, and stories in a text is wasting time—failing to experience real life—or gaining it by making him or herself permanent and indelible through the act of re-presenting, and so repossessing the inner core of the private. Hence, he returns to the obsession with aesthetic autonomy and immortality that we saw in Stephen Dedalus's lecture on *Hamlet.* On the one hand, like Stephen, Malone links aesthetic vision to the possibility of transcendence. On the other hand, unlike Stephen, Malone admits that he could be losing time rather than gaining it even though, as he explains, "aesthetics" are on his side (182). In *Malone Dies,* then, we also see Beckett returning to the problem of temporal recovery and nostalgia that circumscribed the life of the narrator in *First Love.* Following the pattern set up in *Molloy,* however, Malone admits and ruminates about his material and narrative condition rather than seeking a return to the father's time. Malone's notebook acts as a metaphysical space in which to stake out the boundaries of the self. The trick here is that Malone writes with a pencil, not a pen, so the journal recounting his experience is erasable, and he soon begins to conflate his own experiences with those of the characters who occupy the fictional stories he tells himself. Malone's journal foregrounds the fact that repossessing the self through textual fiat does not produce temporal transcendence so much as it imitates the conditions of, and so reproduces, confinement. The autonomy promised by Wilde's theories of art and dialecticized by Joyce's re-envisioning of Wilde qua Stephen Dedalus, is fully negated in this move by Beckett. Here we have a narrator who cannot hope to transcend time by converting consciousness into text like Stephen Dedalus. Instead, Malone's notebook becomes a metaphor of his external confinement while the tool with which he inscribes his identity, his nub of a pencil, gets smaller and smaller. He acknowledges this equation by writing, "this exercise book is my life, [. . .] it has taken me a long time to resign myself to that" (274).

Malone begins by commenting on his "present state," and he indicates that he will continue to remind himself of his whereabouts and of his context throughout his attempt at narrative. Going a step beyond the pattern established in *Molloy, Malone Dies* makes the act of writing and the temporal space—the historicity—of writing itself into the subject of the fiction. Though Malone obsesses about form, the text itself points to the fact that forms are historical. Being trapped within the confines of a certain form also means that one is unavoidably situated within a context or a discourse. Beckett's method of invoking the forms and structures from the past works in opposition to the pattern of aesthetic transcendence hoped for by Stephen Dedalus, then, and the physical setting and historicity of the writer serve to frame Beckett's entire novel. Malone explains:

> Present State. This room seems to be mine. I can find no other explanation to my being left in it. All this time. Unless it be at the behest of one of the powers that be. [. . .] It is not a room in a hospital or madhouse. [. . .] And when I look out of the window it is clear to me, from certain signs, that I am not in a house of rest in any sense

> of the word. No, this is just a plain private room apparently, in what appears to be a plain ordinary house. I do not remember how I got here. (183)

Malone's room, another refigured maternal space like the one that inaugurates *Molloy,* belongs to him—it is his space—and this *intérieur* is in a "plain ordinary house." Malone is quite obsessed with the notion of possession, with what is "his." This theme is reflected in the novel's persistent vivisection of the dialectic of possessing and losing consciousness. Joyce begins *A Portrait of the Artist as a Young Man* with an analysis of the way consciousness unfolds for the newborn Stephen. Stephen's first encounter is with sound, with the story of the "moocow" and "Baby Tuckoo" told by his father, Simon. Hearing brings Stephen into consciousness, and within Joyce's novel, sound quickly translates into music and art, into Stephen's first "Tra la la la, Tra la la lady" (2). If Stephen's bildungsroman ends with his journal, Malone's *Todsroman* is completely circumscribed by one, and Beckett articulates the dissolution of modernism's speculation on the power of consciousness through the figure of sound. In this tale of the loss of consciousness, Beckett's aged artist, Malone, marks out hearing ("I have listened") as his primary mode of orientation to the "present state"(183). He listens to that which transpires outside of his room, in order to attempt some epistemology of his space, and Malone's stories invariably repeat, in one way or another, his initial attempt to produce an epistemology of personal space. As Malone lies in his bed dying, he realizes that he has no real access to the world outside and must rely fully and completely on his senses and on a dialectic of subjectivity and its private meaning. Throughout the novel, Malone seems to evince two great fears regarding subjectivity. On the one hand, he believes that his consciousness will never fully dissolve, that he will continue to be more isolated and progressively less coherent forever. On the other hand, much like Stoker's Jonathan Harker, Malone seems terrified of losing his "little memorandum book and its little special pencil," for it is in this book that he details the failings of consciousness itself (230).

Later in the text, Malone makes this connection between physical and narrative confinement explicit when he complains that "in spite of my stories I continue to fit in this room" (235). Thus, the social dialectic in *Malone Dies* always recedes into an immanent dialectic of Malone's being-toward-death, just as the stories Malone tells always circle back to his own undead subjectivity. As Abbott illustrates, the trope of the threatened notebook has never been quite so unambiguous before nor its fictive author quite so confined. As Malone continually drops his pencil and misplaces his notebook, we witness more physical gaps in the text as, for all intents and purposes, its moribund writer temporarily ceases to be. Like the escape into the private sphere performed by the women of the female Gothic, the escape into form here acts as a paradoxical escape into confinement. Beckett's *Trilogy* demonstrates that the mind is written on and by the body and, once again, that a political and cultural system based on Cartesianism invariably devolves into a Gothic narrative.

V. CONCLUSION: LITERALIZING CONFINEMENT FROM PAGE TO STAGE

In *A Singular Modernity,* Fredric Jameson argues that Beckett's style consciously reflects on as it critiques the formal innovations of his modernist predecessors. Finally, Jameson perceives in Beckett a modernist writer who has moved so far into form that content itself has become excluded (200). Although Jameson's is certainly a valuable and, to a large extent, correct insight, he misses the crucial fact that beginning with the *Trilogy,* Beckett actually allegorizes in the figures of Molloy and Malone the male modernist writer who has begun to identify so entirely with form. Formalism has itself become a metaphor in Beckett. In *The Unnamable,* he renders a figure confined within a jar, obsessed with his own bodily functions, his "virile member," and his long-lost name. The Unnamable has actually become his own text to the extent that, unlike either Molloy or Malone, he really has no stories to tell and no teleology to trace out. At this point in his writing, Beckett has achieved a dialectical *Aufhebung* of content and form, mind and body so thoroughly, that the final text of the *Trilogy* actually represents an attempt to rethink the problem of autonomy in an entirely new way. If autonomy was always already enfolded into confinement, then simply realizing this problem, simply imagining an emblematic character, accurately called the Unnamable, does not bring the story of late-Western notions of subjectivity to a conclusion. Rather, this "character as text" shows precisely how asocial the social world of bourgeois privacy and autonomy has become.

It seems that, for Beckett, the next aesthetic step was to show how life in contemporary capitalist societies nearly always accedes to this logic. While working on the final stages of his *Trilogy,* Beckett began to write *Waiting for Godot,* and to enter into the phase of his career that determined his reputation and brought him international fame. By moving from the page to the stage, Beckett shifted the problematic of spatial confinement, of insularity and autonomy, out of the domestic interiors of his neo-Gothic prose experiments and onto the stage itself.[32] In a sense, the sparse theatrical pieces that followed the trilogy offer in the literal space of the stage the pure formalization—the literalization—of the theme of captivity. The characters in *Godot,* in *Endgame,* in *Happy Days,* in *Not I,* and in *Play* all foreground the fact that their metaphysical and social limitations are fully realized by their actual literal confinement on the stage. Moreover, as we, the audience, move around rather uncomfortably in our seats during the performance of a Beckett play, we become aware of our own confinements, of the discomfort we feel at witnessing a kind of aestheticized form of incarceration. By enfolding this carceral narrative—not just the limitations placed on the artist, but also those placed on the audience—into the experience of his drama, Beckett has made himself and his various audiences into part of the very problem that his plays confront. When he transitions from a writer of prose fiction to a playwright, Beckett imagines the circumscribed space of the theater itself as a metaphor for confinement, and, as such, he places his audience inside of the Cartesian Gothic narrative he has constructed.

EPILOGUE

The Poetics of Fear

Gothic Inheritance at the End of Modernity

I began this study by discussing the dialectics of genre and of how an older literary form like the Gothic was preserved and transformed by the Irish national imaginary in the era of the modernist novel. In *Negative Dialectics,* Theodor Adorno claims that dialectics constitutes a self-conscious exploration of our objective social and contextual delusions (406). Dialectics looks to our ideological and social limitations and critiques them. The main criticism of the dialectical method remains that it is always already inside the very system that it critiques. Dialectics tries to break through and overcome limitations from inside. At its best, in other words, dialectics is a method of immanent critique. By situating Oscar Wilde, James Joyce, and Samuel Beckett inside of the Gothic tradition and inside of the history of colonized Ireland, I have tried to position Irish modernism itself as a dialectical and immanent critique of the Irish Gothic, as a reflection on Ireland's political and national imaginary. Moreover, *Terror and Irish Modernism* comprises an effort to demonstrate that historicism, in all of its various left-political strains, must consider the problem of immanent critique—and so of formalism—seriously and dialectically. Literary forms and genres must be read as part of the movement of history, as elements of the flux of alienation, and as indices of political collectivities, both conscious and unconscious.

Throughout, I have argued that the female Gothic renders explicit the structural dispossession implicit in a patriarchal social economy. Following a basic ideological line, the novels of Anne Radcliffe and her imitators articulate how female sexuality and identity operates within that economy. In texts as diverse as Radcliffe's *The Italian* and Charlotte Brontë's *Jane Eyre,* woman's sexuality, and subsequently her role in society, must be confined to the compulsorily heterosexual, maternal, nondesiring, material, and dependent. Outside of these supposedly safe zones of identity, woman is threatened on the one side by the violence of unfettered male desire and on the other by the vicissitudes madness. To some extent, safe confinement was juxtaposed against unsafe imprisonment. The solution to violent confinement was a kinder, gentler form of confinement. No doubt, to the eighteenth-century society the attraction of this schema of social and physical limitation lay precisely in the fact that it generated both a safe haven in which feminine identity might unfold and public consciousness of the very material problems faced by women who had neither the economic nor the cultural means to find such a haven for themselves. So far, then, my basic arguments about late eighteenth- and early nineteenth-century fiction confirm the fundamental critical premises proposed by Nancy Armstrong's *Desire and Domestic Fiction* (1987) and reasserted by Kate Ferguson Ellis's *The Contested Castle* (1989). But, I have also argued throughout that beginning with the novels of Maria Edgeworth and the manic, Radcliffe-style Unionist Gothic of Charles Robert Maturin, Irish writing began to tailor the Gothic's ambivalence concerning female confinement to the Irish colonial situation. Like the women in England's intimate spheres, the Irish people experienced structural dispossession, the historical disinheritance and disenfranchisement of political subjects by cultural, legal, linguistic, and economic systems.

With the burgeoning of the bourgeois public sphere in the eighteenth century, the family had become the ahistorical cynosure of English national identity. As Edmund Burke claimed in his *Reflections on the Revolution in France,* the British system allowed for "the image of a relation of blood, binding up the constitution of our country with our dearest domestic ties, adopting all our fundamental laws into the bosom of our family affection" (30). The bourgeois family, overseen by a benevolent and fully autonomous patriarch, came to represent both the symbol of England's cultural identity as it entered into the age of imperialist expansion and the apotheosis of the private individual's social identity and freedom. Being a proper family man mattered then as it still matters in most bourgeois societies today. But the longed-for autonomy, the right to govern one's own personal space and affairs that had been promised by the separate spheres, was finally the sole province of men and corresponded directly to the ownership of private property. Subsequently, as I said in chapter 1, in the social economy of desire imagined by the Gothic novels of the day, women figure as objects possessed, never as subjects allowed any real self-possession.

The female-Gothic heroine—Radcliffe's Emily St. Aubert of *The Mysteries of Udolpho* provides a suitable archetype—finds herself perpetually threatened by a premodern, feudal lord who often plans to take both her body and the land entailed to that body by the inheritance, entailment, and dowry systems. At some point, of course, this heroine will be saved by a more affectionate and doting potential patriarch, one who will protect her and allow her some limited form of sovereignty over the intimate sphere that will come to circumscribe her life and her identity. He becomes the modern paterfamilias against which the premodern, feudal lord must be judged. Consequently, however, a certain amount of irremediable fear comes with being a woman or with being identified with the feminine and, so, with the eternally dispossessed, confined, and threatened. This fear animates the Gothic's hallucinatory, paranoiac narrative structure. Fear motivates and controls the dynamic flow of the narrative, and even the figure of the benevolent patriarch cannot fully dispel the abject horrors and potential deracination embodied in Gothic narrative. Hence, Gothic romances in the Radcliffe tradition do not merely end with a marriage, but very often with the birth of an acknowledgeable male heir who can fill the position of future patriarch while also repossessing the body of the mother, at least in a figurative sense. At first glance, this male heir appears as a hybrid who embodies the union of masculine rational authority and feminine corporeal reproduction. Finally, however, the Gothic's male heir points to the desire to ameliorate woman's structural dispossession only as he inevitably reasserts the very male/female binary that his presence intends to resolve. The Gothic male heir does not dispel fear so much as he actually signifies its presence beneath the deceptively placid surface of bourgeois domestic propriety. With the birth of the heir, the system might appear to have solved a problem, but in point of fact it has merely reaffirmed its initial social schema and returned to something resembling a patriarchal status quo.

Following the 1798 rebellion in Ireland led by Theobald Wolfe Tone and the United Irishmen, the rhetoric of unionism was characterized in Irish and English government documents, in newspapers, and in pamphlets as a marriage between a self-threatening, feminized Irish people and the great English patriarch. The supple and convincing rhetoric of the patriarchal family metaphor was stretched to accommodate colonial ideology. In the wake of such rhetoric, Edgeworth wrote her first novel, *Castle Rackrent,* which began to retrofit several of the tropes of the female Gothic romance to the Irish sociopolitical context. By 1807, a mere seven years after the formal passage of the Acts of Union, Maturin's *Fatal Revenge* came to embody not only the tropes of the female Gothic rewritten within an Irish context, but also the attendant male gender anxiety and disorientation that followed the marriage metaphor as it made its way into Ireland. In Maturin's novels, the fear of being identified with the feminine that had animated the Gothic romance was often attached to male characters. The Irish novels that followed in this tradition tended to code masculinity as both threat and threatened, as terrorizing and terrorized, and a certain Irish Gothic poetics of fear was born. Like the Gothic's male heir, this hybrid form, which joined masculine identity to the fears embodied in the confinement narratives of the female Gothic, worked to represent the problems of structural dispossession by showing how men who were confined within traditionally feminine spaces would inevitably transform into terrors. In the Unionist Gothic, men became first the victims and then the victimizers. They became, in other words, justified victims. Following Maturin, writers such as Joseph Sheridan Le Fanu and Bram Stoker wrote Gothic fiction that sought to flee from this disabling double bind. In Le Fanu's "Carmilla" and Stoker's *Dracula,* however, nothing seems more horrifying than being as confined as a woman, and confined male characters work very hard to escape from just such an association. Read in light of the Gothic literary tradition, in fact, Irish history itself had become feminized, a nightmare from which a number of misogynist male writers anxiously, desperately, and sometimes furiously fought to awake.

In chapter 1, I argued that the novels of the Unionist Gothic came to embody not only the contextual problems of the Acts of Union, but also the larger historical and structural crisis of political ressentiment. Defined by Nietzsche in *On the Genealogy of Morality,* ressentiment is, simply put, the hallowing of "revenge under the name of justice—as if justice were basically only a further development of the feeling of being wounded—and retroactively to raise to honor along with revenge the *reactive* affects in general and without exception" (48). For Nietzsche, ressentiment comes from the spirit of *reactive* consciousness, or, that is, from a consciousness incapable of acting on its own, incapable of imagining a positive definition or identity for itself, a consciousness predicated on its own fear, resentment, or envy of the other. Ressentiment has no positive content and can manufacture no active, life-affirming philosophy. It can offer no productive political vision. The historical cycle triggered by ressentiment appears endlessly destructive. Nietzsche's philosophy does not seek to do away with violence but, rather, to do away with the resentful weakness—the logic of the justified victim—that triggers it, for this logic is the real enemy of peace and justice. The logic of the justified victim produces only a social poetics of fear. By donning the cloak of the justified victim, the fictional Montorios and Harkers of the Irish Gothic tradition, as well as real-world neo-imperial states and extrastate actors such as modern-day terrorists, invoke ressentiment, invoke their own weakness, in order to gain support and, paradoxically, to appear strong. Moreover, in being fully *reactive,* this social poetics of fear always comes attached to a sense of urgent immediacy. Such approaches don't need to have a positive vision. They just need to *react* immediately and forcefully when something happens.

In response to this sense of immediacy, to this intensifying of what are finally tried and true positions, I want to offer a quotation from an unlikely source: "The Economist and the present-day terrorists have one common root, namely, *subservience to spontaneity*" (74). The quote comes from V. I. Lenin's 1902 political pamphlet, *What Is to Be Done?* Lenin himself is surprisingly circumspect here, and I read his claim about spontaneity as an insight into the problem of political immediacy and, subsequently, into the Hegelian conception of mediation. Why do entrenched and revolutionary positions often fail? Well, it's because entrenched revolutionaries often fail to take the time to think about the whole picture, to reflect on what's going on in the world, to plan for the future, or to search for innovative solutions. They want immediate action, and they don't bother to think about what final shape that action might take. Blow them all up, they say, and either we or God will sort out the details later. This kind of thinking seems disintegrated, fragmentary, and ignorant of the fact that real political and social change requires an abstract, mediating theory just as much as it requires a concrete, immediate practice. Finally, in dialectical thinking, to mediate means to challenge the sense that everything in the world is immediately open to understanding, apprehension, and comprehension. To mediate is to open up a space in which to contemplate and debate the meaning of an object, an action, or an event and to imagine precisely how one might respond to or negate this object, action, or event.

In the modernist novels of Wilde, Joyce, and Beckett, we encounter writers who attempt to mediate the problems of—and the obsession with—structural disinheritance. Literary modernism works to think through and to critique structural paradigms as much as it works to represent them. Wilde works to achieve this by rendering social conventions subject to the will of the canny aesthete. By acknowledging and manipulating recognized conventions, the aesthete converts a potential weakness like confinement or dispossession into an unexpected strength. Wilde's aesthetes may be confined by social or artistic conventions, but they also display the keen ability to manipulate and expand the horizons of conventionality itself. In mocking the Gothic's primal scene of confinement, Joyce's *Ulysses* invokes the critique of dispossession offered by the Unionist Gothic, only to suggest alternate ways of imagining the narratives that come to us from the past. Joyce's dialectic works to overcome the limitations of the Gothic, and, so, his dialectics, like the optimistic "yes" that concludes the chorus of voices in *Ulysses,* remains affirmative and utopian.

Adorno concludes his *Negative Dialectics* by arguing that an intellectually honest, contemporary dialectical method must make the final move of turning against itself (406). Beckett's fiction makes just such a move. Beckett's writing embraces the limitations of the Gothic in order to allow those limitations to represent the untruth of the contemporary world. As supposedly private individuals, we are willfully confined, asocial, and fearful beings, Beckett tells us. Where Joyce deploys elements of the Gothic's confinement tale to imagine a remarkably open-ended way of approaching history, Beckett converts it into a carefully pared-down critique of the gender politics of modern society. Where Joyce is a liberator, Beckett shows us just how all-encompassing and internalized the social and philosophical machinery of confinement has become.[1] Setting their separate responses to terror and to Ireland's Gothic national imaginary side by side, however, allows us to see two twentieth-century thinkers who struggled to grasp the gendered, colonial, and aesthetic relationship between fear, violence, and personal isolation. This is all to say that Joyce and Beckett connect the problem of structural dispossession to the logic of the justified victim, and so, they provide literary mediations of sociopolitical phenomena. Taken together, Joyce and Beckett both warn us precisely against a social world that allows consciousness to shrink into a detached egoism, into a genus of confinement that produces a mass phenomenon of thoroughly fearful, thoroughly isolated individuals.

Notes

1. GOTHIC DOUBLE BINDS, OR, IRISH TERRORISTS CONFRONT AN UNHOLY UNION

1. In fact, the saint's role as an icon of homoerotic desire owes much to the Renaissance paintings by Reni and by Giovanni Bassi (*Il Sodoma*). The appropriation of Saint Sebastian as a gay icon has a long history, but becomes an explicit subject of intellectual conversation after the 1909 publication of George Eekhoud's article, "Saint Sébastien Dans la Peinture." See George Eekhoud, "Saint Sébastien Dans la Peinture," *Akdemos* 1 (February 15, 1909): 171–75.

2. Chris Baldick's 1989 "Introduction" to the Oxford Classics edition of Maturin's *Melmoth the Wanderer* problematizes the claims about *Melmoth*'s status as the "last—and possibly the greatest—of the Gothic novels in the line from Walpole through Radcliffe and Lewis" (ix). For Baldick, such claims limit the boundaries of the genre and of Maturin's various borrowings from nonGothic sources. Baldick, Chris, "Introduction," *Melmoth the Wanderer* (New York: Oxford UP, 1989): vii–xix.

3. Quoted in Charles Coote, *History of the Union of the Kingdoms of Great Britain and Ireland; With an Introductory Survey of Hibernian Affairs, Traced from the Times of the Celtic Colonisation* (London: S. Hamilton, 1802), 31–32.

4. This is the basic argument of Richard Kearney's "Myth and Motherland," *Ireland's Field Day,* ed. Seamus Deane, 61–80 (Notre Dame, IN: University of Notre Dame Press, 1986).

5. See Theodor Adorno, *Aesthetic Theory,* trans. Robert Hullot-Kentor (Minneapolis: University of Minnesota Press, 1997), 232.

6. If the marriage was a particularly unhappy one for the Irish, it was also a source of anxiety for the British, who, as the economic beneficiaries of the Acts of Union, faced the difficulties of negotiating the contentious, occasionally explosive politics of the "Irish Question" throughout the nineteenth century. For a markedly thorough discussion of the economic repercussions of Irish colonization during the era of the Acts of Union, see R. D. Collison Black's *Economic Thought and the Irish Question, 1817–1870* (London: Cambridge University Press, 1960).

7. My analysis here and throughout draws on Walter Benjamin's discussion of allegory and history in *The Origin of German Tragic Drama* (New York: Verso, 1998), 175.

8. For an overview of the nineteenth-century Irish Gothic, see Julian Moynahan, "The Politics of Anglo-Irish Gothic: Charles Robert Maturin, Joseph Sheridan Le Fanu, and the Return of the Repressed," in *Anglo-Irish: The Literary Imagination in a Hyphenated Culture* (Princeton, NJ: Princeton University Press, 1995), 116.

9. See Luke Gibbons, "Identity without a Centre: Allegory, History and Irish Nationalism," in *Transformations in Irish Culture* (Notre Dame, IN: University of Notre Dame Press, 1996), 134–48.

10. In particular, see L. H. Platt, *Joyce and the Anglo-Irish: A study of Joyce and the Literary Revival* (Atlanta, GA: Rodolpi, 1998); Enda Duffy, *The Subaltern Ulysses* (Minneapolis: University of Minnesota Press, 1994); and Emer Nolan, *James Joyce and Nationalism* (New York: Routledge, 1995), all of whom put a great deal of pressure on the hegemonic position of the Anglo-Irish.

11. See Daniel Corkery's *The Hidden Ireland* (Dublin: M. H. Gill and Son, 1956), as well as Corkery's *Synge and the Anglo-Irish* (New York: Russell and Russell, 1965).

12. For a more intensive and vitriolic version of this argument, see W. J. McCormack's *Dissolute Characters: Irish Literary History through Balzac, Sheridan Le Fanu, Yeats and Bowen* (New York: Manchester University Press, 1993).

13. Nolan's *James Joyce and Nationalism* and Platt's *Joyce and the Anglo-Irish* in particular follow this basic tendency.

14. The arch-example of this kind of counterargument is also at the heart of David Lloyd's *Anomalous States: Irish Writing and the Post-Colonial Moment* (Durham, NC: Duke University Press, 1994). Lloyd suggests that simple notions of nationalism generally rely on a kind of mythic nostalgia.

15. Implicit throughout will be an analysis of how the dialectical kind of formalism recommended by Adorno's writings differs from the recent rise of "New Formalism." See Marjorie Levinson's "What Is New Formalism?" *PMLA* 122, no. 2 (2007): 558–69, for a review of the issues underlying New Formalism. The Marxian dialectical method of critique offered by Adorno—and by Fredric Jameson for that matter—rejects the rigid distinction between form and history that seems to drive much of the writings of the New Formalists. In addition to being a literary history, *Terror and Irish Modernism* works to produce an analysis of how literary forms are themselves always already historical ruins, elements of a history and, inescapably, of a political context. As Adorno's "Cultural Criticism and Society," in *Prisms,* trans. Samuel Webber and Shierry Webber (Cambridge, MA: MIT Press, 1967), 19–34, makes quite clear, the very distinction between form and history, between an internal analysis of the work of art and an external analysis of the context that produced the work, is an act of reification.

16. See Mary Jean Corbett, "Public Affections and Familial Politics: Burke, Edgeworth, and Ireland in the 1790s," in *Allegories of Union in Irish and English Writing, 1790–1870: Politics, History, and Family from*

Edgeworth to Arnold (New York: Cambridge University Press, 2000), 21–50. for a fuller account of the gender politics encoded in Burke's *Reflections.*

17. See Martin Burke's "Piecing Together a Shattered Past: The Historical Writings of the United Irish Exiles in America," in *United Irishmen: Republicanism, Radicalism, and Rebellion,* ed. David Dickson, Daire Keogh, and Kevin Whelan, 297–306 (Dublin: Lilliput, 1993).

18. See R. F. Foster, *Modern Ireland: 1600–1972* (New York: Viking, 1988), 275–76.

19. Quoted in Coote, *History of the Union,* 76–77.

20. In "Marriage Against Inclination: The Union and Caricature," *Acts of Union: The Causes, Contexts, and Consequences of the Act of Union,* ed. Daire Keogh and Kevin Whelan, 140–58 (Portland, OR: Four Courts Press, 2001), Nicholas Robinson collects and discusses an entire series of these political cartoons. The image "Carrying the Union," originally published in March of 1800 by W. Holland, is currently listed in the British Museum's *Catalogue of Political and Personal Satires* (which was published in eleven volumes between 1870 and 1954) as cartoon 9462A.

21. See Jane Elizabeth Dougherty's "Mr. and Mrs. England: The Act of Union as National Marriage" in Keogh and Whelan, *Acts of Union,* 202–15.

22. Eve Kosofsky Sedgwick lays out the basics of these tropes in "The Structure of Gothic Convention," *The Coherence of Gothic Conventions* (New York: Methuen, 1975), 9–36.

23. See Nancy Armstrong. *Desire and Domestic Fiction: A Political History of the Novel* (New York: Oxford University Press, 1987).

24. See Jürgen Habermas, *The Structural Transformation of the Public Sphere: An Inquiry into a Category of Bourgeois Society,* trans. Thomas Burger and Frederick Lawrence (Cambridge, MA: MIT Press, 1991), 55.

25. See my "Formalism and Its Malcontents: Benjamin and de Man on the Function of Allegory," *New Literary History* 35, no. 4 (2004): 663–83.

26. See Robert Miles, "Anne Radcliffe and Matthew Lewis," in *A Companion to the Gothic,* ed. David Punter, 41–57 (New York: Routledge, 2000). See also, Eve Kosofsky Sedgwick's *Between Men: English Literature and Male Homosocial Desire* (New York: Columbia University Press, 1985).

27. See David Lloyd's conception of counternationalism and transvaluation in "Counterparts: *Dubliners,* Masculinity, and Temperance Nationalism," in *Semicolonial Joyce,* ed. Derek Attridge and Marjorie Howes, 128–49 (New York: Cambridge University Press, 2000). See especially, pages 131–34, which deal with Celtic nationalism and the attempt to face a "feminized" identity.

28. In addition to completing my exploration of aesthetic autonomy in *Ulysses,* the Joyce chapter contributes to the growing Jewish studies discussions of Joyce's work represented by Marilyn Reizbaum's *James Joyce's Judaic Other* (Stanford, CA: Stanford University Press, 1999), and Neil Davison's *James Joyce,* Ulysses, *and the Construction of Jewish Identity* (London: Cambridge University Press, 1996).

29. See Eyal Amiran, *Wandering and Home: Beckett's Metaphysical Narrative* (University Park: Penn State University Press, 1993), for one of the fullest accounts of Beckett's role within the European metaphysical tradition. For readings that attempt to balance Beckett-as-aesthetic philosophy with

Beckett-as-political partisan, see James Martin Harding, "Trying to Understand Godot: Adorno, Beckett, and the Senility of Dialectics," in *Adorno and "A Writing of the Ruins": Essays on Modern Aesthetics and Anglo-American Culture* (Albany: State University of New York Press, 1997), 51–64; David Weisberg, *Chronicles of Disorder: Samuel Beckett and the Cultural Politics of the Modern Novel* (Albany: State University of New York Press, 2000).

2. THE WRONG MARRIAGE

1. See James Newcomer's "*Castle Rackrent:* The Disingenuous Thady Quirk," in *Family Chronicles: Maria Edgeworth's* Castle Rackrent, ed. Cóilín Owens, 79–85 (Dublin: Wolfhound, 1987), and Elizabeth Harden's "Transparent Thady Quirk," in Owens, *Family Chronicles,* 86–96.

2. See Julian Moynahan, "The Politics of Anglo-Irish Gothic: Charles Robert Maturin, Joseph Sheridan Le Fanu, and the Return of the Repressed," in *Anglo-Irish: The Literary Imagination in a Hyphenated Culture* (Princeton, NJ: Princeton University Press, 1995), 109–35; and Margot Gayle Backus's *The Gothic Family Romance: Heterosexuality and the Anglo-Irish Colonial Order* (Durham, NC: Duke University Press, 1999).

3. In *Maria Edgeworth's Irish Writing,* Brian Hollingworth calls attention to the double strategies that mark what appears to be the "innocent," straightforward text that is *Castle Rackrent.*

4. See Moynahan, "The Politics of Anglo-Irish Gothic," 116; Norman A. Jeffares, "Maturin the Innovator," in *Images of Invention: Essays on Irish Writing* (Gerrards Cross, UK: Colin Smythe, 1996), 131. Moynahan and Jeffares read *Melmoth* as the apotheosis of the Gothic tradition begun by Horace Walpole's *The Castle of Otranto.* Chris Baldick's 1989 "Introduction" to the Oxford Classics edition of Maturin's *Melmoth the Wanderer* problematizes the claims about *Melmoth*'s status as the "last—and possibly the greatest—of the Gothic novels in the line from Walpole through Radcliffe and Lewis" (ix). For Baldick, such claims limit the boundaries of the genre and of Maturin's various borrowings from nongothic sources.

5. In "Maturin as Innovator," Jeffares reads Maturin's writings in light of Wordsworth's *Lyrical Ballads* in order to claim that, as in *Ballads,* Maturin came "to see Irish resistance to English rule as part of a clash between two cultures, one nationalistic and romantic, based on Gaelic folk tradition and the 'natural' emotions of a native population living in close contact with nature, and the other cosmopolitan and neoclassical, making nature conform to the habits and tastes of society" (131). Moynahan locates in Maturin's texts "both dread of a native revival and some longing for it" (116). In Backus, *The Gothic Family Romance,* Maturin comes to represent the ascendancy's repressed, self-consuming guilt. Nicola Watson's *Revolution and the Form of the British Novel, 1790–1825* (Oxford: Clarendon, 1994) cites an 1819 edition of *Blackwood's* magazine as listing Maturin as one of the undesirably Jacobin authors of the Shelley, Keats, Byron ilk (117).

6. See, in particular, Jacqueline Pearson, "Masculinizing the Novel: Women Writers and Intertextuality in Charles Robert Maturin's *The Wild Irish Boy,*" *Studies in Romanticism* 36 (Winter 1997): 635–50.

7. See Dale Kramer, *Charles Robert Maturin* (New York: Twayne, 1973), 26. Kramer, like most of Maturin's biographers, indicates that Maturin wanted the book to be entitled *The Family of Monotrio,* but that the publisher added the more compelling albeit predictable title *Fatal Revenge.*

8. See Jürgen Habermas's *The Structural Transformation of the Public Sphere*, trans. Thomas Burger (Cambridge, MA: MIT Press, 1991), 43–56.

9. This argument follows the basic thesis of Mary Corbett's *Allegories of Union in Irish and English Writing, 1790–1870* (London: Cambridge University Press, 2000). By 1867, when Matthew Arnold publishes *On the Study of Celtic Literature,* the discourses of science and alterity had changed to allow him to suggest that English "Character" was a racial quality not shared by the Irish, or by anyone else for that matter. Arnold clearly shows some sympathy for the Irish throughout his *Study* and suggests that the "racial" divide between the primitive Irish and the English can be healed by English understanding and by admitting that Ireland can be joined to England by blood ties (177). Arnold's solution resembles something like racial mixing.

10. Readings of *Fatal Revenge* follow the path set out by Nilo Idman's *Maturin: His Life and Works* (London: Constable, 1923), in that they all read the novel based on the ending.

11. Heinz Kosok's "Charles Robert Maturin and Colonialism," in *Literary Inter-Relations: Ireland, Egypt, and the Far East,* ed. Mary Massoud, 228–34 (Gerrards Cross: Colin Smythe, 1996); and Jeffares's "Maturin the Innovator" read the gender relations in Maturin as a potential complication of nationalist sympathies.

12. Maturin placed this footnote in the text in part to defend himself against Samuel Taylor Coleridge, who had given a scathing review to *Bertram.* In *Biographia Literaria,* Coleridge goes so far as to claim that in Maturin's play, "the shocking spirit of Jacobinism seemed no longer confined to politics. The familiarity with atrocious events and characters appeared to have poisoned the taste, even where it had not directly disorganized the moral principles, and left the feelings callous to all the mild appeals, and craving alone for the grossest and most outrageous stimulants" (469).

13. In "Charles Robert Maturin and Colonialism," Heinz Kosok uses the footnote to unpack the problems that colonialism presented to Maturin.

14. See Backus, 132.

15. *British Review* essay cited in Idman, 20.

16. Ibid.

17. See R. F. Foster's "Shipwreck and Deliverance: The Foundations of the Ascendancy," in *Modern Ireland: 1600–1972* (New York: Penguin, 1989), 138–63.

18. In " Diderot and Maturin: Enlightenment, Automata, and the Theatre of Terror," in *European Gothic: A Spirited Exchange 1760–1960,* ed. Avril Horner, 55–69 (New York: Manchester University Press, 2002), Victor Sage interprets Maturin's depictions of the horrors of a mechanized, dehumanized subject as allusions to Denis Diderot's *La Religieuse.*

19. See Pearson, "Masculinizing the Novel"; and Kramer, *Charles Robert Maturin.*

20. Of course, Radcliffe's *The Italian* was, itself, written in response to Matthew Lewis's portrayal of the monk Ambrosio in *The Monk* (1796).

21. See Foster, "Cromwellian Ireland," in *Modern Ireland,* 101–37.

22. See also Julia M. Wright's "Devouring the Disinherited: Familial Cannibalism in Maturin's *Melmoth the Wanderer,*" in *Eating Their Words: Cannibalism and the Boundaries of Cultural Identity,* ed. Kristen Guest, 79–105 (Albany: State University of New York Press, 2001).

23. See Daniel Corkery's *The Hidden Ireland* (Dublin: M. H. Gill and Son, 1956), as well as Corkery's *Synge and the Anglo-Irish* (New York: Russell and Russell, 1965).

24. In "'Unprepared for Sudden Transformations': Identity and Politics in *Melmoth the Wanderer,*" *Studies in the Novel* 26, no. 2 (1994): 173–95, Joseph W. Lew notes the persistent double identities of the characters in Maturin's novel.

25. See R. D. Collison Black's "Private Enterprise and Free Trade," in *Economic Thought and the Irish Question 1817–1870* (London: Cambridge University Press, 1960), 134–58.

26. See W. J. McCormack's complication of this in *Sheridan Le Fanu and Victorian Ireland* (Oxford: Clarendon, 1980), 209.

27. Of course, Le Fanu was also clearly influenced by Charlotte Brontë's depiction of Bertha in *Jane Eyre.*

28. For Ivan Melada, "The sympathy that Le Fanu exhibits towards Irish rebels in such works as the ballad 'Shamus O'Brien' and the novel *Torlogh O'Brien* is an attitude he learned at his mother's knee. As a girl, Emma Lucretia Dobbin was more or less a rebel." Melada, *Sheridan Le Fanu* (New York: Twayne, 1987), 3.

29. See McCormack, *Sheridan Le Fanu and Victorian Ireland,* 209–11.

30. In fact, these products of the Irish literary imagination seem to testify to a case of abjection. In *Powers of Horror,* Julia Kristeva's explains that abjection, figured as a violent breaking away from the phallic mother, involves a "subjective diachrony" (13). Abjection actually precedes the constitution of identity and involves rendering the mother repugnant. Before becoming a subject homologous to or in imitation of the mother, the infant's originary relation with the mother is one of absolute identification. Abjection, then, can never be described as an act of psychic projection because identity finds its very foundation on the site of abjection, on the site from which it must move in order to become a self in the first place. The abject remains situated at the end of the Lacanian *imaginary* and before the entry into the *symbolic* order that helps to determine object relations in the social world. As Kristeva explains, "The abject is not an object facing me which I name or imagine" (1). Far from describing abjection as a mode of projection or a movement toward a unifying identity, Kristeva explains that "the time of abjection is double: a time of oblivion and thunder, of veiled infinity and the moment when revelation bursts forth" (9). That is, Kristeva figures the abject as a kind of "land of oblivion" that is both desired and repugnant. Kristeva's notion of abjection, then, suggests a double move that relinquishes the unifying and integrating identity trajectory implied by Freudian theories of projection and sublimation. She explains that "the abject constitutes a

vortex of summons and repulsion [that] places the one haunted by it literally besides himself" (1). The literary texts that Kristeva recommends in *Powers of Horror,* those of Sade, Proust, Joyce, and Céline, are texts that articulate the breakdown of the self/abject dichotomy. If, however, we situate Maturin and his anxious fictions of nation, masculinity, and terror adjacent to someone like the Marquis de Sade, as Stephen Bruhm does in *Gothic Bodies,* then we read Maturin's Gothic as articulating a similar breakdown of the self/abject dichotomy (5). Many of the readings of the Anglo-Irish colonial order rely on a model in which psychic wholeness becomes both the lost plenitude for which we nostalgically yearn and the singular utopian dream toward which we must move. In opposition to approaches to Irish nationalism that rely on the figure of psychic wholeness, I'd like to suggest that if we append to the Kristevan model a dialectical approach that looks for the ways in which abjection and identity, the horror of the other and the constitution of the self, become inextricably enfolded into each other, interrupted by each other, and, finally, the determinate negation of each other, then we should end up with a model of the modern Irish nation that acknowledges the constitutive character of its double affiliations. In other words, if we begin by interpreting the post-1798 Irish "nation" itself as structured by and around a double bind or double affiliation, then we end up with a *symbolic* order whose anxiety subsists not simply in ridding itself of the abject other in order to constitute a clean and unified identity, but rather in its inability to identify—and so move beyond—the abject in the first place. Thus, in this case we see what Kristeva calls "the violent and clumsy" transition into selfhood that begins with abjection as perennially interrupted (13).

31. Victor Sage's "'Carmilla': I'll Let You Be in My Dream, if I Can Be in Yours," in *Le Fanu's Gothic: The Rhetoric of Darkness* (New York: Palgrave, 2004,) 178–201, emphasizes Le Fanu's appropriation of the idea of spiritual "intermediates" (192).

32. See Backus's remarkable reading of Le Fanu's depiction of abuse and molestation, 127–34.

33. In "'Carmilla,'" Sage claims that through mirroring, Carmilla "makes her main rhetorical bid for control of Laura. It works by confirming Laura's memory from a reversed or mirror-image perspective (so Laura can apparently perform the experiment of transposing it into her own remembered experience—the reader does it alongside her), and thus corroborating it" (183).

34. The pamphlet met with much hostility in England. In "Protestant Ascendancy, 1691–1714," in *A New History of Ireland Vol. IV: Eighteenth-Century Ireland, 1691–1800,* ed. T. W. Moody and W. E. Vaughan (Oxford: Clarendon, 1986), 1–30, J. G. Simms asserts that such books were generally burned by mandate of the English commons (6).

35. See Sage, "'Carmilla,'" 191. Sage depicts Le Fanu's story as a marriage of Darwin and Swedenborg.

36. Christopher Craft's "'Kiss Me with Those Red Lips': Gender and Inversion in Bram Stoker's *Dracula,*" *Representations* 8 (1984): 107–30, elucidates the novel's ambivalent depiction of gender roles and masculine desire while detailing Victorian England's various sexual anxieties.

3. THE REVOLUTION WITHIN

1. It remains important to note that Saint Sebastian's role as a gay icon owes a great deal Renaissance depictions by Giovanni Bassi (*Il Sodoma*) and Guido Reni. Reni's *St. Sebastian* was one of Wilde's favorite paintings. The appropriation of Saint Sebastian as an icon of homoerotic desire is the explicit subject of George Eekhoud's 1909 article, "Saint Sébastien Dans la Peinture" *Akdemos* 1 (February 15, 1909): 171–75.

2. See R. F. Foster, "Ireland Abroad," in *Modern Ireland: 1600–1972* (New York: Penguin, 1989), 345–72; and Foster, "Land, Politics, and Nationalism," 373–99.

3. See Alan Sinfield, *The Wilde Century: Effeminacy, Oscar Wilde, and the Queer Moment* (New York: Columbia University Press, 1994); and Ed Cohen, *Talk on the Wilde Side: Towards a Genealogy of a Discourse on Male Sexualities* (New York: Routledge, 1993).

4. W. J. McCormack contributes the essay "Irish Gothic and After (1820–1945)" to Deane's *Field Day Anthology of Irish Writing,* vol. 2 (New York: W. W. Norton, 1991), 831–54. McCormack, who tends to give Wilde a bit more credit than does Deane, claims that Wilde understood very clearly that "style is a miniature politics," and that his Gothic experiments fit alongside those of other Anglo-Irish Gothic writers (846).

5. Historically speaking, Wilde has long been castigated for willfully losing his Irish accent during his time at Oxford and for writing plays that appealed so directly to the tastes of the English bourgeoisie, so Deane's critique of Wilde comes from a long tradition of similarly posed critiques. But when he spoke to Robert Ross in 1892 while the English censors were considering a ban on performances of *Salome,* Wilde had been quite emphatic about his national identity. He told Ross, "I am not English. I am Irish which is quite another thing." See Richard Ellman, *Oscar Wilde* (New York; Vintage, 1988), 372. See also Davis Coakley, "The Neglected Years: Wilde in Dublin," in *Rediscovering Oscar Wilde,* ed. C. George Sandulescu, 52–60 (Buckingham, UK: Colin Smith Ltd., 1994).

6. See Jeff Nunokawa, *Tame Passions of Wilde: The Styles of Manageable Desire* (Princeton, NJ: Princeton University Press, 2003). Nunokawa convincingly argues that Wilde fuses formal affect with the moral and psycho-sexual content of his writings. In essence, for Nunokawa, Wilde finds a way to market and contain desires that remain outside of the mainstream.

7. In *Vampires, Mummies, and Liberals*: *Bram Stoker and the Politics of Popular Fiction* (Durham, NC: Duke University Press, 1996), David Glover identifies this metonymic element of English Gothic fiction as an elaboration of the Victorian formulation of identity and "character"; "'Character,'" Glover explains, "designated the self-reliant private individual whose ability to take control of his [quintessentially his] own destiny was the cynosure of social and national progress" (59).

8. Theodor W. Adorno's "Universal and Particular," in *Aesthetic Theory,* trans. Robert Hullot-Kentor (Minneapolis: University of Minnesota Press, 1997), observes how modern works of art often come to represent the unreconciled problems of modern bourgeois society.

9. Vicki Mahaffey correctly argues that "what Wilde dislikes about moralism is its complacency." See Mahaffey's *States of Desire: Wilde, Yeats, Joyce and the Irish Experiment* (New York: Oxford University Press, 1998), 56.

10. See Lawrence Danson, "'Each Man Kills the Thing He Loves': The Impermanence of Personality in Oscar Wilde," in *Rediscovering Oscar Wilde*, ed. C. George Sandulescu, 82–93 (Gerrards Cross, UK: Colin Smythe, 1994). Danson argues that "Basil's 'terror' when he first finds himself 'face to face with the young man whose personality had so strangely stirred' him registers the homosexual panic of his *self*-discovery; yet that discovery can only occur through Basil's recognition of Dorian's personality—a personality which cannot exist in Dorian until Basil has first read it into Dorian by projection from the personality he discovers in himself by reading Dorian" (89).

11. This argument follows from a similar one made by Mahaffey in *States of Desire,* but Mahaffey also argues that Dorian has a mother creator in the figure of Basil, and that his libertinism is a result of Basil's repression and sublimation (82–83).

12. See John Paul Riquelme, "Oscar Wilde's Aesthetic Gothic: Walter Pater, Dark Enlightenment, and *The Picture of Dorian Gray,*" *Modern Fiction Studies* 46, no. 3 (2000): 609–31. Riquelme enumerates Wilde's (and Lord Henry's) various appropriations of Pater's writings.

13. See Edouard Roditi, *Oscar Wilde* (Norfolk, VA: New Directions Books, 1947), 113–14.

14. I borrow the term "powers of ubiquity" from Marie-Noëlle Zeender, "John Melmoth and Dorian Gray: The Two-Faced Mirror," in *Rediscovering Oscar Wilde,* ed. C. George Sandulescu, 432–40 (Gerrards Cross, UK: Colin Smythe, 1994).

15. See, in particular, Derek Attridge and Marjorie Howes, eds., *Semicolonial Joyce* (Cambridge: Cambridge University Press, 2000); Seamus Deane, *Celtic Revivals* (London: Faber and Faber, 1985); Enda Duffy, *The Subaltern Ulysses* (Minneapolis: University of Minnesota Press, 1994); David Lloyd, "Adulteration and the Novel," in *Anomalous States* (Durham, NC: Duke University Press, 1993); Emer Nolan, *James Joyce and Nationalism* (London: Routledge, 1995).

4. OVERCOMING ALLEGORY

1. A similar structure supplies much of the drama in two of Yeats's more powerfully realized dramas, "Cathleen ni Hoolihan" and "Purgatory." See W. B. Yeats, "Purgatory," in *Eleven Plays of William Butler Yeats,* ed. Norman Jeffares (New York: Macmillan, 1964), 199–206; see also Yeats, "Cathleen ni Hoolihan," in Jeffares, *Eleven Plays,* 221–31. Curiously enough, Elizabeth Bowen's novel *The Last September,* first published in 1929, depicts the Gothic narrative from the inside. See Elizabeth Bowen, *The Last September* (New York: Anchor, 2000).

2. In imagining Jane's writing as her child and heir, Charlotte Brontë's *Jane Eyre* finds an innovative solution to this problem.

3. Montoni is the primary archetype here, but we find analogous clerical figures in Radcliffe's *The Italian* and in Matthew Lewis's *The Monk*.

4. See Kate Ferguson Ellis's *The Contested Castle: Gothic Novels and the Subversion of Domestic Ideology* (Urbana: University of Illinois Press, 1989).

5. The idea of a feminized Ireland is, of course, quite common in the critical literature. For a look at how Joyce deals with it, check out Joseph Valente, "'Neither Fish nor Flesh'; or how 'Cyclops' Stages the Double-Bind of Irish Manhood," in *Semicolonial Joyce,* ed. Derek Attridge and Marjorie Howes, 96–127 (Cambridge: Cambridge University Press, 2000); and David Lloyd, "Counterparts: *Dubliners,* Masculinity, and Temperance Nationalism," in Attridge and Howes, *Semicolonial Joyce,* 128–49. See also Christine van Boheemen-Saaf, "The Primitive Scene of Representation: Writing Gender," in *Joyce, Derrida, Lacan, and the Trauma of History: Reading, Narrative, and Postcolonialism* (New York: Cambridge University Press, 1999), 120–54.

6. In his analysis of the Irish Free State movement, *Britain and Irish Separatism: From the Fenians to the Free State, 1867–1922* (Washington, DC: Catholic University Press, 1984), Thomas E. Hachey claims that the league's primary purposes were to halt evictions, reduce land rents, and "ultimately, to make tenant farmers the owners of their land" (22). Parnell and Davitt wanted to oust the exploitative inheritance and ascendancy class systems overseen by the British and the Anglo-Irish landlords. Though the league's primary function was to use boycotts to achieve its ends, in following the basic structure of nineteenth-century Irish political engagement it often resorted to violence against the offending landlords and their farms. Gladstone's Parliament in London offered a conciliatory Bill. When Parnell rejected it, he was imprisoned under the auspices of the British Coercion Bill, and in 1881 the Land League was outlawed.

7. Home rule bills were finally passed by the English Parliament in 1914 and 1920.

8. See Malcolm Brown, "Literary Parnellism," in *The Politics of Irish Literature: From Thomas Davis to W. B. Yeats* (Seattle: University of Washington Press, 1972), 371–90.

9. In fact, in the "Oxen of the Sun" episode Joyce mocks Gothic writing and the Gothic's rule of *Lex Talionis,* when he has Haines the Englishman whom Stephen entertains and despises in the opening chapter, appear behind a secret panel with a phial of poison and a "portfolio of Celtic literature" (412).

10. See my "Formalism and Its Malcontents: Benjamin and de Man on the Function of Allegory," *New Literary History* 35, no. 4 (2004): 663–83.

11. See Walter Benjamin, *The Origin of German Tragic Drama* (New York: Verso, 1998).

12. This separates allegory from its much-preferred sibling, the symbol, which always tries to imagine a way to transcend the simplicity of overt representation.

13. Benjamin, *The Origin of German Tragic Drama,* 178.

14. Likewise, in the 1939 version of his essay, "Paris, Capital of the Nineteenth Century," reprinted in *The Arcades Project,* Benjamin claims that "the singular debasement of things through their signification, something characteristic of seventeenth-century allegory, corresponds to the singular debasement of things through their price as commodities" (22).

15. In this sense, Benjamin's notion of allegory dovetails with Marxian conceptions of the commodity in *Capital* and with Marx's arguments about idealist philosophy in *The German Ideology*. Allegory, like commodity capitalism, erases historical and natural specificity..

16. In *James Joyce and the Question of History*, James Fairhall attempts to balance Fredric Jameson's conceptions of narrative and poststructuralist notions of language in order to provide a notion of how we should read history. Fairhall's study allows for a powerful account of the manner in which *Ulysses* deconstructs the boundary between fiction and history (252). However, the basic structure of Fairhall's argument relies on a narrative conception of history. That is, to use his own words, for Fairhall, as for Jameson, "we perceive the world in the shape of stories" (7). Although these stories are invariably subject to transformation and interpretation, and thus, in some sense, open to revision, this version of knowing history remains inextricably bound to the consecutive and linear arrangement of narrative. Joyce's mode of figuration presents us with a confrontation between opposing ways of thinking history, between allegory and accumulation. For Joyce, these opposing methods finally provide very different approaches to confronting the dual problems of nationalism and political identity.

17. See, for instance, the debates concerning the Citizen in the "Cyclops" episode. See Emer Nolan's *James Joyce and Nationalism* (London: Routledge, 1995); and Joseph Valente's response, "'Neither Fish nor Flesh."

18. Translation altered.

19. See Karen Lawrence's "Paternity as Legal Fiction in *Ulysses*," in *James Joyce, the Augmented Ninth: Proceedings of the Ninth International James Joyce Symposium*, ed. Bernard Benstock, 233–43 (Syracuse, NY: Syracuse University Press, 1988).

20. In *Joyce and the Anglo-Irish*, Len Platt argues that Joyce's treatment of Eglinton in "Scylla and Charybdis" is somewhat unfair. After all, Eglinton generally opposed the Revival's emphasis on mythic history. As Eglinton himself says in "The Irish Mythological Cycle," reprinted in *Anglo-Irish Essays* (New York: John Lane, 1918), 35–40, "Had the Celt ever permitted himself to doubt, had he ever called in the aid of reason, his history would have been different" (40). It's likely that Eglinton's mockery of Stephen in the "Scylla and Charybdis" episode parallels his arguments about the spiritualism of the Revivalists.

21. Joyce's use of the terms "vegetable philosophy" and "vegetable verse" represents a denigration of the superstitious nature of revivalism by relating the movement to Russell's commitment to vegetarianism.

22. F. S. L. Lyons, *Charles Stewart Parnell* (New York: Oxford University Press, 1977), 616. See also Joseph Valente's "The Manliness of Parnell." *Eire Ireland* 41, no 1 (2006): 64–121.

23. In a more critical sense, Parnell also stands in for the problem of political action itself. In other words, between the hopes of what Joyce once called the "senile conscience" of English parliamentary politics and the anguish and defeat of the physical-force tradition in Ireland stands the ghost of Parnell (*The Critical Writings* 223).

24. See, in particular, Seamus Deane's "The Provincial Intellectual," in *Celtic Revivals: Essays in Modern Irish Literature* (Boston: Faber, 1985); and Emer Nolan's *James Joyce and Nationalism* (New York: Routledge, 1995).

25. See Don Gifford and Robert J. Seidman, *Ulysses Annotated: Notes for James Joyce's* Ulysses (Berkeley and Los Angeles: University of California Press, 1989), 256.

26. See Norman Cohen, *Warrant for Genocide: The Myth of the Jewish World Conspiracy and the Protocols of the Elders of Zion* (New York: Harper and Row, 1966); and Neil R. Davison, *James Joyce,* Ulysses, *and the Construction of Jewish Identity* (New York: Cambridge University Press, 1998), 19.

27. In *The Sense of an Ending: Studies in the Theory of Fiction* (New York: Oxford University Press, 1967), Frank Kermode distinguishes between these notions of historical time in terms of the Greek *chronos* and *kairos* (47).

28. These are only a few of the many distinctions. The documents of the dual Torah also include, among others, Tosefta, Yershalmi (Talmud of the Land of Israel), Balvi (Talmud of Babylonia), the Midrash compilations, and the Siddur and Mahzor.

29. See, in particular, the Rashi-Rambam debates. In these debates Ramban (Nachmanides) interrogates Rashi's Midrash on Shemoth (Exodus). Rashi cites a passage from the written Torah concerning God's command to build the Tabernacle and the sin of the Golden Calf. Following the Scripture, Rashi writes, "There is no 'earlier' or 'later' in the Torah—The event of the Calf (Exodus Ch. 32) preceded the command to build the Tabernacle (Exodus Ch. 25) by many days" (9). Hence, Rashi makes the building of the Tabernacle consequent to the Israelites' sin of idolatry with the Golden Calf. The Tabernacle becomes a symbol of and place for repentance. Rashi continually challenges the chronology of the Torah itself, claiming that events are presented out–of sequence. Ramban disagrees, and glosses Rashi's Midrash by claiming that the events occurred in the order stated in Scripture and that the Tabernacle is not simply intended for repentance, for it also reflects the glory of God (10). Here we get a disagreement that appears to alter the text without altering it. The Rashi and Ramban Midrashic glosses present arguments about the written Torah that work both to disrupt and to maintain what is described in the text. They lay out reasons for, and judge the ways in which the Tabernacle had an effect on everyday practice. In this fashion we see how and what the Tabernacle means for the times of Rashi and of Ramban, but we also see how collective memory, the remembered and recited Midrash presents a conflict that in some sense disrupts the text itself. Though, admittedly, in the case of Talmudic commentary, such disruptions generally refer to events and commands that have transcendental as well as material implications. Primarily, as in the Rashi-Ramban debate, Midrash discusses what has been left out.

30. In this way, Midrashic memory can be seen to line up with the concept of "temporal accumulation" recommended by Ian Baucom in "The Sea Is History: On Temporal Accumulation," in *Specters of the Atlantic: Finance Capital, Slavery, and the Philosophy of History* (Durham, NC: Duke University Press, 2005), 309–33.

31. See Max Horkheimer and Theodor Adorno," The Concept of Enlightenment," in *Dialectic of Enlightenment* (New York: Continuum, 1995), 3–42.

32. Reprinted in Paul Mendes-Flohr and Jehuda Reinharz, *The Jew in the Modern World* (New York: Oxford University Press, 1995), 219–21.

33. Reprinted in Mendes-Flohr and Reinharz, 282–84.

34. See Davison's *James Joyce,* and Ira B. Nadel's *Joyce and the Jews* (Iowa City: University of Iowa Press, 1989).

5. ENGENDERING A CARTESIAN GOTHIC

1. See Theodor W. Adorno, "Trying to Understand Endgame," in *Notes to Literature: Volume One,* ed. Rolf Tiedeman, trans. Shierry Weber Nicholsen, 241–76 (New York: Columbia University Press, 1991); Georg Lukács, "The Ideology of Modernism," in *The Lukács Reader,* ed. Arpad Kadarky, 187–209 (New York: Blackwell Press, 1995).

2. Recent scholarship has attempted to fill, or at least account for, this empty space. David Weisberg's *Chronicles of Disorder: Samuel Beckett and the Cultural Politics of the Novel* (New York: State University of New York Press, 2000), argues that Beckett's fiction occupies a space between modernist autonomy and postwar commitment by reading Beckett's work in light of European and literary history. Likewise Tyrus Miller's "Dismantling Authenticity: Beckett, Adorno and the 'Post-War,'" *Textual Practice* 8, no. 1 (1994): 43–57, reads Beckett in a similarly political, Adorno-inflected fashion. However, both Weisberg and Miller pay little attention to Beckett's rethinking of experience in light of his Irish background. The more recent volume of essays entitled *Engagement and Indifference: Beckett and the Political,* ed. Henry Sussman and Christopher Devenney (New York: State University of New York Press, 2001), demonstrates precisely the difficulties of reading for Beckett's politics. Deploying the basic maneuvers of European poststructuralist language theory, Sussman's introduction seems particularly illuminating as it lays out the differences between reading Beckett in terms of "language-based" systems and "subject-based" ones (2). For Sussman, language-based theories remain apprehensive about any codes deposited in language that betray an "interest." Hence, the poststructuralist tradition of reading Beckett that Sussman invokes tends to look with suspicion not only on the ideologies toward which Beckett's work responds but also on ideological approaches to Beckett's work.

3. Though there certainly is no dearth of scholarship on the Joyce/Beckett relationship, the thoughtful account of it detailed in James Knowlson's *Damned to Fame: The Life of Samuel Beckett* (New York: Simon and Schuster, 1996), makes for a good starting place. Seamus Deane begins to unpack the postcolonial implications of this relationship in "Joyce and Beckett," in *Celtic Revivals: Essays in Modern Irish Literature, 1880–1980*. Winston-Salem, NC: Wake Forest University Press, 1985), 123–34.

4. See Eyal Amiran, *Wandering and Home: Beckett's Metaphysical Narrative* (University Park: Penn State University Press, 1993), for one of the fullest accounts of Beckett's role within the European metaphysical tradition.

5. Anthony Uhlmann, *Beckett and Poststructuralism* (Cambridge: Cambridge University Press, 1999).

6. See "Three Dialogues by Samuel Beckett and Georges Duthuit," in *Samuel Beckett: A Collection of Critical Essays,* ed. Martin Esslin, 17 (Englewood Cliffs, NJ: Prentice-Hall, 1965).

7. This negative dialectical move also remains at the heart of Seamus Deane's reading of Beckett, in "Joyce and Beckett." See James Martin Harding, "Trying to Understand Godot: Adorno, Beckett, and the Senility of Dialectics," in *Adorno and "A Writing of the Ruins": Essays on Modern Aesthetics and Anglo-American Culture* (Albany: State University of New York Press, 1997), 51–64, as well.

8. Tyrus Miller's "Dismantling Authenticity: Beckett, Adorno and the 'Post-War,'" goes a long way toward clarifying many of the concerns that Adorno's criticism seems to share with Beckett's antisocial art. In reading Beckett's *Endgame* and "The Lost Ones" together with *Aesthetic Theory,* Miller convincingly argues that both thinkers understand negativity, autonomy, and the problematic nature of art in modernity in profoundly similar ways (44–45). Both resist theories of art that call either for the final reconciliation of opposites in the figure of some historical meta-subject or for reductive notions of political commitment. Miller also takes care to connect Beckett to Adorno's persistent attacks on existentialism and on the concomitant notion of authenticity [*Eigenlichkeit*]. For the most part, Miller is also correct in attaching Adorno to Beckett's postwar writings. As I demonstrate, in the years before 1947, Beckett's capacity to read literary genres themselves as the indices of historical macroproblems lines up—in a rough way—with many of the ideas that drive Lukác's *Theory of the Novel.* For more recent assessments of Beckett's politics, see Alain Badiou, *On Beckett*, ed. Alberto Toscana and Nina Power (Manchester, UK: Clinamen Press, 2003); and Terry Eagleton, "Political Beckett?" *New Left Review* 40 (July/August 2006): 67–74.

9. Ironically, both Lukács and the existential-absurdist school embodied by, say, Martin Esslin's *Theater of the Absurd* (New York: Doubleday, 1961), agree in representing Beckett's work as the ultimate realization of enlightened liberal subjectivity.

10. See Amiran's *Wandering and Home.*

11. In essence, then, when we read novels, in this case Gothic ones, specifically in terms of generic form, we must remember that the form is not just a simple representation of some idea. Instead, generic motifs manifest immanent and reflexive demonstrations of the ideologies and conceptual constellations by which they are informed.

12. See Linda Ben-Zvi's "Feminine Focus in Beckett," in *Beckett in Dublin,* ed. S. E. Milmer, 55–61 (Dublin: Lilliput Press, 1992). See also Mary Bryden, *Women in Samuel Beckett's Prose and Drama: Her Own Other* (New York: Barnes & Noble, 1993). When we begin surveying the prose fictions of this period from the standpoint of Nancy Armstong's assertions (See *Desire and Domestic Fiction: A Political History of the Novel* [New York: Oxford University Press, 1987]). about the ideological structure of the British private sphere and the rise of the figure of the "domestic woman," we see in late eighteenth- and early nineteenth-century British fiction the groundwork

for the construction of a new kind of woman. We also become privy to the architecture of a modern bourgeois consciousness built upon the desire for domesticity and for the hearth rather than upon something as abstract as the individual's civil rights or as uncontrollable as regional, communal, or sectarian loyalty.

13. In the preceding chapter, I define structural dispossession as "the historical dispossession and disenfranchisement of political subjects by cultural, legal, and economic systems." Both chapter 1, "Gothic Double Binds," and the Joyce chapter (chap. 4), "The Uncreating Conscience," provide more detailed discussions of the implications and dynamics of structural dispossession.

14. This is all to say that Beckett's modernism admits the limits of aesthetic autonomy by suggesting that autonomy does not produce an artist with the capacity for transcendence so much as it produces a figure whose life has been converted into and confined by a corporeal and vulnerable text. In essence, I am arguing that in *Molloy* and *Malone Dies,* Beckett begins to fuse his re-vision of the female Gothic with a markedly critical reflection on the failings of modernism itself. Chronologically speaking, then, it is only with these two texts that Beckett's writing begins to fit more precisely with the negative dialectics recommended by Adorno's theories of art and reaffirmed by critics like David Weisberg and Tyrus Miller.

15. See Elizabeth Grosz's *Volatile Bodies: Toward a Corporeal Feminism* (Bloomington: Indiana University Press, 1994), 6.

16. See Iain Wright's " What Matter Who's Speaking?': Beckett, the Authorial Subject and Contemporary Critical Theory" *Southern Review* 16, no. 1 (1983): 59–86. Wright's essay is one of the first to assert the connections and disconnections between the poststructuralist and humanist versions of Beckett. On the specifically Cartesian aspects of *Murphy,* see Samuel Mintz's very early piece, "Beckett's *Murphy:* A 'Cartesian Novel,'" *Perspective* 2, no. 3 (1959): 156–65. More recently, P. J. Murphy's "Beckett and the Philosophers," in *The Cambridge Companion to Samuel Beckett,* ed. John Pilling, 222–40 (Cambridge: Cambridge University Press, 1994), provides a thoughtful overview of how philosophically oriented criticism has attempted to deal with Beckett's influences and implications.

17. This is Begam's particular locution. See *Samuel Beckett and the End of Modernity* (Stanford, CA: Stanford University Press, 1996), 42.

18. Rita Felski's *The Gender of Modernity* (Cambridge, MA: Harvard University Press, 1995), and Susan Bordo's *The Flight to Objectivity: Essays on Cartesianism and Culture* (Albany: State University of New York Press, 1987) both make similar arguments about mind/body dualism and masculine culture. See also Alice Jardine, *Gynesis: Configurations of Woman and Modernity* (Ithaca, NY: Cornell University Press, 1985).

19. See Jürgen Habermas, *The Structural Transformation of the Public Sphere: An Inquiry into a Category of Bourgeois Society,* trans. Thomas Burger and Frederick Lawrence (Cambridge, MA: MIT Press, 1991).

20. My reading of *Murphy* in terms of Gothic confinement corresponds to the philosophical reading of him in terms of the Leibnizian Monad. See David Hesla, *The Shape of the Chaos: An Interpretation of the Art of Samuel Beckett* (Minneapolis: University of Minnesota Press, 1971), 74–75.

21. See, in particular, "Madness and the Cogito in *Murphy*" in Begam's *Samuel Beckett and the End of Modernity,* 40–65.

22. Though written shortly after World War II, *First Love* [*Premier Amour*] was only published in 1969 after Beckett won the Nobel Prize. Beckett translated the work into English in early 1973.

23. For a more psychoanalytically inflected reading, see Julia Kristeva's "The Father, Love and Banishment," in *Desire in Language: A Semiotic Approach to Literature and Art,* ed. Leon S. Roudiez, trans. Thomas Gora, Alice Jardine, and Leon S. Roudiez, 148–58 (New York, Columbia University Press, 1980).

24. In fact, one of Weisberg's central claims is that "Beckett never lets an emphasis on aesthetic form become detached from the material content through which form becomes manifest. From Murphy's dilemma deciding the order in which he will eat the assorted biscuits of his impoverished lunch, to the mathematical permutations of Watt feeding the famished dog, to Molloy's need to suck his stones in an aesthetically pleasing manner, the 'mania' for an artful order, for a principle of distinction, is always contrasted with the condition of poverty and privation" (84). Weisberg's book comes significantly closer than most other Beckett criticism to articulating the full political implications of Beckett's ambivalent writing style. In rejecting postcolonial readings of Beckett *tout-court,* however, Weisberg not only overlooks one of the grounding conditions of Beckett's ambivalence, he also effectively cuts Beckett off from Irish literary traditions that helped to form the discursive field in the first place.

25. Beckett seems far more comfortable with allegory than does Joyce. As Adorno points out, however, Beckett nearly always emphasizes the negative or reductive elements of allegory in order to demonstrate how human social consciousness moves toward reductive and singular readings of the world.

26. Both David Lloyd's "Writing in the Shit: Beckett, Nationalism and the Colonial Subject," in *Anomalous States: Irish Writing and the Post-Colonial Moment* (Durham, NC: Duke University Press, 1993), 41–58, and Revathi Krishnaswamy's "Reading Colonial Erotics," *Effeminism: The Economy of Colonial Desire* (Ann Arbor: University of Michigan Press, 1998), tend to interrogate the sex and gender implications of British colonialism along these lines. To see how this type of problem applies to *Jane Eyre,* see Gayatri Chakravorty Spivak, "Three Women's Texts and a Critique of Imperialism," *Critical Inquiry* 12, no. 1 (1985): 235–61.

27. With Beckett's help, Patrick Bowles translated *Molloy* into English. The English translation was published in 1955 in Paris by Olympia Press and in New York by Grove Press.

28. See the entry "Molloy" in *The Grove Companion to Samuel Beckett: A Reader's Guide to His Works, Life, and Thought,* ed. C. J. Ackerley and S. E. Gontarski (New York: Grove Press, 2004), 376–79.

29. And, if we follow the basic Lacanian conception of subject formation and observe the instant in which the infant begins to transition away from identification with the mother and to attach him or herself to external reality via the mirror phase, we must admit, with Lacan, that such a development "leads us to oppose any philosophy issuing from the *Cogito*" (93). In fact,

the Lacanian approach conceives of the mirror phase as "*an identification* in the full sense which analysis gives to the term: namely, the transformation which takes place in the subject when he assumes an image" or *imago* (94). For Lacan this is the beginning of the subject's misrecognition, of the subject's capacity to imagine him or herself as a singular, unified agent who can and must resolve the sense of discord that he or she feels with the external world.

30. For Weisberg, this problem in Beckett "recapitulates a persistent aporia of modernism, that an inner reality and an outer reality exist separately, and can be evaluated and gauged as such, as on an 'index.' On the other hand, it expresses the choice facing the artist in the 1930s: respond to the 'colossal fiasco' either by engaging it, by making 'contact,' or by escaping into the freedom of the imagination, even if the escape courts madness" (32).

31. In his review of the 1989 English-language translation of Theodor Adorno's *Kierkegaard,* Peter Fenves draws attention to Adorno's use of the term "*wörtliche Metapher*" or "literal Metaphor" (104). In *Kierkegaard: Construction of the Aesthetic* (Minneapolis: University of Minnesota Press, 1989), Adorno claims that in reading Kierkegaard's metaphors literally, "the mythical content of his philosophy breaks through" (12). For Adorno, analyzing the metaphorical language that a philosopher uses is an appropriate method for demonstrating how the material world subtends all philosophical speculation. In other words, the metaphors that Kierkegaard employs betray both his background and the social world in which he wrote. Literal metaphors are, as Fenves explains, "phenomenalized figures, figures reduced to their phenomenological content and, to this extent, divorced from the systematic, rationalistic, and idealistic intentions to which they were put to use. Literalization [is] the reduction of each figure to its original lexical position" (104–5). See Peter Fenves, "Image and Chatter: Adorno's Construction of Kierkegaard," *Diacritics* 22, no. 1 (1992): 100–14.

32. I have to thank Jed Esty for pointing this out to me during a conversation about Beckett's use of forms of confinement.

EPILOGUE

1. The fact that the Irish Gothic persists well past Beckett and into the more recent novels of John Banville and Seamus Deane indicates that Gothic modes of confronting the traumas of history continue to have some resonant, if not to say undead, force in the Irish imaginary. See, in particular, Banville's 1973 novel, *Birchwood* (New York: Vintage, 1997), and Deane's *Reading in the Dark* (New York: Vintage, 1995).

Bibliography

Abbott, H. Porter. "The Harpooned Notebook: Malone Dies and the Conventions of Intercalated Narrative." In *Samuel Beckett: Humanistic Perspectives,* edited by Morris Beja, S. E. Gontarski, and Pierre Astier, 71–79. Columbus: Ohio State University Press, 1983.

Ackerley, C. J., and S. E. Gontarski. *The Grove Companion to Samuel Beckett: A Reader's Guide to His Works, Life, and Thought.* New York: Grove Press, 2004.

Adorno, Theodor W. *Aesthetic Theory.* Translated by Robert Hullot-Kentor. Minneapolis: University of Minnesota Press, 1997.

———. *Kierkegaard: Construction of the Aesthetic.* Minneapolis: University of Minnesota Press, 1989

———. *Minima Moralia: Reflections from Damaged Life.* Translated by E. F. N. Jephcott. New York: Verso, 1997.

———. *Negative Dialectics.* Translated by E. B. Ashton. New York: Continuum, 1973.

———. *Prisms.* Translated by Samuel and Shierry Weber. Cambridge, MA: MIT Press, 1967.

———. "Trying to Understand *Endgame.*" In *Notes to Literature: Volume One,* 241–75. Translated by Shierry Weber Nicholson. New York: Columbia University Press, 1991.

Amiran, Eyal. *Wandering and Home: Beckett's Metaphysical Narrative.* University Park: Penn State University Press, 1993.

Arata, Stephen D. "The Occidental Tourist: Dracula and the Anxiety of Reverse Colonization." *Victorian Studies* 33 (1990): 621–45.

Armstrong, Nancy. *Desire and Domestic Fiction: A Political History of the Novel.* New York: Oxford University Press, 1987.

Attridge, Derek and Margorie Howes, eds. *Semicolonial Joyce,* Cambridge: Cambridge University Press, 2000.

Backus, Margot Gayle. *The Gothic Family Romance: Heterosexuality, Child Sacrifice, and the Anglo-Irish Colonial Order.* Durham, NC: Duke University Press, 1999.

Badiou, Alain. *On Beckett.* Edited by Alberto Toscana and Nina Power. Manchester, UK: Clinamen Press, 2003.

Bakhtin, Mikhail. *The Dialogic Imagination: Four Essays.* Translated by Kenneth Brostrom. Austin: University of Texas Press, 1982.

Baldick, Chris. "Introduction" to *Melmoth the Wanderer.* London: Oxford University Press, 1998.

Banville, John. *Birchwood.* New York: Vintage, 1997.

Bataille, Georges. "Molloy's Silence." Translated by John Pilling. In *On Beckett: Essays and Criticism,* edited by S. E. Gontarski, 131–39. New York: Grove Press, 1986.

Baucom, Ian. "'The Sea Is History': On Temporal Accumulation." In *Specters of the Atlantic: Finance Capital, Slavery, and the Philosophy of History,* 309–33. Durham, NC: Duke University Press, 2005.

Beckett, Samuel. "Censorship in the Saorstat." In *Disjecta: Miscellaneous Writings and a Dramatic Fragment,* edited by Ruby Cohn, 84–88. New York: Grove Press, 1995.

———. "Dante . . . Bruno . Vico . . Joyce." *Our Exagmination Round His Factification for Incamination of Work in Progress.* Paris: Shakespeare, 1929.

———. *Endgame: A Play in One Act, Followed by Act without Words, a Mime for One Player.* New York: Grove Press, 1958.

———. "The Essential and the Incidental: Sean O'Casey." In *Disjecta: Miscellaneous Writings and a Dramatic Fragment,* edited by Ruby Cohn, 82–83. New York: Grove Press, 1995.

———. "First Love." *The Complete Short Prose, 1929–89,* edited by S. E. Gontarski, 25–45. New York: Grove Press, 1995.

———. *Molloy Malone Dies the Unnamable.* New York: Grove Press, 1958.

———. *Proust.* New York: Grove Press, 1970.

———. *Waiting for Godot.* New York: Grove Press, 1954.

———. *Watt.* New York: Grove Press, 1959.

Begam, Richard. *Samuel Beckett and the End of Modernity.* Stanford, CA: Stanford University Press, 1996.

Benjamin, Walter. "Experience." In *Selected Writings: Volume 2, 1927–1934,* 553. Translated by Rodney Livingstone. Cambridge, MA: Harvard University Press, 1999.

———. *Illuminations.* Translated by Harry Zohn. New York: Schocken, 1968.

———. *The Origin of German Tragic Drama.* Translated by John Osborne. New York: Verso, 1998.

———. *Reflections: Essays, Aphorisms, Autobiographical Writings.* Translated by Edmund Jephcott. New York: Schocken, 1978.

Ben-Zvi, Linda. "Feminine Focus in Beckett." In *Beckett in Dublin,* 55–61. Dublin: Lilliput Press, 1992.

Birkhead, Edith. *The Tale of Terror: A Study of the Gothic Romance.* New York: Russell & Russell, 1963.

Black, R. D. Collison. "Private Enterprise and Free Trade." In *Economic Thought and the Irish Question 1817–1870,* 134–58. London: Cambridge University Press, 1960.

Blanchot, Maurice. "Where Now? Who Now?" Translated by Richard Howard. In *On Beckett: Essays and Criticism,* edited by S. E. Gontarski, 141–49. New York: Grove Press, 1986.

Bonchek, Avigdor. *What's Bothering Rashi? A Guide to In-Depth Analysis of His Torah Commentary*. New York: Feldheim, 1999.

Bordo, Susan. *The Flight to Objectivity: Essays on Cartesianism and Culture*. Albany: State University of New York Press, 1987.

Bowen, Elizabeth. *The Last September*. New York: Anchor, 2000.

Brontë, Charlotte. *Jane Eyre*. Edited by Beth Newman. New York: Bedford/St. Martin's, 1996.

Brown, Malcom. "Literary Parnellism." In *The Politics of Irish Literature: From Thomas Davis to W. B. Yeats*, 371–90. Seattle: University of Washington Press, 1972.

Bruns, Gerald. *Hermeneutics Ancient and Modern*. New Haven, CT: Yale University Press, 1992.

Bryden, Mary. *Women in Samuel Beckett's Prose and Drama: Her Own Other*. New York: Barnes & Noble, 1993.

Burke, Edmund. *A Philosophical Enquiry into the Origin of Our Ideas of the Sublime and the Beautiful*. New York: Oxford University Press, 1990.

———. *Reflections on the Revolution in France*. Edited by J. G. A. Pocock. Indianapolis, IN: Hackett, 1987.

———. "Tract on the Popery Laws." In *The Portable Burke*, edited by Isaac Kramnick, 295–309. New York: Viking, 1999. .

Burke, Martin. "Piecing Together a Shattered Past: The Historical Writings of the United Irish Exiles in America." In *United Irishmen: Republicanism, Radicalism, and Rebellion*, edited by David Dickson, Daire Keogh, and Kevin Whelan, 297–306. Dublin: Lilliput Press, 1993.

Callanan, Frank. *The Parnell Split: 1890–91*. Dublin: Cork University Press, 1992.

Coakley, Davis. "The Neglected Years: Wilde in Dublin." In *Rediscovering Oscar Wilde*, edited by C. George Sandulescu, 52–60. Gerrards Cross, UK: Colin Smythe.

Cohen, Ed. *Talk on the Wilde Side*. New York: Routledge, 1992.

Cohen, Norman. *Warrant for Genocide: The Myth of the Jewish World Conspiracy and the Protocols of the Elders of Zion*. New York: Harper and Row, 1966.

Coleridge, Samuel Taylor. *Biographia Literaria* in *Samuel Taylor Coleridge: A Critical Edition of the Major Works*. Edited by H.J. Jackson, 155–482. New York: Oxford University Press, 1992.

Connor, Stephen. *Samuel Beckett: Repetition, Theory and Text*. New York: Blackwell, 1988.

Coote, Charles. *History of the Union of the Kingdoms of Great Britain and Ireland; With an Introductory Survey of Hibernian Affairs, Traced from the Times of the Celtic Colonisation*. London: S. Hamilton, 1802.

Corbett, Mary Jean. *Allegories of Union in Irish and English Writing, 1790–1870*. London: Cambridge University Press, 2000.

Corkery, Daniel. *The Hidden Ireland*. Dublin: M. H. Gill and Son, 1956.

———. *Synge and the Anglo-Irish*. New York: Russell and Russell, 1965

Craft, Christopher. "'Kiss Me with Those Red Lips': Gender and Inversion in Bram Stoker's *Dracula*." *Representations* 8 (1984): 107–30.

Curtis, L. P. *Apes and Angels: The Irishman in Victorian Caricature.* New York: Smithsonian, 1997.

Danson, Lawrence. "'Each Man Kills the Thing He Loves': The Impermanence of Personality in Oscar Wilde." In *Rediscovering Oscar Wilde,* edited by C. George Sandulescu, 82–93. Gerrards Cross, UK: Colin Smythe, 1994.

Davison, Neil. *James Joyce,* Ulysses, *and the Construction of Jewish Identity.* London: Cambridge University Press, 1996.

Deane, Seamus. *Celitc Revivals: Essays in Modern Irish Literature 1880–1980.* London: Faber, 1985.

———. *Field Day Anthology of Irish Writing.* 5 vols. New York: W. W. Norton, 1991.

———. *A Short History of Irish Literature.* Notre Dame, IN: University of Notre Dame Press, 1986.

———. *Reading in the Dark.* New York: Vintage, 1995.

———. *Strange Country: Modernity and Nationhood in Irish Writing Since 1790.* London: Oxford University Press, 1997.

Descartes, Rene. *Discourse on the Method of Rightly Conducting Reason, and Seeking Truth in the Sciences.* Translated by John Veitch. Chicago: Open Court, 1960.

Dougherty, Jane Elizabeth. "Mr. and Mrs. England: The Act of Union as National Marriage." In *Acts of Union: The Causes, Contexts, and Consequences of the Act of Union,* edited by Daire Keogh and Kevin Whelan, 202–15. Portland, OR: Four Courts Press, 2001.

Duffy, Enda. *The Subaltern Ulysses.* Minneapolis: University of Minnesota Press, 1994.

Duthuit, George. "Three Dialogues by Samuel Beckett and Georges Duthuit." *Samuel Beckett: A Collection of Critical Essays,* edited by Martin Esslin, 17. Englewood Cliffs, NJ: Prentice-Hall, 1965.

Eagleton, Terry. *Heathcliff and the Great Hunger: Studies in Irish Culture.* New York: Verso, 1995.

———. "Political Beckett?" *New Left Review* 40 (July/August 2006): 67–74.

Edgeworth, Maria. *Castle Rackrent.* New York: Oxford University Press, 1999.

Eekhoud, George. "Saint Sébastien Dans la Peinture." *Akdemos* 1 (February 15, 1909): 171–75.

Eglinton, John. "The Irish Mythological Cycle." In *Anglo-Irish Essays,* 35–40. New York: John Lane, 1918.

Ellis, Kate Ferguson. *The Contested Castle: Gothic Novels and the Subversion of Domestic Ideology.* Urbana: University of Illinois Press, 1989.

Ellman, Richard. *James Joyce.* New York: Oxford University Press, 1982.

———. *Oscar Wilde.* New York: Vintage, 1988.

Esslin, Martin. *The Theatre of the Absurd.* New York: Anchor Books, 1969.

Fairhall, James. *James Joyce and the Question of History.* London: Cambridge University Press, 1993.

Fanon, Frantz. *The Wretched of the Earth.* Translated by Constance Farrington. New York: Grove Press, 1963.

Felski, Rita. *The Gender of Modernity*. Cambridge, MA: Harvard University Press, 1995.

Fenves, Peter. "Image and Chatter: Adorno's Construction of Kierkegaard." *Diacritics* 22, no. 1 (1992): 100–14.

Foreman, J. B., ed. *The Complete Works of Oscar Wilde: Stories, Plays, Poems & Essays*. New York: Harper Perennial, 1989

Foster, R. F. *Modern Ireland: 1600–1972*. New York: Penguin, 1988.

Fraser, Graham. "'No More Than Ghosts Make': The Hauntology and Gothic Minimalism of Beckett's Late Work." *Modern Fiction Studies* 46, no. 3 (2000): 772–85.

Garvin, Tom. *1922: The Birth of Irish Democracy*. Dublin: Gill and Macmillan, 1996.

Gibbons, Luke. "Identity without a Centre: Allegory, History and Irish Nationalism." In *Transformations in Irish Culture,* 134–48. Notre Dame, IN: University of Notre Dame Press, 1996.

Gifford, Don, and Robert J. Seidman. *Ulysses Annotated: Notes for James Joyce's* Ulysses. Berkeley and Los Angeles: University of California Press, 1989.

Glover, David. *Vampires, Mummies, and Liberals: Bram Stoker and the Politics of Popular Fiction*. Durham, NC: Duke University Press, 1996.

Gordon, Lois. *The World of Samuel Beckett: 1906–1946*. New Haven, CT: Yale University Press, 1996.

Grosz, Elizabeth. *Volatile Bodies: Toward a Corporeal Feminism*. Bloomington: Indiana University Press, 1994.

Habermas, Jürgen. *The Structural Transformation of the Public Sphere*. Translated by Thomas Burger. Cambridge, MA: MIT Press, 1991.

Hachey, Thomas E. *Britain and Irish Separatism: From the Fenians to the Free State, 1867–1922*. Washington, DC: Catholic University Press, 1984.

Hansen, Jim. "Formalism and Its Malcontents: Benjamin and de Man on the Function of Allegory." *New Literary History* 35, no. 4 (2004): 663–83.

Harden, Elizabeth. "Transparent Thady Quirk." In *Family Chronicles: Maria Edgeworth's* Castle Rackrent, edited by Cóilín Owens, 86–96. Dublin: Wolfhound, 1987.

Harding, James Martin. "Trying to Understand Godot: Adorno, Beckett, and the Senility of Dialectics." In *Adorno and "A Writing of the Ruins": Essays on Modern Aesthetics and Anglo-American Literature and Culture,* 51–64. Albany: State University of New York Press, 1997.

Harrington, John P. *The Irish Beckett*. Syracuse, NY: Syracuse University Press, 1991.

Hegel, G. W. F. *Science of Logic*. Translated by A. V. Miller. New York: Prometheus, 1989.

Henke, Suzette. *James Joyce and the Politics of Desire*. New York: Routledge, 1990.

Hesla, David. *The Shape of the Chaos: An Interpretation of the Art of Samuel Beckett*. Minneapolis: University of Minnesota Press, 1971.

Hollingworth, Brian. *Maria Edgeworth's Irish Wrriting*. New York: Palgrave Macmillan, 1997.

Horkheimer, Max, and Theodor W. Adorno. *Dialectic of Enlightenment.* Translated by John Cumming. New York: Continuum, 1973.

Idel, Moshe. *Kabalah: New Perspectives.* New Haven, CT: Yale University Press, 1988.

Idman, Nilo. *Maturin: His Life and Works.* London: Constable, 1923.

James, Lawrence. *The Rise and Fall of the British Empire.* New York: St. Martin's, 1994.

Jameson, Fredric. "Modernism and Imperialism." *Nationalism, Colonialism, and Literature,* edited by Seamus Deane, 43–66. Minneapolis: University of Minnesota Press, 1990.

———. *The Political Unconscious: Narrative as a Socially Symbolic Act.* Ithaca, NY: Cornell University Press, 1984.

———. *A Singular Modernity: Essay on the Ontology of the Present.* New York: Verso, 2002.

Jardine, Alice. *Gynesis: Configurations of Woman and Modernity.* Ithaca, NY: Cornell University Press, 1985.

Jeffares, Norman A. "Maturin the Innovator." In *Images of Invention: Essays on Irish Writing,* 131–49. Gerrards Cross, UK: Colin Smythe, 1996.

Joyce, James. *The Critical Writings.* Edited by Ellsworth Mason and Richard Ellman. Ithaca, NY: Cornell University Press, 1989.

———. *Letters of James Joyce,* vol. 1. Edited by Richard Ellman. New York: Viking, 1966.

———. *A Portrait of the Artist as a Young Man.* New York: Penguin, 1992.

———. *Ulysses.* New York: Random House, 1961.

Kant, Immanuel. *Critique of Judgment.* Translated by James Creed Meredith. Oxford: Clarendon, 1952.

Kearney, Richard. "Myth and Motherland." In *Ireland's Field Day,* edited by Seamus Deane, 61–80. Notre Dame, IN: University of Notre Dame Press, 1986.

Kenner, Hugh. *Dublin's Joyce.* Boston: Beacon, 1956.

———. *Samuel Beckett: A Critical Study.* Berkeley and Los Angeles: University of California Press, 1968.

Kermode, Frank. *The Sense of an Ending: Studies in the Theory of Fiction.* New York: Oxford University Press, 1967.

Kierkegaard, Søren. *Concluding Unscientific Postscript.* Translated by David F. Swenson and Walter Lowrie. Princeton, NJ: Princeton University Press, 1968.

———. *Either/Or: A Fragment of Life,* vol. 1. Translated by David F. Swenson and Lillian Marvin Swenson. Princeton, NJ: Princeton University Press, 1971.

Knowlson, James. *Damned to Fame: The Life of Samuel Beckett.* New York: Simon and Schuster, 1996.

Kosok, Heinz. "Charles Robert Maturin and Colonialism." In *Literary Inter-Relations: Ireland, Egypt, and the Far East,* edited by Mary Massoud, 228–34. Gerrards Cross, UK: Colin Smythe, 1996.

Kramer, Dale. *Charles Robert Maturin.* New York: Twayne, 1973.

Krishnaswamy, Revathi. *Effeminism: The Economy of Colonial Desire.* Ann Arbor: University of Michigan Press, 1998.

Kristeva, Julia. "The Father, Love and Banishment." In *Desire in Language: A Semiotic Approach to Literature and Art,* edited by Leon S. Roudiez, 148–58. Translated by Thomas Gora, Alice Jardine, and Leon S. Roudiez. New York: Columbia University Press, 1980.

———. *Powers of Horror: An Essay on Abjection.* New York: Columbia University Press, 1982.

Lane, Fintan. *The Origins of Modern Irish Socialism.* Dublin: Cork University Press, 1997.

Lawler, Donald. "The Gothic Wilde." *Rediscovering Oscar Wilde,* edited by C. George Sandulescu, 249–68. Gerrards Cross, UK: Colin Smythe, 1994.

Lawrence, Karen. "Paternity as Legal Fiction in *Ulysses.*" In *James Joyce, the Augmented Ninth: Proceedings of the Ninth International James Joyce Symposium,* edited by Bernard Benstock, 233–43. Syracuse, NY: Syracuse University Press, 1988.

Le Fanu, Joseph Sheridan. "Carmilla." In *In a Glass Darkly: Stories by Sheridan Le Fanu,* edited by V. S. Pritchett, 222–288. London: John Lehmann, 1947.

Lenin, V. I. *What Is to Be Done? Burning Questions of Our Movement.* Translated by Joe Fineberg and George Hanna. New York: International, 1988.

Levinson, Marjorie. "What is New Formalism?" *PMLA* 122. No. 2 (2007): 558–69.

Lew, Joseph W. "'Unprepared for Sudden Transformations': Identity and Politics in *Melmoth the Wanderer,*" *Studies in the Novel* 26, no. 2 (1994): 173–95,

Lewis, Matthew. *The Monk.* New York: Oxford University Press, 1980.

Lloyd, David. *Anomalous States: Irish Writing and the Post-Colonial Moment.* Durham, NC: Duke University Press, 1993.

———. "Counterparts: *Dubliners,* Masculinity, and Temperance Nationalism." In *Semicolonial Joyce,* edited by Derek Attridge and Marjorie Howes, 128–49. New York: Cambridge University Press, 2000.

Lukács, Georg. "The Ideology of Modernism." *The Lucáks Reader,* edited by Arpad Kadarky, 187–209. New York: Blackwell, 1995.

Lyons, F. S. L. *Charles Stewart Parnell.* New York: Oxford University Press, 1977.

Mahaffey, Vicki. *States of Desire: Wilde, Yeats, Joyce and the Irish Experiment.* New York: Oxford University Press, 1998.

Marx, Karl. *The German Ideology.* New York: Prometheus Books, 1998.

———. *Grundrisse: Foundations of the Critique of Political Economy.* Translated by Martin Nicolaus. New York: Penguin, 1993.

Maturin, Charles Robert. *The Fatal Revenge: The Fatal Revenge; Or, The Family of Montorio,* 3 vols. London: Longman, Hurst, Rees, and Orme, 1807.

———. *Melmoth the Wanderer.* London: Oxford University Press, 1998.

Maxwell, T. Henry. *The Irish Land Acts, 1903 to 1909.* Dublin: John Falconer, 1910.

McCormack, W. J. *Dissolute Characters: Irish Literary History through Balzac, Sheridan Le Fanu, Yeats and Bowen.* New York: Manchester University Press, 1993.

———. "Irish Gothic and After (1820–1945)." *Field Day Anthology of Irish Writing,* edited by Seamus Deane, vol. 2, 831–54. New York: Norton, 1991.
———. *Sheridan Le Fanu and Victorian Ireland.* Oxford: Clarendon, 1980.
Melada, Ivan. *Sheridan Le Fanu.* New York: Twayne, 1987.
Mendes-Flohr, Paul and Jehuda Reinharz, eds. *The Jew in the Modern World.* New York: Oxford University press, 1995.
Mercier, Vivian. *Beckett/Beckett.* New York: Oxford University Press, 1979.
Miles, Robert. "Anne Radcliffe and Matthew Lewis." *A Companion to the Gothic,* edited by David Punter, 41–57. New York: Routledge, 2000.
Miller, Tyrus. "Dismantling Authenticity: Beckett, Adorno and the 'Post-War.'" *Textual Practice* 8, no. 1 (1994): 43–57.
Mintz, Samuel. "Beckett's *Murphy:* A 'Cartesian Novel.'" *Perspective* 2, no. 3 (1959): 156–65.
Moers, Ellen. *Literary Women.* New York: Oxford University Press, 1985.
Moynahan, Julian. *Anglo-Irish: The Literary Imagination in a Hyphenated Culture.* Princeton, NJ: Princeton University Press, 1995.
Murphy, P. J. "Beckett and the Philosophers." In *The Cambridge Companion to Samuel Beckett,* edited by John Pilling, 222–40. Cambridge: Cambridge University Press, 1994.
Nadel, Ira B. *Joyce and the Jews: Culture and Texts.* Iowa City: University of Iowa Press, 1989.
Neitzsche, Friedrich. *On the Genealogy of Morality.* Translated by Maudemarie Clark and Alan J. Swenson. New York: Hackett, 1998.
Neusner, Jacob. *Classic Judaism: Torah, Learning, Virtue.* New York: Peter Lang, 1993.
———. *How Judaism Reads the Torah, III/IV.* New York: Peter Lang, 1993.
Newcomer, James. "*Castle Rackrent:* The Disingenuous Thady Quirk." In *Family Chronicles: Maria Edgeworth's* Castle Rackrent, edited by Cóilín Owens, 79–85. Dublin: Wolfhound, 1987.
Nicholsen, Shierry Weber. *Exact Imagination, Late Work: On Adorno's Aesthetics.* Cambridge, MA: MIT Press, 1997.
Nolan, Emer. *James Joyce and Nationalism.* London: Routledge, 1995.
Nunokawa, Jeff. *Tame Passions of Wilde: The Styles of Manageable Desire.* Princeton, NJ: Princeton University Press, 2003.
O'Brien, Connor Cruise. *Parnell and His Party: 1880–90.* New York: Oxford University Press, 1957.
O'Brien, Eoin. *The Beckett Country: Samuel Beckett's Ireland.* New York: Arcade, 1993.
Pearson, Jacqueline. "Masculinizing the Novel: Women Writers and Intertextuality in Charles Robert Maturin's *The Wild Irish Boy.*" *Studies in Romanticism* 36 (1997): 635–50.
Platt, L. H. *Joyce and the Anglo-Irish: A Study of Joyce and the Literary Revival.* Atlanta, GA: Rodolpi, 1998.
———. "The Voice of Esau: Culture and Nationalism in 'Scylla and Charybdis.'" *James Joyce Quarterly* 29, no. 4 (1992): 737–50.
Punter, David. *Gothic Pathologies: The Text, the Body, and the Law.* New York: St. Martin's, 1998.

Radcliffe, Anne. *The Italian*. New York: Oxford University Press, 1998.

———. *The Mysteries of Udolpho*. New York: Oxford University Press, 1970.

Ratzinger, Joseph. *Catechism of the Catholic Church*. Liguori, MO: Liguori, 1994.

Reizbaum, Marilyn. *James Joyce's Judaic Other*. Stanford, CA: Stanford University Press, 1999.

Riquelme, John Paul. "Oscar Wilde's Aesthetic Gothic: Walter Pater, Dark Enlightenment, and *The Picture of Dorian Gray*." *Modern Fiction Studies* 46, no. 3 (2000): 609–31.

———. "Toward a History of Gothic and Modernism: Dark Modernity from Bram Stoker to Samuel Beckett." *Modern Fiction Studies* 46, no. 3 (2000): 585–605.

Robinson, Nicholas. "Marriage Against Inclination: The Union and Caricature." *Acts of Union: The Causes, Contexts, and Consequences of the Act of Union*, edited by Daire Keogh and Kevin Whelan, 140–58. Portland, OR: Four Courts Press, 2001.

Roditi, Edouard. *Oscar Wilde*. Norfolk, VA: New Directions Books, 1947.

Rosensweig, Franz. "Jewish Learning and the Return to Judaism." *The Jew in the Modern World*, edited by Paul Mendes-Flohr and Jehuda Reinharz, 282–84. New York: Oxford University Press, 1995.

Ryan, William Patrick. *The Irish Literary Revival: Its History, Pioneers, and Possibilities*. New York: Lemma Press, 1970.

Sage, Victor. " Diderot and Maturin: Enlightenment, Automata, and the Theatre of Terror." In *European Gothic: A Spirited Exchange 1760–1960*, edited by Avril Horner, 55–69. New York: Manchester University Press, 2002.

———. "'Carmilla': I'll Let You Be in My Dream, if I Can Be in Yours." *Le Fanu's Gothic: The Rhetoric of Darkness*. New York: Palgrave, 2004.

Said, Edward W. *Orientalism*. New York: Vintage, 1979.

Sampson, William. *Memoirs of William Sampson*. New York: George Forman, 1807.

Scholem, Gershom. *Kabbalah*. New York: Penguin, 1978.

———. *On the Possibilities of Jewish Mysticism and Other Essays*. Translated by Johnathan Chipman. Philadelphia: Jewish Publication System, 1997.

Sedgwick, Eve Kosofsky. *Between Men: English Literature and Male Homosocial Desire*. New York: Columbia University Press, 1985.

Simms, J. G. "Protestant Ascendancy, 1691–1714." In *A New History of Ireland*, Vol. 4, *Eighteenth-Century Ireland, 1691–1800*, edited by T. W. Moody and W. E. Vaughan. Oxford: Clarendon, 1986.

Sinfield, Alan. *The Wilde Century: Effeminacy, Oscar Wilde, and the Queer Moment*. New York: Columbia University Press, 1994.

Spenser, Edmund. "A View of the Present State of Ireland." In *Field Day Anthology of Irish Writing*, edited by Seamus Deane, vol. 1. New York: W. W. Norton, 1991. 175–202.

Spivak, Gayatri Chakravorty. "Three Women's Texts and a Critique of Imperialism." *Critical Inquiry* 12, no. 1 (1985): 235–61.

Stoker, Bram. *Dracula*. New York: Bantam, 1989.

Sussman, Henry. "Introduction: The Politics of Language-Based Systems." In *Engagement and Indifference: Beckett and the Political*, edited by Henry Sussman and Christopher Devenney. Albany: State University of New York Press, 2001. 1–10.

Uhlmann, Anthony. *Beckett and Poststructuralism*. Cambridge: Cambridge University Press, 1999.

Ulrich-Mohr, Hans. "Wandering Jew (Ahasuerus)." In *The Handbook to Gothic Literature*, edited by Marie Mulvey-Roberts, 249–51. New York: New York University Press, 1998.

Valente, Joseph P. *Dracula's Crypt: Bram Stoker, Irishness, and the Question of Blood*. Urbana: University of Illinois Press, 2001.

———. "'Neither Fish nor Flesh'; or How 'Cyclops' Stages the Double-Bind of Irish Manhood." In *Semicolonial Joyce*, edited by Derek Attridge and Marjorie Howes, 96–127. Cambridge: Cambridge University Press, 2000.

van Boheemen-Saaf, Christine. "The Primitive Scene of Representation: Writing Gender." In *Joyce, Derrida, Lacan, and the Trauma of History: Reading, Narrative, and Postcolonialism*, 120–54. New York: Cambridge University Press, 1999.

Walpole, Horace. *The Castle of Otranto*. New York: Dover, 1966.

Watson, Nicola. *Revolution and the Form of the British Novel, 1790–1825*. Oxford: Clarendon, 1994.

Weisberg, David. *Chronicles of Disorder: Samuel Beckett and the Cultural Politics of the Modern Novel*. Albany: State University of New York Press, 2000.

Wilde, Oscar. "The Critic as Artist." In Foreman, *The Complete Works of Oscar Wilde*, 1009–1159.

———. "The Decay of Lying." In Foreman, *The Complete Works of Oscar Wilde: Stories, Plays, Poems & Essays*, 970–92.

———. *De Profundis*. In Foreman, *The Complete Works of Oscar Wilde*, 873–957.

———. "An Ideal Husband." In Foreman, *The Complete Works of Oscar Wilde*, 482–551.

———. "The Importance of Being Earnest." In Foreman, *The Complete Works of Oscar Wilde*, 321–84.

———. *The Picture of Dorian Gray*. In Foreman, *The Complete Works of Oscar Wilde*, 17–167.

———. "The Soul of Man Under Socialism." In Foreman, *The Complete Works of Oscar Wilde*, 1079–1104.

Wolf, Immanuel. "On the Concept of a Science of Judaism." In *The Jew in the Modern World*, edited by Paul Mendes-Flohr and Jehuda Reinharz, 219–20. New York: Oxford University Press, 1995.

Wright, Iain. "'What Matter Who's Speaking?': Beckett, the Authorial Subject and Contemporary Critical Theory." *Southern Review* 16, no. 1 (1983): 59–86.

Wright, Julia M. "Devouring the Disinhereited: Familial Cannibalism in Maturin's *Melmoth the Wanderer*." In *Eating Their Words: Cannibalism and the Boundaries of Cultural Identity,* edited by Kristen Guest, 79–105. Albany: State University of New York Press, 2001.

Yeats, William Butler. *Eleven Plays of William Butler Yeats,* edited by Norman Jeffares, 199–206. New York: MacMillan, 1964.

———. *Essays and Introductions.* New York: Collier, 1961.

———. *The Poems.* Edited by Daniel Albright. London: Everyman, 1994.

———. *A Vision.* New York: Collier, 1965.

Zeender, Marie-Noëlle. "John Melmoth and Dorian Gray: The Two-Faced Mirror." *Rediscovering Oscar Wilde,* edited by C. George Sandulescu, 432–40. Gerrards Cross, UK: Colin Smythe, 1994.

Zunz, Leopold. "On Rabbinic Literature." In *The Jew in the Modern World,* edited by Paul Mendes-Flohr and Jehuda Reinharz, 221–28. New York: Oxford University Press, 1995.

Index

Abbott, H. Porter, 161, 163, 165
Adorno, Theodor W., 1, 4, 10, 11, 20, 50, 59, 66–68, 84, 109, 115, 125, 127, 160–61, 169, 173, 175n5, 176n15, 177–78n29, 182n8, 186n31, 187nn1, 2, 188nn7, 8, 189n14, 190n25, 191n31
  Aesthetic Theory, 1, 50, 59, 109, 160–61, 175n5, 182n8, 188n8
  "Cultural Criticism and Society," 176n15
  Dialectic of Enlightenment, 115, 186n31
  Kierkegaard, 166–68, 191n31
  Minima Moralia, 84
  Negative Dialectics, 169, 173
  "Trying to Understand *Endgame*," 127, 187n1
Amiran, Eyal, 129, 177n29, 187n4, 188n10
Arata, Stephen D., 8, 71
Armstrong, Nancy, 19, 170, 177n23
Attridge, Derek, 125, 177n27, 183n15, 184n5
Auerbach, Nina, 55
Austen, Jane, 25, 30, 41, 130, 159

Backus, Margot Gayle, 10–12, 33, 37, 47–48, 51, 178nn2, 5, 179n14, 181n32
Badiou, Alain, 188n8
Bakhtin, Mikhail, 7
Balzac, Honoré de, 81
Baldick, Chris, 47, 175n2, 178n4,
Banville, John, 191n1
Bassi, Giovanni (Il Sodoma), 175n1, 182n1
Bataille, George, 157
Baucom, Ian, 186n30
Baudelaire, Charles, 81
Beckett, Samuel, 3, 4, 6–8, 18, 24, 25–26, 52, 85, 123 125–167, 169, 173–74, 187n2, 188n8, 189n14, 190nn25, 27
  "Censorship in the Saorstat," 142–44, 148, 150
  "Dante . . . Bruno.Vico. .Joyce," 138
  Endgame, 127, 166, 187n1, 188n8
  "Essential and the Incidental," 128
  First Love, 25, 132, 140–51, 153, 154, 155, 156, 158, 164, 200n22
  Malone Dies, 25, 129, 131, 151, 153, 161–66, 189n14
  Molloy, 52, 125, 129, 131, 151–61, 164, 165–66, 189n14, 190nn27, 28
  Murphy, 25, 131, 132, 133–41, 142, 143, 144, 147, 148, 150, 153, 155, 156, 158, 189nn16, 20, 21, 190n24
  Unnamable, The, 127, 129, 131, 153, 166
  Waiting for Godot, 138, 144, 148, 166, 178n29, 188n7
Beckford, William, 21, 40
Begam, Richard, 125–126, 134, 189nn17, 21

Benjamin, Walter, 9–10, 11, 21, 93–94, 110, 176n7, 177n25, 184nn11, 13, 14, 185n15
The Arcades Project, 184n14
The Origin of the German Mourning Play, 21, 93–94, 110, 176n7, 177n25, 184nn11, 13
Ben-Zvi, Linda, 130, 132, 188n12
Birkhead, Edith, 41–42
Black, R.D. Collinson, 175n6, 180n25
Blanchot, Maurice, 127, 160
Boheemen-Saf, Christine van, 184n5
Bordo, Susan, 189n18
Bowen, Elizabeth, 176n12, 183n1
Brontë, Charlotte, 18, 130, 139, 169, 180n27, 183n2
Jane Eyre, 19, 139, 152, 153, 169, 180n27, 183n2, 190n26
Brown, Malcolm, 184n8
Bruhm, Stephen, 181n30
Bruns, Gerald L., 114
Bryden, Mary, 188n12
Bunyan, John, 89
Burke, Edmund, 4, 7, 12–15, 16, 17, 19, 20, 22, 40, 41, 46, 108, 141, 170, 176–77n16
Reflections on the Revolution in France, 12–15, 40, 41, 46, 141, 170, 176–77n16,
"Tract on the Popery Laws," 13
Burke, Martin, 14, 177n17

Clare, John, 17
Cohen, Ed, 62, 182n3
Cohen, Norman, 186n26
Coleridge, Samuel Taylor, 179n12
Collins, Michael, 141
Collins, Wilkie, 154
Connor, Stephen, 151
Corbett, Mary Jean, 27, 46, 176n16, 179n9
Corkery, Daniel, 9, 144, 176n11, 180n23
Cosgrave, W.T., 141
Craft, Christopher, 181n36
Curtis, L.P., 10

Danson, Lawrence, 183n10
Davison, Neil, 113, 177n2, 186n26, 187n34
Davitt, Michael, 57, 60–61, 72, 184n6
Deane, Seamus, 8, 10, 24, 25, 62–65, 68, 72, 102, 126, 175n4, 182nn4, 5, 183n15, 185n24, 187n3, 188n7, 191n1
Celtic Revivals, 8, 10, 126, 183n15, 185n24, 187n3
Field Day Anthology, 8, 63, 175n4, 182n4
Short History of Irish Literature, 62
Strange Country, 8
Derrida, Jacques, 125, 126, 127
Descartes, Rene, 126, 134–36, 139
De Valera, Eamon, 141–42
Dickens, Charles, 72, 159
Dougherty, Jane Elizabeth, 16, 177n21

Eagleton, Terry, 8, 188n8
Eekhoud, George, 175 n. 1, 182n1
Edgeworth, Maria, 5, 24, 27–31, 33, 37, 71, 74, 170, 171, 176–77n16, 178nn1, 3
Belinda, 31
Castle Rackrent, 5, 27–31, 33, 171, 178nn1, 3
Eglinton, John, 99, 101, 119, 185n20
Eliot, George, 159
Eliot, T.S., 75, 126
Ellis, Kate Ferguson, 19, 34, 41, 89, 170, 184n4
Ellman, Richard, 126, 182n5
Esslin, Martin, 188nn6, 9

Fairhall, James, 185n16
Fanon, Frantz, 16, 150–51, 162
Felski, Rita, 189n18
Fenves, Peter, 67, 191n31
Forster, E.M., 126, 159
Foster, John, 17
Foster, R.F., 39, 177n18, 179n17, 180n21, 182n2
Freud, Sigmund, 53–55, 180n30

Gibbons, Luke, 8, 176n9
Gilbert, Sandra, 21
Gladstone, William, 9, 51, 61, 90, 184n6
Glover, David, 182n7
Godwin, William, 40
Gordon, Lois, 126

Gramsci, Antonio, 8
Grattan, Henry, 17
Grosz, Elizabeth, 135–36, 189n15
Gubar, Susan, 21

Habermas, Jürgen, 162, 177n24, 179n8, 189n19
Hachey, Thomas E., 61, 184n6
Harden, Elizabeth, 178n1
Harding, James Martin, 178n29, 188n7
Harrington, John, 25, 126, 142
Hesla, David, 126, 134, 189n20
Hegel, G.W.F., 24, 87, 94–95, 120, 138–39, 173
Holland, W., 17, 177n20
Hollingworth, Brian, 178n3
Horkheimer, Max, 115, 186n31
  Dialectic of Enlightenment, 115, 186n31
Howes, Marjorie, 125, 177n27, 183n15, 184n5
Huysman, Karl, 78, 81, 82

Idman, Nilo, 32, 37, 41, 179nn10, 15

Jameson, Fredric, 7, 91, 126, 166, 176n15, 185n16
  Political Unconscious, 7, 91, 126
  Singular Modernity, 166
Jardine, Alice, 189n18, 190n23
Jeffares, Norman A., 37, 178nn4–5, 179n11, 183n1
Joyce, James, 4, 6–8, 9, 10, 18, 24, 25, 52, 62–63, 75, 84–86, 87–123, 125–26, 131, 132, 134, 136, 138, 142, 144, 145, 156, 158, 159, 164, 165, 169, 173–74, 181n30, 184nn5, 9, 185nn16, 21, 23, 190n25
  Portrait of the Artist as a Young Man, 86, 92, 105, 136, 143, 165
  Ulysses, 4, 9, 23, 24, 25, 52, 75, 86, 87–123, 134, 143, 159, 173, 185n16

Kearney, Richard, 141, 175n4
Kenner, Hugh, 125–29, 131, 134
Kermode, Frank, 186n27
Kierkegaard, Søren, 66–68, 69, 161, 191n31
Kosok, Heinz, 179nn11, 13
Knowlson, James, 187n3
Kramer, Dale, 41, 179nn7, 19
Krishnaswamy, Revathi, 190n26
Kristeva, Julia, 53, 90, 93, 97, 103, 127, 180–81n30

Lawler, Donald, 74
Lawrence, Karen, 98, 185n19
Lefanu, Joseph Sheridan, 5, 7, 8, 11, 18, 24, 25, 28, 31, 47, 50–58, 98, 172, 180n27, 181nn31, 33, 35
  "Carmilla," 31, 51–57, 98, 172, 181nn31, 33, 35
  In a Glass Darkly, 50, 52, 53,
  Uncle Silas, 51
  Wyvern Mystery, 51
Lenin, V.I., 173
Levinson, Marjorie, 176n15
Lewis, Matthew, 21, 29, 30, 32, 40, 73, 95, 117–18, 175n2, 177n26, 178n4, 180n20, 183n3
  The Monk, 21, 29, 30, 40, 95, 117–18, 180n20, 183n3
Lloyd, David, 25, 126, 127, 144–45, 150, 163, 176n14, 177n27, 183n15, 184n5, 190n26
Lukács, Georg, 125, 127–28, 131, 151, 157, 187n1, 188nn8–9
Lyons, F.S.L., 106, 185n22

Mahaffey, Vicki, 63–65, 183nn9, 11
Marx, Karl, 110, 120, 185n15
Maturin, Charles Robert 1–8, 11, 12, 18, 22–23, 24, 25, 27–50, 51, 52, 55, 56, 57, 60, 64, 70, 71, 74, 81–84, 89–90, 117–18, 131, 132, 134, 141, 145, 146, 158, 162, 170, 171–72, 175n2, 179n12
  Albigenses, 33
  Bertram, 34, 179n12
  Fatal Revenge, 6, 22–23, 24, 29–31, 33–35, 37–50, 64, 70, 90, 146, 171, 179nn7, 10
  Melmoth the Wanderer, 1–3, 22, 25, 29, 30, 33, 36, 40, 47–50, 57, 64, 81–84, 91, 92, 117–18, 185n2

Milesian Chief, 29, 35
Wild Irish Boy, 46
Melada, Ivan, 180n28
McCormack, W.J., 52, 176n12, 180nn26, 29, 182n4
Mercier, Vivian, 126
Miles, Robert, 22, 177n26
Miller, Tyrus, 127, 187n2, 188n8, 189n14
Mintz, Samuel, 189n16
Moers, Ellen, 18, 21
Molyneux, William, 56
Moynahan, Julian, 51, 176n8, 178nn2, 4, 5
Murphy, P.J., 189n16

Nadel, Ira, 187n34
Neusner, Jacob, 114
Newcomer, James, 178n1
Nietzsche, Friedrich, 15–16, 71, 75, 172
On the Genealogy of Morality, 15–16, 71, 172
Nolan, Emer, 176nn10, 13, 183n15, 185nn17, 24
Nunokawa, Jeff, 65, 182n6

O'Brien, Conor Cruise, 106
O'Brien, Eoin, 25, 126
O'Casey, Sean, 129, 132, 142
O'Connell, Daniel, 34, 51
Ovid, 75–76, 84

Parnell, Charles Stewart, 57, 60–61, 72, 90–91, 105–107, 109, 119–122, 184nn6, 8, 185nn22, 23
Pearson, Jacqueline, 37, 40, 178n6, 179n19
Pitt, William, 17
Platt, L.H., 100–01, 176nn10, 13, 185n20
Proust, Marcel, 139, 145, 153, 181n30
Punter, David, 95, 130, 177n26

Radcliffe, Anne, 5, 18, 20, 21, 25, 29, 31, 32, 34, 36, 37–40, 42–43, 49–50, 53, 73, 87–89, 130–31, 146, 151–52, 169–71, 175n2, 177n26, 178n4, 180n20, 183n3
Italian, 31, 42, 169, 180n20, 183n3
Mysteries of Udolpho, 5, 29, 38, 73, 87–89, 131, 170
Ranke, Leopold Von, 115
Reizbaum, Marilyn, 118, 177n28
Reni, Guido, 1, 175n1, 182n1
Richardson, Samuel, 53, 72, 153, 159, 161, 162
Riquelme, John Paul, 75–76, 183n12
Robinson, Nicholas, 177n20
Roditi, Edouard, 81, 183n13
Rosensweig, Franz, 116
Ross, Robert, 182n5
Rousseau, Jean-Jacques, 2
Russell, George (A.E.), 100–01, 108
Ryan, William Patrick, 100

Sage, Victor, 54, 56, 179n18, 181nn31, 33, 35
Said, Edward W., 16, 126
Sampson, William, 14–15, 22, 108
Scholem, Gershom, 113–14
Sedgwick, Eve Kosofsky, 21–22, 177nn22, 26
Shakespeare, William, 68, 76, 95–96, 99, 101–109, 119–122
Hamlet, 95–96, 98–109, 111, 122, 163
Sheridan, Richard Brinsley, 17, 19, 22
Sickert, Walter, 59–60, 62
Simms, J.G., 181n34
Sinfield, Alan, 62, 77–78, 182n3
Spenser, Edmund, 3, 22 .
A View of the Present State of Ireland, 3, 22
Spivak, Gayatri Chakravorty, 190n26
Stoker, Bram, 6–7, 8, 10–11, 18, 20, 22, 24, 47, 52, 57–58, 71–74, 86, 89, 130, 131, 134, 158, 162, 165, 172
Dracula, 8, 10–11, 20, 22, 24, 57–58, 65, 71–74, 89, 162, 172
Sussman, Henry, 187n2
Swift, Jonathan, 3

Tone, Theobald Wolf, 4, 105, 171

Valente, Joseph, 10–12, 72, 184n5, 185n17

Walpole, Horace, 21, 29, 32, 95, 175n2, 178n4
Watson, Nicola, 32, 178n5
Weisberg, David, 127, 145, 151, 159, 178n29, 187n2, 189n14, 190n24, 191n30
Wilde, Oscar, 1–4, 6–8, 18, 22, 24–25, 52, 57–58, 59–86, 88, 91–93, 97, 99, 108, 121, 130, 131, 132, 134, 145, 156, 158, 164, 169, 173, 182nn4–5
  "Critic as Artist," 80, 85
  "Decay of Lying," 69, 80, 85
  De Profundis, 58, 66
  Ideal Husband, 68, 156
  Importance of Being Earnest, 64, 76, 91
  Lady Windermere's Fan, 69
  Picture of Dorian Gray, 24, 57, 64–66, 74–84, 91–92, 99, 121, 183n12–14
  "Soul of Man Under Socialism," 69
Wohlwill, Immanuel, 116
Wright, Iain, 189n16
Wright, Julia M., 37, 180n22

Uhlmann, Anthony, 126, 187n5

Yeats, W.B., 8, 10, 23, 61, 62, 84, 85, 91, 100–01, 132, 141, 145, 183n1
  Cathleen Ni Hoolihan, 23, 141, 183n1
  Purgatory,
Yershalmi, Yosef, 113, 186n28

Zeender, Marie-Noële, 82, 183n14